"This is the best kind of travel memoir— [barcode] of a journey made years ago. The older a himself as a young man and the result is an account of the world, then and now, that is eloquent, rueful, and profound."

—Elizabeth Hay, Scotiabank Giller Prize winner
and author of *All Things Consoled: A Daughter's Memoir*

"This delightful blend of travelogue and memoir swept me away to a foreign land: the late seventies. Youthful and privileged, Abley and his travel companion understand little of the decolonizing world and people they meet. But with his signature wit, critical candour, and empathy, Abley's older self offers context and the wisdom of hindsight. An absorbing portrait of regions in rapid transformation and a couple of young outsiders bemused by hospitality, sights, and sounds they encounter on their trip of a lifetime."

—Shauna Singh Baldwin, author of
What the Body Remembers and *The Tiger Claw*

"A wonderful book about travel during a time on the threshold of change in the world. *Strange Bewildering Time* lives up to its name and Mark Abley writes of his travels from Istanbul to Kathmandu, and everywhere in between, with eloquent detail, wit, and wisdom."

—David Farley, author of *An Irreverent Curiosity*

"Open this book and you'll get wafts of sandalwood and spices, of sun-baked roads and thumb-worn pages, and a touch of hippie sweat. Mark Abley's *Strange Bewildering Time* is a gauge of how people have shaped the world and how the world shaped a wide-eyed poet. There's nostalgia, humour, and melancholy throughout this story, warm and honestly told. And as much as it is a look at how a young man changed, how relationships and experience can sometimes make the past seem foreign, I felt the older man very much alive in this—not so much a tale of someone looking back at a former self but of someone eloquently showing that if we keep our desire to search and express, the best parts of youth don't die."

—Colin McAdam, Scotiabank Giller Prize finalist
and author of *Black Dove*

Strange
Bewildering
Time

Istanbul to Kathmandu in the
Last Year of the Hippie Trail

Mark Abley

ANANSI

Published in Canada in 2023 and the USA in 2023 by House of Anansi Press Inc.
houseofanansi.com

House of Anansi Press is committed to protecting our natural environment.
This book is made of material from well-managed FSC®-certified forests, recycled materials,
and other controlled sources.

House of Anansi Press is a Global Certified Accessible™ (GCA by Benetech) publisher.
The ebook version of this book meets stringent accessibility standards and is
available to students and readers with print disabilities.

27 26 25 24 23   1 2 3 4 5

Library and Archives Canada Cataloguing in Publication

Title: Strange bewildering time : Istanbul to Kathmandu in the last year of
the Hippie Trail / Mark Abley.
Names: Abley, Mark, author.
Description: Includes bibliographical references.
Identifiers: Canadiana (print) 20220285713 | Canadiana (ebook) 20220285810 |
ISBN 9781487009663 (softcover) | ISBN 9781487009670 (EPUB)
Subjects: LCSH: Abley, Mark—Travel. | LCSH: Middle East—Description and travel. |
LCSH: Southeast Asia—Description and travel.
Classification: LCC DS10 .A25 2023 | DDC 915/.04427—dc23

Cover design: Jennifer Lum
Cover photograph: Two peaks of Mt Ararat from the Turkish/Iranian border, 1970,
© Neil Rawlins, neilrawlins.blogspot.com
Text design and typesetting: Alysia Shewchuk
Cartography: Bill Nelson

Every reasonable effort has been made to trace ownership of copyright materials. The publisher
will gladly rectify any inadvertent errors or omissions in credits in future editions.

*House of Anansi Press respectfully acknowledges that the land on which we operate is the
Traditional Territory of many Nations, including the Anishinabeg, the Wendat, and the
Haudenosaunee. It is also the Treaty Lands of the Mississaugas of the Credit.*

 Canada Council   Conseil des Arts   ONTARIO ARTS COUNCIL
for the Arts   du Canada   CONSEIL DES ARTS DE L'ONTARIO
                                                          an Ontario government agency
                                                          un organisme du gouvernement de l'Ontario

With the participation of the Government of Canada |  Canadä
Avec la participation du gouvernement du Canada

*We acknowledge for their financial support of our publishing program
the Canada Council for the Arts, the Ontario Arts Council, and the Government of Canada.*

Printed and bound in Canada

MIX
Paper from
responsible sources
FSC
www.fsc.org   FSC® C103567

This ocean of the world is hard to cross:
its waters are very deep.
—KABIR

When the uncertain future becomes the past,
the past in turn becomes uncertain.
—MOHSIN HAMID, *Moth Smoke*

Je est un autre.
—ARTHUR RIMBAUD

Contents

Prologue

I was standing outside a cheap hotel in Shiraz when the Shah of Iran appeared.

It was a warm spring afternoon, full of the competing scents of roses and diesel. Two hours earlier I'd left the hotel to see the sumptuous tomb of a much-loved Persian poet, and as I strolled back I was still thinking about the copper dome, the blossoming orange trees, the blaze of rose bushes around the shrine. When I turned a street corner, I came upon a crowd of smartly dressed children, each of them clutching a small green, white, and red flag. Were the girls and boys celebrating May Day? It seemed unlikely.

The closer I got to the hotel, the more the sidewalks were alive with adults and excited children. The din of traffic had dwindled to a distant murmur. I found Clare, my travelling companion, seated on a hard chair outside the hotel's front door, looking as demure as possible.

"What's going on?" I asked.

"The Shah is coming. They say he's opening a factory today."

"But why are you out here on the sidewalk?"

"The manager told me to leave the room. I didn't want to go. But he insisted — the police won't allow anyone near an upstairs window."

Five minutes later, a police car drove past. More cars followed, then Jeeps with armed soldiers poised at the ready — in recent months violent protests against the Shah had broken out across much of Iran. Motorcycles arrived next, and a few bulky cars adapted to hold running boards; the men perching on them scanned the crowd. In their wake came a milk-coloured Cadillac, its windows wide open. Flags fluttered wildly in the children's hands.

A grey-haired man sat alone in the back of the Cadillac, his white uniform dripping ribbons and medals. Not just a king but a self-anointed emperor, he displayed his honours on his chest. The Shah offered a stiff wave as the car passed, his head turned in our direction. I noticed the dark-rimmed glasses on his face but not the expression of his lips. Within a year he would flee into exile and his kingdom would become a religious republic. In two years, he would be dead.

Further motorcycles thundered along, then another pair of cars equipped with running boards and watchful men. A final car sped by, and the motorcade was gone.

The hotel manager thanked Clare as the talkative crowd dispersed. He picked up her chair and invited us to follow him into a small courtyard behind the lobby. There he seated us at a rickety table with elaborate care. Bringing us each a glass of mint tea, he demonstrated a Persian way to drink: put a sugar lump between your teeth and sip the tea through it.

THE YOUNG MAN WHO saw the Shah go by on that first afternoon of May 1978 is almost as foreign to me now as the temples and mosques he explored across Asia, the bazaars he haunted, the street stalls where he purchased doner kebab or aloo chaat. He was an observer, an idealist. He worried that a God-shaped emptiness was growing inside him, and he hoped a three-month journey overland from Istanbul to Kathmandu might help to fill the hole. He was more innocent than he realized; more ignorant, too.

He wrote nearly every day on the journey, filling two unlined notebooks and half-filling a third. The notebooks, which were the colour of ripe tomatoes, said "Plain" on the front. He had bought them in the WHSmith shop on Cornmarket Street in Oxford, and every time he pulled one out of his backpack he felt a twinge of nostalgia. In the future, or so he hoped, Asian images, sensations, and memories would infuse his poetry. He wanted to be a great poet. (Later, he would have been happy to be a good poet.) I forgive his ambition. I admire his tenacity. I'm embarrassed by his awkwardness.

It's not only the hair loss, the beard's greying, the growth of body fat that make the young man a stranger to me today. It's everything I've done since 1978, and everything that has been done to me. It's becoming a husband, a father. It's working for many years in publishing and journalism. It's meeting people from a multitude of cultures and nations, and hearing the stories they tell. It's understanding the extreme privilege I enjoyed as a young man and realizing how much I took for granted. It's opening my eyes—or having them prised open—to much that escaped me at the time.

Who are you? the members of The Who would ask—

repeatedly—in the title song of their 1978 album. Who was I? When I set off for Istanbul, I was twenty-two and greedy for enlightenment. My mind overflowed with questions. Oxford had given me all the love, friendships, and ideas I could ask for, but I was a glutton: I wanted more.

I was living in a foreign country then. I don't mean England: I mean the past.

WE HAD REACHED SHIRAZ on a whim and a dare. Clare's whim; my dare.

"I'm rather keen on travelling to India in the spring," she casually remarked one afternoon as a massive horse chestnut tree shed its gold-brown leaves on the lawn outside an eighteenth-century college window. We were eating chocolate biscuits in the room of a mutual friend and sipping cups of milky tea. "Would you like to come?"

Would I? Of course I would. I had grown up in western Canada, and in my imagination India was a glamorous blur, redolent of incense, resonant with sitars. At first the blur had involved Rudyard Kipling's *Jungle Book* and *Kim*, which I read with baffled curiosity in a high-school English class in Saskatoon. Later my vision of India stretched to include the pacifist heroics of Mohandas Gandhi and the power politics of Indira Gandhi, his unrelated namesake. I knew nothing, however, about Orientalism; Edward Said's acute and dismaying book by that name would not be published until the final months of 1978. Said, a Palestinian intellectual, would diagnose a harmful vision of reality—Orientalism—in which, to Western eyes, "Orientals lived in their world, 'we' lived in ours.

The vision and material reality propped each other up, kept each other going. A certain freedom of intercourse was always the Westerner's privilege; because his was the stronger culture, he could penetrate, he could wrestle with, he could give shape and meaning to the great Asiatic mystery."

I plead guilty. Except my younger self craved something a little different: I hoped that Asia could give shape and meaning to the mystery of my own life.

At Oxford, where I spent long days on an aesthetic high with the potency of hash, I took yoga lessons from a lean and brilliant Ghanaian, the son of an exiled prime minister. I learned the rudiments of Tai Chi in a fire station turned arts centre. Having been brought up devoutly Anglican, I also made my communion at an Anglo-Catholic church where the clouds of incense matched the sermons in importance and surpassed them in intensity. On a retreat in Nashdom Abbey, a monastery of Anglican Benedictines, I bought a small replica of a Byzantine fresco and wondered, briefly, if I should become a monk. Yet apart from the troubling demand for chastity and the equally difficult call for obedience, a monastic life would have required me to accept doctrines I could no longer quite believe. Perhaps the vision and material reality of India would prop me up—or bring me down with a thud.

"We'd have to go overland, of course," Clare said. "I'm excited at the idea of visiting the superb mosques in Turkey and Iran. I imagine you would be, too."

She was a graduate student in history, and one of those Englishwomen who tend to conceal the intimidating breadth of their knowledge behind a façade of jaunty cheerfulness. In truth I knew nothing about the mosques of Turkey and Iran, superb or otherwise. Clare didn't propose the journey for the sake of her degree—Asian travel was a desire on her part, an urge rather than a need. While she loved fine art and architecture, she looked with skepticism on all religions. She was intrepid, inquisitive, and occasionally prone to sarcasm.

Unlike Clare, I lacked the money to embark on the trip with confidence. A generous scholarship was supporting me in Oxford, but I had never bothered to put much of the money aside, and my meagre savings would propel me only a little way across Asia. My parents struggled to pay their bills; I couldn't ask them for help. Unless I could raise hundreds of pounds in short order, India would remain the culmination of a road untravelled.

Then I saw that *Punch*—a venerable humour magazine that cluttered up the waiting rooms of English dentists and accountants—had launched a nationwide writing competition for students. The theme was life in 2001. *I'm a poet*, I thought, *not a humorist*. But alas, no poetry journal anywhere was sponsoring a contest with a first prize of five hundred pounds.

"All right," I told Clare. "I'll enter the competition. The odds are terrible. But if I win, I'll go with you to India."

I SUSPECTED THAT MOST of the other contestants would produce a comic variation on *2001: A Space Odyssey*. They might submit an entry in the clinical voice of HAL, explore the pleasures of waltzing on the moon, or insert a bone-throwing ape into a plate-glass Liverpool. I settled on a different approach.

In those autumnal weeks of 1977, with Margaret Thatcher little more than a cloud on the damp horizon, the dominant rhetoric in Britain was one of inexorable lament. The Empire was over and done with; the Irish Republican Army seemed able to bomb and assassinate at will; inflation quivered in constant double digits. "It has been a matter of supreme regret to me," wrote a former Conservative cabinet minister, the aptly named Quintin Hogg, "that my public life has taken place in a period of national humiliation and decline." I decided to carry this uniquely British dolefulness into the future, and so I composed a Christmas letter from an Englishman to a cousin abroad, satirizing a nation I knew mainly from Oxford, fragments of London, and the ever-anxious columns of *The Guardian*.

How would 2001 feel, I wondered, in a Britain where things had kept on getting worse? The country had staggered into the new century in the grip of an epidemic. Queen Elizabeth opened an oil museum, the North Sea having run out of fuel. The Post Office announced a plan to reduce its service, describing this as a "further improvement." England's football team failed to qualify for the World Cup after a 5–1 defeat at the boots of Luxembourg. Graham Greene celebrated his ninety-seventh birthday by publishing *The Frontiers of Gloom*, although the Nobel Prize eluded him yet again. And Shah-in-Shah Enterprises — formerly known as Harrod's — had begun to erect a giant red, white, and blue mosque opposite the Institute of Contemporary Arts.

This forlorn squib won first prize. I was wrong about the Shah, of course. But on the strength of my prophetic grumbling, I could just about afford to accompany Clare to India.

Contrary to the prevailing mood in Britain, I felt modestly hopeful about the future. The long nightmare of the Vietnam War had ended, and in China the Cultural Revolution had crashed to a halt. Nearly all the former colonies in Africa and the Caribbean had won their independence, and most of them were functional democracies. Europe had recovered from the devastation of Hitler's war with no renewed support for fascism and only a grey-cheeked dullard in the Kremlin. In the United States, a humane and honest Democrat held sway in the White House, allowing the corrupt debacle of Republican rule to fade into memory. Nothing as bad, surely, could happen again.

You may say I was a dreamer: I was not the only one. Admittedly rock had given way to punk and disco. But in other respects, the world appeared to be revolving smoothly.

I HAD BACKPACKED THROUGH various European countries, yet I'd never set foot in what was then called the "Third World": nations beyond the grip of both the United States and the Soviet Union, and supposedly free to find their own way forward. In the serious press, much ink flowed about the challenges of "underdevelopment." At Oxford I'd met a few students from subtropical cities in what many people still referred to as the *British* Commonwealth, but my dealings with them had been superficial. Back in Canada I knew nobody who was Indigenous. My father and mother—immigrants from Britain—owned no buildings or land in either country. It was easy for me to avoid thinking about my own links to colonialism.

I had no idea that St. John's College in Oxford, where I'd spent two and a half glorious years immersed in English literature, had welcomed benefactions from men who made a fortune off slavery. Among the college's small treasures is a cigar box of wood and beaten silver showing the Hindu gods Vishnu and Lakshmi, both floating in a divine sea of milk.

The cigar box once belonged to the 1st Viscount Kitchener of Khartoum — a butchering general in Sudan, an overseer of concentration camps in South Africa, and a commander-in-chief of the British Army in India.

Although I hadn't laid hands on the cigar box, I had spent my share of time in Rhodes House. Indeed the money sustaining me in Oxford ultimately came from the exorbitant profits that Cecil Rhodes had snatched from the gold and diamond mines of southern Africa, some of them still producing cash for a racially segregated, white-ruled nation by the name of Rhodesia. Rhodes, like Kitchener, took little interest in women; they played no part in his scheme of the imperial future except as the mothers of talented sons. The scholarships he founded were, when I arrived in Oxford, open only to young men. In Rhodesia and South Africa, they were open only to young *white* men. I had enjoyed vast privilege based on vast injustice.

In his last will and testament, Rhodes outlined an assortment of qualities he wanted his scholars to display, including "fondness of and success in manly outdoor sports such as cricket football and the like." (I'm still not sure how I qualified.) He also mapped out a visionary goal for the twentieth century: "The furtherance of the British Empire, for the bringing of the whole uncivilised world under British rule...making the Anglo-Saxon race but one Empire." The Rhodes Trust, at that time still riddled with aristocrats and merchant bankers, gave all its newly minted scholars a pamphlet celebrating the founder's achievements; it spoke of "the savage barbarism of Southern and Central Africa before the advent of the European." The savage oppression in the diamond mines went unmentioned. The Trust was echoing its founder, who had urged the white-run Cape

Colony to adopt a system of "despotism in our relations with the barbarians of South Africa."

I had fed off this legacy for years, and I had not protested.

AFTER WE AGREED TO TRAVEL, Clare and I fell in love, though not with each other. Our timing was terrible—except that Annie was in the last year of an undergraduate program and her all-important final exams would take place in June. In her springtime Oxford, I told myself, I would be a black-bearded distraction with a Canadian accent. By June I should have crossed through Turkey, Iran, Afghanistan, and Pakistan, reaching northern India or even Nepal.

"Go ahead," she insisted. "Make the trip." Clare's new boyfriend said the same.

Distance would serve as a test. If Annie and I could survive three months apart, perhaps we could survive decades together.

So Clare and I endured a barrage of checkups, vaccinations, dental work, X-rays, and gamma globulin injections. We booked one-way train tickets from London to Istanbul, and one-way flights from Delhi back to London. In between, nothing was fixed. Our itinerary would be up to fate—we made no detailed plans. We knew only that we would travel by local bus and train, shunning Magic Bus, Swagman Tours, Budget Bus, Top Deck, and other such companies whose vehicles plied a bumpy route between western Europe and Nepal, deciding where their shaggy passengers could go and what they could see.

"It might get quite hot in India," Clare said. "They say it always does, before the monsoons."

"As long as we don't run into any riots or *coups d'état*," I replied.

"Oh, I wouldn't worry about that."

For much of the journey we would be following the Hippie Trail, a route taken by hundreds of thousands of young Westerners in the previous fifteen years. Not that either of us saw ourselves as hippies — or "freaks," to use the favoured term of the day. (The informal terminus of the trail was a passageway in the heart of Kathmandu known to foreign visitors as Freak Street, not Hippie Street.) We were overlanders, with less of a hunger for illicit substances and more of a taste for architectural marvels than the lion's share of Western travellers. We were also students, having reached an age when most people in western and southern Asia had long since left school and begun to earn a living or had already borne children. And we were tourists, who squirmed away from the label. Serious-minded travellers never like to confess they are perpetrating tourism.

We had enough self-assurance to ignore the risks of the trip. Malaria was said to be rampant in parts of Pakistan, India, and Nepal. Rabid dogs could bite anywhere. Even if our shots in the arm kept typhoid and hepatitis at bay, they could not protect us from dysentery. I bought a money belt to secure my passport, cash, and travellers' cheques: we knew that budget hotels and hostels could be a magnet for thieves. But there was nothing new or surprising about all this. I felt more worried about the future of my relationship with Annie than I did about any hardships I might face in the Khyber Pass. My childhood faith in the Christian God had started to erode at Oxford, yet I retained a sturdy (and perhaps imperial) belief in my ability to roam the world without harm. Admittedly, some backpackers came to grief. Mick Jagger, in his stylish impersonation of the devil, had promised to set traps for troubadours who would die before they reached Bombay. But we would stay alert for traps, and we intended to skip Bombay.

Our route would be established by improvisation and common sense, spiced with an occasional dash of guidebook insight. In the 1970s, Lonely Planet was in its infancy and Rough Guides were still unborn. We relied on a mustard-coloured paperback that Clare had bought: the 1976 edition of *Student Guide to Asia*, written and published in Australia. The further east we travelled, the more helpful it would become. The book devoted only five pages to Turkey, nearly all of them on İstanbul, compared to its seventeen pages on Singapore and fifty-six on Indonesia. While most of its chapters were no use to us, we took note of a stern and salutary warning in the introduction: "To many Asians, the continuing influx of young Western travellers resembles nothing so much as a passing parade of outlandishly dressed tramps and trollops." Anyone who wears a backpack, the guidebook said, meets with scorn. "In short, travellers have managed to get themselves a bad name. They are tolerated in most countries, but only just."

By 1978, overlanders were sporting fewer bangles and bandanas than a few years earlier, and a tightening enforcement of drug laws across the continent meant travellers were also less likely to shoot up or smoke up. What endured was a dismay at Western materialism and a desire to imagine Asia as a contin-ent of the spirit. Decades before the Hippie Trail emerged, Hermann Hesse conjured the hope that would inform it in his novella *The Journey to the East*. Hesse's narrator, speaking for all of Europe's fresh-faced wanderers, explains: "Our goal was not only the East, or rather the East was not only a country and something geographical, but it was the home and youth of the soul." He declares that "we conquered the war-shattered world by our faith and transformed it into Paradise." Such extravagant claims go a long way toward explaining Hesse's popularity: he elevated youthful illusions into literature.

As historical movements go, the Hippie Trail was a brief one. Born in the early 1960s, it would expire by 1979. It was both a by-product and a casualty of politics. The Western students and vagabonds who took to Asia's roads and railways had come of age at a time when wealth and expectations were rising in tandem. We enjoyed the luxury of contemplating the busy planet and our own place in it, confident that jobs would always be there for the taking, eventually, if we needed them. Many of us — sidestepping any thought of what our parents had suffered when they were young — scoffed at their shiny cars and appliances, their conventional beliefs and prejudices. We focused on the dulling misery beneath. Theirs was a fate, a quagmire, we were determined to avoid. Surely the ancient wisdom of Asia might reveal a more fulfilling way of life. Or if not, the dope would be cheap.

Who are you? We were on the road to become ourselves.

We knew little about where we were going: for many of us, until we hit the road, Asia was an alluring blank. We dreamed about the intoxicating effect that Afghanistan, India, and other countries would have on us. We never thought about the sobering impact of our presence on people there.

THE MATERIAL WORLD HAS been transformed since the collapse of the Hippie Trail. Less obvious are the profound changes in realms of the mind. Picking up the trio of red notebooks and leafing through them for the first time in decades, I noticed the lack of countless phrases and words that English speakers take for granted today. *Social media, email, website*: none of these terms existed in 1978. Neither did *AIDS* or *safe sex*. *Twitter* was a verb referring to songbirds. *Hip hop* was something rabbits did in children's books. *CDs*— antiquated objects now— belonged to the future then. What on Earth could *Wi-Fi* mean? Smartphones, spreadsheets, laptops, bitcoin: unimaginable, all. Nobody worried about climate change or global heating; *biodiversity* wasn't even a term. Neither was *alt right*.

By travelling overland through Asia, Clare and I placed ourselves profoundly out of touch with the people we loved. We were on our own to an extent that nowadays may be hard to imagine. For all the crowds, noise, and confusion it entails, travel can be a quest for solitude. If so, Clare and I succeeded at our task. International phone calls would have been complex to arrange and, for us, brutally expensive. Our only word from home came in the letters and cards we picked up in the central post offices of a few Asian cities by means of Poste Restante (a term that has vanished in the decades since). Those shiny postcards and flimsy blue airmail letters reminded us of what we'd left behind. They also bolstered our faith in what lay ahead. Otherwise we were immersed in a river of sudden, uncertain currents.

Bliss was it in that dawn to be alive... Well, maybe not. It had its blissful moments, to be sure. But while this book describes a journey I made through physical space, its pages are also a modest attempt to evoke a juncture in history. Certain places Clare and I visited in the final year of the Hippie Trail are almost inaccessible to Westerners now. Others I would find unrecognizable if I were ever to return. What we heard in parts of Asia seems like a ragged, discordant prelude to the shattering music of the future. Some of our experiences on the road from Istanbul to Kathmandu may shed an oblique light on events that have occurred since 1978, and on processes still at work today. Or cast a shadow.

At points in Asia, I tried to be a camera. I thought that as I filled my notebooks with details of the hour, I would capture small truths about people and places. Yet the details were simply impressions: written in my own language, laden with my own values, pervaded by my own biases. Places and people endure and evolve, but time disappears. When I open the notebooks now, I don't see the alleyways of India or the gardens of Iran: I see scribbled imprints of a lost era. Perhaps my journals are a photograph of time.

THE HOTEL MANAGER STOOD UP, excusing himself with grace. We could hear the noise of the Shiraz traffic regaining its usual volume. Clare and I stayed a few minutes longer in the court-yard, sipping our glasses of tea. The afternoon—the journey itself—seemed vibrant with hope.

"Did you get a good look at the Shah?" she asked.

"Yes. Ridiculous number of medals. What is he trying to prove?"

"I wonder if we'll run into anyone else who's famous."

"That's highly unlikely," I said. I put a new lump of sugar in my mouth and drew the tea up through it.

A siren blared in the distance. An engine backfired on the street.

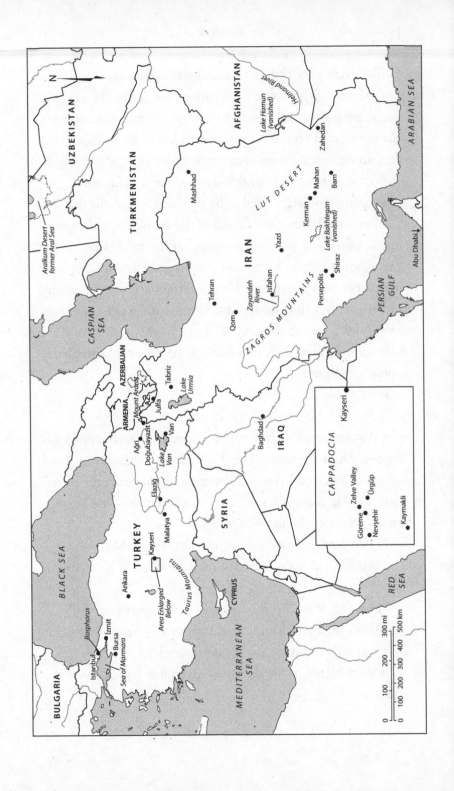

1.

Turkey

"You wouldn't want to know"

Clare and I hugged our partners goodbye at Oxford station. The time had come. Trapped in a clump of commuters with neckties and briefcases, I tried to look confident; Clare succeeded in looking determined. Doubts battered me. What was I doing? How could this trip, any trip, justify a wilful absence from love?

I heaved my navy blue backpack and sleeping bag onto my shoulders and found a pair of seats on the train. It was a cold grey day: along Port Meadow the morning river drank up the sky. Oxford's intricate pattern of spires and domes retreated all too fast. A woman sitting near us spent the hour to London Paddington poring over a copy of *The Times* — a copy that was four weeks old. In April's infancy, the beeches and oaks by the Thames stood bare. London was a Tube-smelling blur. Twice, without thinking, I stretched out to hold Clare's hand and managed to pull back in time.

We crossed the English Channel by ferry and climbed aboard a waiting train in France. A few years earlier I would have felt overjoyed to alight in the country; now it scarcely registered in my mind. *Un croque monsieur, s'il vous plaît*—dreams of India and Nepal kept flickering behind my eyelids—*et un café au lait.* I could imagine the sleekly flowing Ganges and the soaring Himalayan peaks we hoped to see after two months on the road. I could not imagine the chained bear, the belly-dancing teenagers, the drunk driver, or the truckloads of riot police we would encounter in the first two weeks.

France gave way to Switzerland. Hours later, the train having chugged into a town in northern Italy, a passenger raised a window, stretched out an arm and snapped off a sprig of pine. He set it down on a narrow shelf—its sharp, fresh scent filled the compartment until we rolled to a halt beside the Grand Canal. The champagne splendours of the Orient Express, with its murders and sofas and wood-panelled sleeping cars, were no more: indeed, a direct Paris-to-Istanbul train had made its final run a year earlier. I didn't mind. Before heading east again, we gave ourselves a night and day in the amphibious pomp of Venice. A pair of stone lions that we noticed at the entrance to its ancient shipyard commemorate a victory over the Ottoman Empire—through the long centuries when the city was a sovereign republic, it fought seven wars against the Turks and launched a disastrous crusade. Like so much of Europe, Venice had defined itself in opposition to Islam and the Orient.

I hadn't bothered to obtain a Yugoslav visa, assuming it would be simple to buy one on the next leg of the journey. But an hour shy of midnight, after the train shuddered to a

halt at Italy's eastern border, a beetle-browed guard seized my
Canadian passport and held on to it.

"This way," he said. "Come."

I stepped down into a chilly darkness. The guard strode off
between two sets of railway tracks past the front of the train.
He disappeared into a small, dimly lit building, leaving me
alone outside. I stood there, conscious that my ticket was still
in my backpack and my backpack was still on the train. Time
slipped by. A bemused Australian girl on her way to a Greek
island joined me at the door. Our talk lapsed into silence. A few
other passengers arrived, their voices clearer than their faces in
the moonless night. What if the train moved off without us?

But once the door creaked open, the visas were distributed
quickly and free of charge. My relief felt as vast as Europe.

I repaid the Yugoslav officials by smuggling a new pair of
jeans into their country. Clare did the same. A couple from
Belgrade asked us to do this: they would earn a handsome profit
if we helped them sidestep the country's import laws. Paul, a
young artist from London with a sketchpad and a determined
gaze, found room to stash away two pairs of jeans and a pocket
calculator. The Yugoslav couple beamed at us all.

Was the train muscling through Slovenia or Croatia as a
grey dawn broke? In 1978, who outside the Balkans thought a
question like that could ever matter? Warfare in eastern Europe
surely belonged to the past. For an hour the train shadowed
a copper-coloured river, magpies and hooded crows flapping
heavily away toward a chain of burly mountains. A shepherd
holding a crook oversaw a flock of dark-faced sheep. The
massive high-rise blocks of Belgrade loomed into sight; the
smiling Yugoslav couple wobbled out of our compartment

and staggered off the train, their arms full of jeans and other Italian purchases. I dozed through the limestone hills of eastern Serbia and woke to a fox, its mouth full of some small bird or mammal, standing in a muddy field and watching the train pass. The trees wore a sumptuous formal attire of white and pink blossoms.

At the Bulgarian frontier, the guard inspecting our documents turned out to be a football fan. He picked up Clare's British passport: "England! Bobby Charlton. Bobby Moore." He must, judging by his looks, have been a teenager in 1966 when an English squad won the World Cup for the first and only time. "Geoff Hurst," I said. Barely glancing at my Canadian passport, he replied: "Gordon Banks." Damn, who else was on the team? I rummaged the depths of my memory—"Martin Peters!" The guard was relentless: "Alan Ball." I lifted my empty hands. He nodded his head in triumph. So much for the Iron Curtain.

Border followed border. After a long wait at the final one, we crossed into Turkey and a young, clean-shaven lab technician took an empty seat nearby. He came from a town in the recently divided island of Cyprus—a Turkish invasion in 1974 had sliced it in two, preventing the entire nation from being forcibly incorporated into Greece. Clare and I had no Turkish lira. Discovering this, Emir bought us each a sesame-seed pastry. For him, the price of a secure homeland was the absence of a country: his passport, though issued by Turkey, had a blank in the space marked "nationality." This hampered his ability to travel. He'd married an Englishwoman, he told us, but when he arrived at the port of Dover to meet her family, the British authorities refused to let him in.

"Why?" he asked. "She is my wife."

Clare and I made sympathetic noises.

Emir wanted to talk. Moving on from the tale of his own life, he recounted a story that has circulated in Turkey, Iran, and central Asia for hundreds of years. You can see the hero, Nasreddin Hodja, as a holy fool, a trickster, a wise man, or all three. He is a mullah—a highly unorthodox one.

In the story, a wealthy neighbour named Aslan tries to play a mean joke on Nasreddin. The mullah is praying for money—he and his wife, Fatima, survive amid empty shelves—when Aslan delivers a bagful of gold coins. Nasreddin thinks, or pretends to think, that the gold is a payment from God. But Aslan soon demands the money back, and he takes the mullah to court. At this point, Nasreddin devises a plan to outwit his neighbour. And a judge, having heard both men speak, tells the mullah to hold on to the gold.

That's how the story usually goes. Yet that's not quite what Emir told us as the train rattled across the plains of western Turkey. His Nasreddin was a proud Turk, the rich neighbour a businessman from Athens.

"So you see," Emir said, "the Turk keeps the money."

He flashed a broad smile—I saw a glint of metal between his lips. A timeworn Nasreddin story had become a parable of national honour.

It's curious that in the traditional telling, the neighbour's name is Aslan. Generations of English-speaking children have grown up reading the Narnia novels by C. S. Lewis and knowing Aslan as the righteous lion—Jesus with four legs and a mighty roar. The word *aslan* is, in fact, Turkish for "lion." But in *The Lion, the Witch and the Wardrobe*, the first of the Narnia

books to be published, Edmund falls into sin when he greed-
ily devours some morsels of Turkish Delight. A later novel in
the series, *The Horse and His Boy*, features villainous horsemen
of an arid land who brandish scimitars, possess slaves, wear
turbans, and obey a grand vizier. Those images match what
a few of Shakespeare's characters say about Turks: "malignant
and turbaned," "the circumcised dog," and "never trained to
offices of tender courtesy."

The Narnia books, like *Othello* and *The Merchant of Venice*,
point up the uneasy, menacing place Turkey has filled in the
Western imagination. Its religion, its army, its culture, its system
of government all provoked scorn and fear. For centuries, the
folk plays that were performed at Christmastime in England,
Ireland, and Newfoundland took St. George as the hero and
a Turkish knight as his dastardly foe. Taken to a nightmarish
extreme, this sense of foreign threat saturates *Midnight Express*,
a Hollywood movie about the sufferings of an American student
in a Turkish jail. The warders, the policemen, and the prisoners
are sadistic, boorish, or both. *Midnight Express* would receive
its world premiere at the Cannes Film Festival six weeks after
our arrival in Istanbul.

The final railway guard to check our tickets noticed a pack
of Camels protruding from Paul's jacket. A second pair lay in
his bag, beside some art supplies. The guard offered to buy the
cigarettes and quoted an excellent price. The men stepped into
the corridor to complete the deal. But a Turkish soldier was
loitering there and the guard walked away, entering the next
compartment without a word.

"What just happened?" Paul asked as he slumped down
again.

"The soldier would take the cigarettes," Emir said, "but he would not pay." He did not seem surprised. "I was two years in the army," he added. "I did not enjoy."

The staccato rhythm of wheels echoed through my head: *Impatiently, impatiently*... My limbs felt cramped and sore from so much train-sitting. I found it impossible, as another night ebbed, to read more than a single paragraph of V. S. Naipaul. In the seat across from me, Clare was chewing her fingernails. Neither of us wanted to admit our nervousness. We were at last approaching the Bosphorus—the strait that divides Europe from Asia. Its name is Greek, meaning "ox ford."

A watery sun dawned over pastures and rugged farmland. Twenty or more storks stood motionless on a patch of plowed earth. Their white necks and red legs shone in the early light.

DECADES LATER I CAN'T remember the storks, but I trust my journal. I would fail to understand a lot of people on the trip and would miss the meaning of certain events, but I'm confident I got the birds right. The notebooks sketch a telling portrait of the young man I was: a poet, a birdwatcher, a worrier, a lapsing Christian. My backpack had no room for a pair of binoculars, and my funds did not extend to an expensive camera. But I looked on my journal as a kind of lens. Sometimes I turned it on myself.

Even when the backpack didn't weigh my shoulders down, I stood apart from the cultures around me. Privilege gave me the power to interpret what I saw as a spectacle, a sort of technicolour pageant, and to judge it accordingly. "The Orientalist," Edward Said was soon to write, "poet or scholar, makes the

Orient speak, describes the Orient, renders its mysteries plain
for and to the West. He is never concerned with the Orient
except as the first cause of what he says." The other travellers on
the Hippie Trail shared the privilege of detached judgment; the
local people we met did not. We might scrutinize a mosque or
temple for its age and beauty; they would worship in it.

Our vision quests overlapped with their everyday lives. What
to us seemed exotic was merely normal in their eyes. But the
reverse is also true: many of the youthful Westerners in Asia
were brightly coloured birds of passage, and our garish plumage
could attract both envy and derision. We had taken flight; we
had fled the nest. Few of the overlanders had reached the age
of thirty. We felt a hunger to explore or escape, and we had
enough money to appease our curiosity. (*To live in one land*,
wrote the poet John Donne, *is captivity*.) We also enjoyed the
luxury of time. Money and time allowed some of us to finish
growing up on the road.

But enough of "we." I don't want to speak for anyone else,
not even (or especially) Clare. Her journey through Asia was
not the same as mine. It was shaped by her knowledge of history and her resolutely English perspective. It was shaped by
being a woman. It was shaped, most of all, by the experience
of travelling with me.

ISTANBUL PROVED TO BE full of 1950s Dodges and DeSoto
Diplomats. Clare and I emerged from a vaulted, high-ceilinged
railway station and skirted the morning crowds. The finned cars
were trundling past horse-drawn carts on muddy streets that
pushed up from the banks of the Bosphorus. If we'd landed

here a thousand years earlier, we would have been standing in the heart of a Christian city named Constantinople, the capital of the Byzantine Empire, gazing with awe on marble-walled thoroughfares, towering columns, public baths, a chariot-racing stadium, and, I suppose, similarly humble carts pulled by equally weary horses.

Abode of Happiness. Sublime Porte. Second Rome. City of the World's Desire. To these ancient monikers for Constantinople and Istanbul, I thought a new one could be added: *Ringer of Ears.* The engines, mufflers, and blurting car horns all but drowned out the muezzins' calls to prayer. Yet the amplified muezzins all but silenced the foghorns in the Bosphorus, where ships were tracing a careful passage between the Mediterranean and the Black Sea. By the ornate arches of Istanbul University's main gate, shielded from some of the city's noise, an old man sat on the ground and played a set of Turkish bagpipes: more flutelike than their Scottish counterpart, and without such a robust drone.

We stayed in a rundown coldwater hotel, where I woke in the half-light from a nagging dream: I'd been attempting to change trains in a station outside London while clutching a salmon sandwich. Any four-footed private in Istanbul's army of slender cats would have loved a meal like that. I saw and heard a pair of them mating outside the hotel, ten feet up a budding tree. Two males waited optimistically at the base of the trunk.

In the stripped hulk of the Church of St. Irene—built in what I would have called the Dark Ages—a soft flutter of wings mingled with the cooing of pigeons and the babble of sparrows. A rooster crowed from a nearby yard. At one end of the church stood an assortment of cannons—the silent residue of recent centuries when the building served as an arsenal, a warehouse, and a weapons museum. "I sometimes think myself unlucky," the novelist Orhan Pamuk would write in *Istanbul,* his loving portrait-cum-memoir, "to have been born in an aging and impoverished city buried under the ashes of a ruined empire. But a voice inside me always insists this was really a piece of luck." The floor had birdshit on it.

We arrived in Rustem Pasha, a small mosque four centuries old, during a time of prayer. Clare knew she would need to conceal her long hair and remove her shoes before venturing inside, but to my surprise I too had to find a head covering. A sign set out the rules and added "Thank you for your coordination." About twenty men were already inside, each of them praying separately. Then an imam moved forward and knelt at the blue-tiled mihrab — a niche in the wall signifying the direction of Mecca. The men lined up behind him, facing south-southeast, as the imam began to chant. I felt as if the magnificent tilework was echoing with prayer.

Heavy leather curtains took the place of doors in Rustem Pasha, and scents drifted in from a spice market: ginger, cinnamon, mace. Outside the mosque Clare fed a few dried berries to a stray mongrel with a broken leg. A black-and-white cat approached us too, but we had nothing for her. She lay down anyway beside the dog — they must have been old friends.

The following day a much fatter cat lingered by my ankles while Clare and I ate stuffed peppers in a freak hangout known to foreigners as the Pudding Shop — a modest restaurant whose menu juxtaposed Turkish cuisine with Western food. It warranted a couple of mentions in *Student Guide to Asia.* Amid the torn jeans, ankle bracelets, and occasional kurtas in the

Pudding Shop, I scanned the messages from travellers, most of them in English, pinned on a bulletin board. The complaints, invitations, pleas, and recommendations were an authentic foretaste of the Hippie Trail — Emily from Adelaide praised a hotel in Kabul and added five hearts after her name — but was this the kind of authenticity I wanted? A man with bushy sideburns emerged from a phone booth and lurched through the restaurant in a daze.

With their pipes and sandals, their free-range hair and beards, some of our fellow Westerners in Asia drew immediate attention to themselves. Maybe they were born to run. Patrick Marnham, in *Road to Katmandu*, an early and jaundiced description of life on the Hippie Trail, evoked "these displaced persons, fugitives from the social and economic wars of Europe and North America" — he forgot Australia and New Zealand, which provided a disproportionately high number of overlanders. Marnham compared the travellers he met to deserters: "Most of them had not yet taken their first job and already they needed another chance; they were searching for a way out of the snare which their lives had become. And so, like men in a panic, they ran."

His account holds a grain of harsh truth, although it ignores the women on the road. But while Marnham heightened the edgy desperation, he underplayed the joy of adventure and, in many of us, the idealism. What I sensed in the Pudding Shop was not panic but camaraderie, as if young people from a host of Western countries had come together to share a mutual dream. I felt a mixture of elation and annoyance: Were these hungry travellers my tribe, my community? And hadn't I set off for Asia to get away from them all?

"The most characteristic mark of the tourist," wrote the American historian Eric J. Leed, "is the wish to avoid tourists and the places they congregate." Accordingly, Clare and I quit the Pudding Shop and wandered off to a less crowded site for coffee (I overcame my initial urge to ask for "Greek coffee"). We were sitting at an outdoor table near the grand bazaar when a coffin moved slowly past. Arabic calligraphy adorned its green velvet cover. Every few yards the four men who were carrying the coffin stopped to put it down, and four others stepped up to replace them. Finally the coffin vanished into the bazaar.

LIKE MANY OF THE little shops in Istanbul, the café kept a photograph of Kemal Atatürk on display. In the decades after the First World War, Atatürk had lifted his country from the decrepit shambles of the Ottoman Empire and moulded it into a modern, secular state. His face—hawklike, big-nosed, unsmiling—lent a constant air of gravitas to whatever wall it occupied. He was a field marshal before the presidency beckoned; but for his victories on the battlefield, Turkey would be a smaller, weaker nation now.

Atatürk expressed scorn for organized religion—he may well have been an atheist. "The Turkish Republic cannot be the country of sheikhs or dervishes," he declared. "If we want to be men, we must carry out the dictates of civilization." As his idea of civilization was a staunchly Western one, the Muslim calendar gave way to its European counterpart and Arabic lettering, in which Turkish had been written for centuries, surrendered to the Latin alphabet. The nation's laws were redrafted in light of Italian, Swiss, German, and French models. Women gained full legal and political rights, and a man could no longer have several wives. Sufi dervishes and other religious leaders faced imprisonment; and the fez, a symbol of Ottoman manhood, was banned under a Hat Law of 1925 that obliged men to wear Western-style hats in public.

Thanks to Atatürk's fierce secularism, Hagia Sophia—the central building of the city through fourteen centuries—closed as a mosque and reopened as a museum. I'd been yearning to see it. Gold-encrusted, marble-columned, high-domed, breathtaking in scale and ambition, Hagia Sophia had been the grandest church in Christendom from the moment of its consecration in 537 under the Byzantine emperor Justinian. Its name means "holy wisdom" in Greek. A self-referential mosaic in a vestibule shows the Virgin Mary and a miniature Jesus flanked, on the one hand, by Justinian holding a model of the church and, on the other, by the emperor Constantine gripping a model of the city.

"There's a legend about Hagia Sophia," Paul had told us on the train. "If you stand in just the right place under the dome and close your eyes, you'll see things that are happening in all four corners of the globe." (I tried this, but it didn't work.) "Because this is the focal point. This is the heart of it all."

At its height of wealth and prestige, Hagia Sophia employed seven hundred clergy. Its capture by the Ottomans in 1453 symbolized the final collapse of Constantinople: Islam was now supreme in an empire that would soon stretch from northwest Africa and central Europe all the way down the Red Sea to the Gulf of Aden. The conquerors transformed Hagia Sophia into a mosque, and so it remained until Atatürk set to work. He didn't remove the minarets or the massive wooden discs the

Ottomans had added to Hagia Sophia. But he forbade religious services of any kind to be held in what had been a mosque for half a millennium, and he ordered the resplendent Byzantine frescoes and mosaics, long since painted over, to be uncovered and exposed again to light and air. Exploring an upper gallery in Hagia Sophia, I came upon the golden original of the icon I'd bought in Nashdom Abbey: Jesus standing between his mother and a sombre John the Baptist, offering a blessing to the world, serene, beyond all hurt.

Clare and I left Hagia Sophia and found a young brown bear muzzled and chained near the main steps. A camera-happy throng surrounded its owner: a Romany man with a furrowed red face, a tawny moustache, and a white beard. If we'd handed him some coins, he would have forced the bear to dance.

NIGHT BROUGHT A HIGH wind and a raucous thunderstorm. Next morning Clare and I caught a ferry to Asia (or, less grandly, "We went to a different part of Istanbul"). There we ate flatbread and salted lemons in an outdoor café, and ambled through a hilly impoverished neighbourhood where the donkeys, men, and horses all carried daunting loads on their backs. Some of the women wore headscarves and black robes, leaving only part of their faces visible. Plangent music pealed from radios in every second shop. A venerable Dodge transporting a newly married couple — or a couple about to be married — sported a cascade of red and white carnations.

"You're taking an awful lot of notes," Clare said.

We were still getting used to each other. She knew I wanted to be a writer, yet she may have felt bemused at the volume of words I could cram onto a page and the amount of time I spent doing so. Besides, she had an excellent memory; mine was leaky and erratic. Apart from its potential use as a resource for future poems, notetaking allowed me to sift through events and weigh their meaning. It gave me a tool to manage my growing sense of culture shock.

Clare and I observed a white-and-lion-coloured cat surveying the city from a tiled roof. The cat must have had a terrific view of all the tea brewers, cassette vendors, stamp traders, and broom sellers, not to mention the men who squatted on Istanbul pavements with nothing before them but a pair of scales, hoping for someone or something to weigh. Or, perhaps, hoping for a donation, the gift of alms being a pillar of Islam. Dust from a half-built garage flew at my face; it lodged behind my contact lenses and raked my eyes until tears flowed to relieve the pain.

"Hello," children playing in a schoolyard called out to us. "Hello. Hello! Goodbye."

Then we sailed back across the Bosphorus to a vibrant realm of florists and cobblers and a lost world of hammered gold and gold enamelling, dreaming of what was past, and passing, and to come.

ATATÜRK WAS AN AUTOCRAT: he ruled a one-party state. Seven years would elapse after his death in 1938 before Turkey began to wobble toward a Western-style democracy. When Clare and I arrived in the nation, its prime minister was a poet and former journalist named Bülent Ecevit. A canny politician, and the longtime head of Turkey's social democratic party, Ecevit had translated T. S. Eliot into Turkish. *That sounds good*, I thought. I assumed that Turkey, like its NATO allies, would pursue a secular path. I imagined its future would be European.

Too simple. Whether in artistic, social, spiritual, or economic terms—not just geographical ones—Turkey is Asian as well as European. Indeed the country is a fulcrum, a pivot, a perpetual high-wire act. I didn't realize that the military had carried out coups in 1960 and 1971 before lending power back to the politicians. Nor did I know that on May Day in 1977, dozens of left-wing demonstrators in the commercial heart of Istanbul had been killed in an unprovoked attack. The murderers escaped. Weeks before we reached the city, seven students at Istanbul University died and forty-one suffered injuries in an assault by the Grey Wolves, a paramilitary force that fused Turkish nationalism with hardline Islamist beliefs.

I thought Ecevit represented the future: democratic and liberal. I was wrong. The Grey Wolves, emboldened by atrocity, would grow in membership and influence. Two years after our trip, a further military coup put a halt to all political life. Although the generals did not retain power for long, the ensuing decades have depleted Atatürk's humanist vision and worn away his secular reforms. Hagia Sophia's role as a national museum would be among the casualties. In 2020, Turkey's president, Recep Tayyip Erdoğan, announced the building would revert to a previous identity. "Hopefully it will serve as a mosque until eternity," he said. He recited verses from the Quran on Hagia Sophia's first day of formal prayers in nearly a century. Henceforth, every Friday, Jesus and the saints would be invisible, the Byzantine mosaics hidden from view.

Turkey's identity now hangs in the balance. Atatürk

once described Islam as "the absurd theology of an immoral Bedouin." But Erdoğan has suggested Islamic law should govern the country. "For us," he explained, "democracy is a means to an end."

ISTANBUL HAD LONG BEEN a glamorous destination in the minds of roving Europeans and North Americans — the climax and finale of the Orient Express. Yet for overlanders on the Hippie Trail, the city functioned instead as a gateway, a departure point. It marked a definitive farewell to Europe.

Clare and I left in a mist of cologne and a fog of music. The cologne came from a spray bottle wielded by a teenage conductor just before the sleek bus pulled out of the station. He walked down the aisle, squirting a sweet lemon fragrance onto the hands of women and men alike. The music was whatever the driver's favourite radio station chose to provide. The station interspersed Turkish pop with a smatter of European and American items: the *Pink Panther* theme, a syncopated update of a Mozart symphony, and "London Bridge Is Falling Down" banged out on a xylophone. "Hello, children," a woman said in a honeyed English voice as the nursery rhyme ended. "How are you all today?"

We were still in the city's outskirts at that point, overlooking the Sea of Marmara and its fleet of steel-grey Turkish warships. I marvelled at the sprawl. Fuelled by a recent migration of families from small towns and villages, the Istanbul we saw had swelled to house 2.7 million people. A large city, though not the size of London, Paris, or Berlin. In years to come, the rural economy would fray and the migration become more intense.

The Turkish novelist Elif Shafak, grieved at the way her beloved city had turned into a giant construction site, would compare it to "a bloated goldfish," already having gobbled too much for its own good yet still searching for food. By 2022, Istanbul would easily be Europe's biggest city (if you include those living east of the Bosphorus), with sixteen million residents.

İzmit, briefly the capital of the eastern Roman Empire, passed in a haze of oil refineries and cement works. Clare and I perched near the front of the bus, giving us a fine prospect not only of the industrial landscape but also of the plastic heart, the plastic crescent moon, and the red plastic flowers hanging down the windshield. The driver, polite and amiable when passengers boarded, behaved like a tyrant at the wheel, manoeuvring the bus past cars and vans even when the oncoming lane was busy, and forcing slow-moving vehicles onto the roadside. He used his horn so often, it sounded a fitful brass accompaniment to the radio tunes.

"Do you think the driving will always be like this?" Clare said.

"Probably," I replied. I'd never had much trouble believing the worst. Clare and I were feeling more at ease with each other now, more at ease with Turkey as well.

The driver, satisfied with his loud progress, pulled the bus over for a short break at a café by the Sea of Marmara. The café's name: Aberdeen Steak House.

Hours later, the bus ride receding into memory, we sat on a hilltop, the city of Bursa spread out below us. Clare counted twenty-five minarets in a minute. Red-roofed, white-tiled houses stretched out toward a green plain richly fed by thermal springs. "Bursa consists of nothing but water!"—or so wrote a seventeenth-century traveller named Evliya Çelebi, so impressed by the city's fountains that he indulged in wild overstatement. As we peered at it from above, Bursa seemed beyond the ravages of time.

The extinct volcano to the south had once been the home of a Byzantine saint. A swineherd and soldier in his youth, Joannicius lived alone as a hermit monk. I doubted the tale that he could render himself invisible, but I half-believed the claim that he could levitate; in the 1970s, the Maharishi Mahesh Yogi made the same assertion. The story I wanted to believe tells how Joannicius was eating a humble dinner with a fellow monk when a huge brown bear, neither muzzled nor chained, arrived at the hermitage door. The saint called to the bear, who padded over and lay beside him. The second monk was terrified—until the saint asked the bear to recline at his friend's feet instead. "At the time of creation," Joannicius said, "animals revered human beings, as we were made in the image of God. We had no fear of them. The reason we're afraid now is because we've broken God's commandments." The story fails to disclose whether the gentle bear shared the men's meal, as it ends on a flat note: "The monk departed, greatly edified."

That evening we dined in a small restaurant. The owner shook our hands as if we were dignitaries. His wife, daughter, and two sons took turns bringing us bowls and glasses and cutlery, saucers and platefuls of food. Clare liked to keep her sandy-coloured hair tied up at the back, but to appease the curiosity of the owner's daughter, she let her hair down and shook it out. The girl's eyes widened and she put a hand in front of her mouth, attempting to hide a smile. I felt like a spectator in a ritual of elaborate courtesy.

"Here," the restaurant owner told us, "your names are Mustafa and Leyla."

Renamed if not reinvented, we caught a bus the next morning to Ankara, the nation's capital. A jagged line of snow-topped mountains glowed in the early light. The soundtrack was an upmarket radio station, one that played European classical music as a backdrop for ads: local melodies would yield to a snatch of Rodrigo or Rachmaninoff, followed by a sales pitch in Turkish. Having crossed a high pass, the bus careered down into sweeping farmland, the distant towns and villages speckled with minarets. The further east we travelled, the more I thought of the Canadian prairies. Trees were scarce. Alkali flats appeared and disappeared. The land had an uncompromising feel, and for long miles the highway barely curved. The scale of the rolling country was immense. But in Turkey sheep and goats far outnumbered the cattle, and what farmer in Alberta or Saskatchewan would stride alone across a field, sowing seed by hand?

STUDENT GUIDE TO ASIA told us nothing about Ankara, or indeed anywhere between Istanbul and Iran. We were relying on our wits, which required me to pay a slow visit to a bank and make a cumbersome trip to the Consular Section of the Imperial Iranian Embassy. There a framed, unsmiling Shah, dressed in ceremonial regalia with a hodgepodge of medals, badges, ribbons, and stars on his chest, stared down from the wall behind the visa officer's head.

"You are Canadian but living in England," the visa officer said. I couldn't tell if this was a statement or a question.

"That's right."

"Have you ever been associated with a political party?"

"No, never," I lied. It seemed unlikely that the files on his desk or the contents of his metal cabinet would reveal that I had once been an ardent member of the Saskatchewan Young New Democrats.

"Very good," he said.

Passport stamped with the necessary visa, I left the embassy happy. A middle-aged man who helped me find the correct bus introduced himself as a policeman. If so, he was dressed in plain clothes.

Amid Ankara's jostle and bustle, Clare and I found the Museum of Anatolian Civilizations a welcome respite. Housed in a medieval trading post, it elongated my sense of the past: the Byzantines, even the Romans, now felt like newcomers. I saw a miniature bronze-and-silver stag that a servant or grieving relative had laid in a royal tomb four thousand years ago. An unflinching clay sculpture of a mother goddess is even older; she sits naked, legs apart, on a chair whose armrests are the heads of leopards or lionesses. The museum was mostly empty. I wandered through it with amazement, half-hearing the caged finches singing in every gallery. From roughly 1800 to 1200 B.C., I learned, this region was the core of the Hittite Empire — the stony remnants of its capital lie east of Ankara. A bas-relief of a winged lion with a human head left me breathless. Another bas-relief showed the ancient hero Gilgamesh ringed by lions, a stag, and a bull.

Sudden interest in a dead civilization did not induce us to spend a night in Ankara's Hittite Hotel or to exchange money at the state-owned Hittite Bank.

UNTIL I VISITED ANKARA, Hittites were just a vague biblical name to me — uttered in the same breath as the Kenizzites, the Kadmonites, the Girgashites, and no more real than any of them. Yet in truth, the Hittite Empire rivalled Egypt in size and scope. Its capital, Hattusa, boasted palaces and human-made ponds, fortified walls and open-air temples, buried granaries and sculptured friezes. The Hittites were masters of silverwork and chariots.

What brought them down? The usual answer involves the rise of Assyria in the east and lethal raids by the mysterious Sea People in the west. But that's a partial story. When the Hittite Empire began to falter, it had to import grain to stave off famine. The empire suffered fatal turmoil while Greece and Egypt were going through convulsions of their own. Lately the whole era has acquired a scholarly nickname: Late Bronze Age Collapse. The Hittites, it's now understood, were victims of climate change. Fossilized pollen from the Sea of Galilee shows that droughts afflicted the region for a century and a half. Crops failed repeatedly. Forests around the eastern Mediterranean dwindled and perished. The Late Bronze Age Collapse was a political calamity only because it was first an ecological one.

One of the surviving Hittite myths tells of how Telipinu, the god of fertility and agriculture, vanished. Without him, animals and plants became infertile. Smoke and mist obscured human settlements. Mountain slopes, forests, and meadows dried up. Starvation ensued. Other gods went looking for Telipinu and could not find him. He had travelled far and fallen into a profound sleep, from which a bee sting woke him at last. But in his fury at being wakened so painfully, he lashed out, inciting storms and floods, shattering buildings, altering the course of rivers. It took the intervention of Kamrusepa, the goddess of healing—using a special cream that mingled figs and grapes, olive oil and honey, sesame seeds and essence of cedar—and the sacrifice of a dozen rams before Telipinu was appeased. The underlying meaning, I suspect, is that Hittite storytellers were aware of the need to preserve the natural realm from drought, flood, and fire. Otherwise, they sensed, their civilization would fall.

But who pays attention to storytellers? The lion, the cheetah, the tiger; the Asian elephant; the Persian fallow deer: in Hittite times, all these animals roamed the land that Turkey now covers. None of them does so today. South of Ankara, the second-largest lake in the country would shrivel into dust in 2021, carcasses of nesting flamingos littering the salt flats. A few leopards are rumoured to survive in a fragment of wilderness. Brown bears, for the moment, endure.

THAT EVENING CLARE AND I sauntered up a hill and entered a square dominated by the Haci Bayram Mosque and Mausoleum. The complex takes its name from a Sufi saint and poet of the fifteenth century—dervishes once lived where his tomb now stands. A Roman temple lies in ruins nearby. We sat down at an outdoor café for a glass of tea. Three or four boys were playing football in the square. Darkness had already fallen, the crescent moon gleaming above a single star. A young waiter took our modest order and walked back to the counter through a forest of vacant chairs. When the strong clear tea and some lumps of sugar had arrived on a silver tray, the manager came over to our table and began a conversation. A bald, broad-shouldered man, he wore an impressive moustache. Like many Turks, he spoke German more fluently than English — hundreds of thousands of Turks had migrated to West Germany as "guest workers" over the previous decade — and I struggled to express some thoughts in my basic German. The manager refused to accept payment for the tea; indeed, he ordered a second glass for each of us and paid for that too.

After a time he excused himself and went off to the Haci Bayram Mosque. Other men were walking in the same direction. The smooth-cheeked waiter, who had introduced himself as Naim, offered me a cigarette. Then the muezzin began his call to worship. *Hasten to the best of deeds: prayer is better than sleep*... Soon we could hear the ancestral call echoing through the streets of Ankara. The prayer, delivered simultaneously from several minarets, seemed a part of the living city, suspended like moonlight in the cool spring air.

When we rose to leave, the football-playing boys in the square ran over to shake our hands.

PINNACLES AND HOODOOS — fairy chimneys, to use the British phrase — dot the Cappadocia region of central Turkey, a four-hour ride southeast of the capital. Erosion of the soft volcanic rocks has fashioned an extraordinary landscape, gnarled with crumbling beauty. Into the pale stone, through a span of nine hundred years, the Byzantine Greeks cut an intricate network of churches, monasteries, and villages.

Clare and I were heading to the dusty town of Nevşehir. "*Vous êtes les seuls visiteurs*," said a man across the aisle on the bus from Ankara; he had laboured for some years in Marseille.

The man was exaggerating, though not by much. His friend, a car mechanic, spoke little English and no French, but when the bus made a pit stop, he unexpectedly bought our lunch. Small islands appeared to be floating in the air off a lake's treeless shore. Far to the south, sunlight glittered on the white-crowned volcanic peaks of the Taurus Mountains.

In Nevşehir, the donkey carts outnumbered the cars. "Tonight, will you go with me to disco folklore?" asked a young clerk in the almost empty hostel. A sign promised: "Restaurant, Bar, Lobby, Roof." We declined his request.

Instead we set out for Göreme, the spiritual heart of Byzantine Cappadocia. We were tramping down a country road when the driver of a pickup truck screeched to a stop. The truck was on its way to a mill, and when we jumped off after a five-minute ride, I discovered that flour had coated my clothes. The flour matched the colour of the pumice cliffs where the chapels nestled. I found it a momentary shock, having grown used to the elegant abstract geometries of mosque decoration, to discover human faces on walls and ceilings. Saints on the lower walls had been defaced or despoiled by graffiti. Higher up, the survival rate is better.

The frescoes are an intense composite of angels, saints, and biblical scenes, amplified by flowers and vines. In the so-called Dark Church, which survived centuries as a Turkish pigeon house, the newborn Jesus flutters in mid-air while the heads of an ox and a donkey loom over his crib. If a beard is painted green, so be it. If the Virgin Mary is twice as tall as an adjacent saint, so be it. Some of the paintings are sophisticated; others are what art experts would call naive. Yet to my exulting eyes, the artists' technical limitations were irrelevant to the soul of the place. Wandering from grotto to grotto, chapel to chapel, I felt touched by joy. Three times, without understanding my own impulse, I ran my right hand over a cross carved in the compliant stone.

Exaltation gave way to hunger: we ordered kebabs in a café down the road. A class of teenage girls on a weekend excursion from Ankara hurried over to greet us. They spoke enough English to ask us where we came from and to shake our hands — mine as well as Clare's.

"How many children do you have?" one of them asked.

"We're not married," Clare said.

The girls fell silent. They giggled a little, embarrassed. Most of them retreated across the room to the long table where a teacher was sitting. But the piped-in music was Turkish — a stringed instrument, played solo — and two of the girls remained near our table and began to dance. I might have been less shocked if I'd known that in the 1970s one of Turkey's most famous albums — it sold well over a million copies — was the work of a belly dancer: *How to Make Your Husband a Sultan*. The girls swayed in the aisle beside us and their teacher did not intervene.

An easygoing young man named Adnan befriended us the next day on a sandy corner. An aspiring engineer, he wanted to practise his English, which was already excellent. When he wasn't inquiring about opaque idioms or details of syntax, he was pointing out an orchard of apricot trees or explaining that a handsome, raven-eyed woman was wearing Kurdish traditional dress. He told us he was a socialist.

"I have not travelled like you," he said. "Can you tell me, is Cappadocia truly interesting to foreign people?"

I hoped he believed my answer. I felt sad that he needed to ask.

Clare and I were walking through Göreme with Adnan when an open jeepload of soldiers sped past us on the road. I asked him where they were going.

"They are going... You wouldn't want to know."

We saw another couple in the distance who looked, I thought, pretty much like us. "Hippie tourists," Adnan said in a dismissive tone. I wasn't sure what made him use that phrase. Perhaps the man's hair was somewhat longer than mine; perhaps Adnan felt annoyed by the woman's jeans. The couple had done nothing to provoke his scorn. But it wasn't a question of what they did; it was who, in Adnan's eyes, they were. I bit my tongue when I noticed him tossing away a cigarette pack in a frescoed cave and goalkicking a matchbox over a ledge.

He accompanied us to the Zelve Valley, an area of red-gold cliffs and abrupt slopes that required some tortuous climbing and had no other visitors. We clambered with him up a dry, winding watercourse. I was starting to think of Cappadocia as Christian badlands. Adnan showed us the domed, cross-shaped church of El Nazar, carved into an otherworldly rock formation, dozens of frescoes surviving on its upper levels. Saints in heavy halos watched us from on high. Geckos sprinted along the inner walls, their tongues licking out for tiny prey. Outside the church a flock of swallows and swifts, newly back from Africa, skittered and veered through the air. By a precipice slowly collapsing into pebbles and dust, some tawny-furred ground squirrels scurried to and fro above their burrows. Two golden eagles flew low as we strolled back toward the main road, patches of white on their great wings contrasting with their dark-feathered bodies.

To me the presence of all these animals emphasized a sort of wildness in Cappadocia—a defiance, or an absence, of life in human terms. The cave churches are not isolated in space: modern Turkey prospers or struggles around them in all its dieselled contradictions. But the churches remain set apart in time. Only as tourist attractions for moneyed foreigners do they have any connection with the bustling culture that encircles them. I had visited cathedrals in Britain and Europe where prayers have been uttered continually over hundreds of years, the gradual changes to the fabric casting a thick overlay on the work of the first artists. Cappadocia has no such overlay. In a tiny, empty chapel I could stand face to face with St. George on a white stallion, and feel spirit to spirit with the anonymous, long-dead painter who imagined a holy warrior, a horse, a dejected dragon. I even wondered if the God-shaped emptiness inside me was on the verge of closing up.

Later Clare and I played dominoes with Adnan in a café. We ate a salad of raw carrot and red cabbage, sipped a sweet, hot, orange-flavoured beverage, and watched men kick a football around an open space, shouting with laughter or dismay. Then we exchanged addresses, pretending we would stay in touch.

IT WAS A SATURDAY NIGHT, after all; we were young; the trip was going well. Putting our misgivings aside, Clare and I agreed to try the "disco folklore" we'd been offered the previous day. The event would take place in a medieval caravanserai — one of a string of large, fortified inns built for traders across swaths of central Asia, the Middle East, and North Africa. The caravanserais provided food, drink, safety, and shelter to camels and humans alike: they were essential to the functioning of the Silk Road linking Europe and China. This one stood north of the town of Ürgüp, on the far side of Göreme. The hostel clerk said that a friend would be joining the three of us—a friend with a car.

He arrived late. Clare and I took the back seats, with the men riding in front. The driver set off at a clip through the unlit streets of Nevşehir, braking only slightly to insert a cassette in the tape deck. It played Turkish music accompanying a woman's voice. She wasn't singing, though; she was panting, sighing, moaning, gasping, crying out. The men laughed. Clare looked at me with her eyebrows raised in dismay. The woman took a few miles of hilly countryside to come. Then she repeated the task.

Inside the hulking, stone-arched caravanserai, we sat down by a small table under a familiar Toulouse-Lautrec poster: a cabaret singer in Paris, red-scarfed, black-caped. The poster beyond it showed a European or American nude—I didn't investigate. We had hoped to find ourselves in a friendly circle of young Turkish men and women. Instead the crowd consisted of eight men, myself included, and Clare. Her face fell as she understood a tourist was now the attraction. At least the inn provided lots of room to dance. Had silk merchants done so in the thirteenth century? The dancing entailed much stretching of arms, regardless of whether the soundtrack was Turkish or European—Édith Piaf, Elton John, the Stones—but when a middle-aged man stopped wiggling his hands and started draping them around Clare's shoulders, she ran back to her chair.

"Drink! Cheers! Drink!"

Some dance to remember, some to forget. I could cope with the raw wine that began the evening. But then a tall bottle of raki—an aniseed-flavoured Turkish spirit—joined it on the table. And if raki on its own offered a robust challenge, the mixture of raki and red wine in a single glass posed an even greater one.

"Drink! Cheers! Drink!"

Our driver spoke little English, but he knew those words by heart. As a woman Clare was exempt from the need to participate in an endless series of toasts; she could cast a vague, beneficent smile and peer through her glasses into the middle distance. As a man, I was not exempt. Or, in such a lovely place, was I simply too weak to say *no*? Maybe we were all just prisoners here, of our own device. The hours stretched into the night like dynasties.

"Drink! Cheers! Drink!"

On the ride back to Nevşehir, I realized the driver was even more drunk than me. He decided to show off his skill at the wheel, or frighten us, or both. He took a blind curve on a hill without slowing. He waved his hands to and fro as if he were still on the dance floor. He put his right foot up in the air, far from the brake pedal. He veered into the opposite lane and stayed there, chortling. He turned off the headlights when another car approached. Worst of all, he kept looking backwards over his shoulder, laughing, watching. Our fear added to his fun. Clare burst into tears and I gripped her hand tightly. This made him drive all the faster.

When we checked out of the hostel two days later, we found that we'd been charged a fee for disco folklore.

SUNDAY MORNING BROUGHT a vicious headache.

"Drank too much, didn't you?" said Clare mercilessly. "Get up, it's time to be off."

Somehow we made it to the underground city of Kaymakli. Or, to use the Greek name, Anakou—for the people who first hid out in this labyrinth of warrens, tunnels, and rock-carved chambers were Byzantine Greeks. They wanted to elude marauding Arabs or Mongols. Centuries later, their descendants hoped to avoid the westward-marching Turks. The softness of the limestone allowed the Greeks to live in modest discomfort far below the feet and hooves of invaders. Kaymakli remained in use, at least occasionally, until the 1923 expulsion of Greeks from Turkey and Turks from Greece: ethnic cleansing at its mutual vilest. The city burrows down several levels—past kitchens, stables, storage rooms, a church—deep into the welcoming earth.

I was full of naive enthusiasm for the builders of Kaymakli. Apart from my usual fondness for the underground and the underdog, I saw it as a place where the West had fended off the East. Over the ensuing weeks I would come to perceive history through a very different lens. Besides, as Clare explained to me, it would be wrong to idealize the Byzantine Greeks. True, they created some fabulous art and architecture. But the empire thrived on cruelty and many of its leaders were incompetent. Some Byzantine emperors died a natural death, especially if you consider gangrene natural, but the reign of a remarkable number ended when an emperor was beheaded, castrated, poisoned, strangled, lynched, or—a favourite punishment—blinded and packed off to expire in a monastery. Several emperors had their noses amputated. One died of exhaustion after playing polo.

Another was murdered in his bath by an underling who hit him with a bucket. "A fish begins to stink at its head," observed Rumi—the great Persian-language poet who watched empires rise and fall in what Westerners call the thirteenth century.

Clare and I had squeezed and scrambled to the bottom level of Kaymakli—at least, the lowest level at which visitors were allowed—when the lights went out. Without emergency lamps, the blackness was total: not an absence of light so much as a quality in its own right, a presence, a force. Five or six other people found themselves stranded in the same chamber, and none of us felt able to move. Sound and touch were the only senses. Even a whisper seemed loud. The ventilation shafts did not require light, so we could breathe normally, but could we think normally? A woman let out a half-strangled cry. Involuntarily I turned in the direction of the noise and saw only a network of veins inside my eyes. After a time I realized that time itself was at risk of losing its authority: Had darkness gripped us for two minutes, or five, or ten? I was near panic when light resumed.

We returned to Nevşehir by minibus and were recovering over soup in a threadbare restaurant when Abdullah walked in and greeted us. He was the mechanic who had bought our lunch two days earlier. Now, with the taste of lentils still on our lips, he took us to have tea with a friend of his, a mournful tailor. Then he showed us a mosque, insisting all three of us should climb up to the women's gallery. And then, as rain began to fall, he brought us to his own little house. We took off our shoes at the door and stepped inside to meet his wife, Pinar, his sister, and four small children.

Abdullah wanted to tell us so much. He knew perhaps seventy or eighty words in English, but the language kept failing him. He would write a Turkish word on a piece of paper and hand it to us, as if our hearing, not our linguistic competence, was miserably lacking. But our Turkish limped no further than *yes* and *no*, *please* and *thank you*, *hello* and *goodbye*. My comprehension skills were, if anything, even less adequate. When he introduced himself, I heard him say "Ben Abdullah" and I kept calling him Ben. In fact, *ben* is Turkish for "I."

Unable to engage in much conversation, we drank more tea and looked at an illustrated schoolbook that belonged to his oldest child. We turned the pages of a picture book about Ali Baba and the forty thieves. And we watched television: a large TV set was the showpiece of the home, and Abdullah took great pride in it. An obese man with slick hair and thick glasses belted out unrecognizable pop songs in English. I tried not to show what I thought. Clare avoided the three-chinned singer by retreating into an adjoining room with Pinar. She reappeared wearing a pair of the baggy, pyjama-like trousers favoured by many women in Cappadocia. The rest of us applauded. After Clare had changed back into English costume, Pinar produced a green headscarf. She walked over to Clare, bowed slightly, and presented it to her with a smile.

What could we give Pinar or her family? In my jacket I had a snapshot of Annie with my mother and father, taken a few months earlier in a sunlit meadow near the English Channel. It was the only picture of my parents that I'd brought on the trip. I gave it to Pinar's children. They smiled out of delight, or duty.

We walked back toward our hostel in thick rain. Abdullah insisted on accompanying us—perhaps he thought that in Cappadocia we should never walk alone. Just before we reached the hostel, a car stopped. Osman, a friend of Abdullah and a fellow mechanic, was cruising the streets. I would have preferred to spend the rest of the afternoon inside, but after the exquisite hospitality Clare and I had enjoyed, how could we refuse a ride now? Osman drove out of Nevşehir and, in a nearby village, parked at a roadside store. A few minutes later, he and Abdullah emerged carrying two bottles of wine, four bottles of beer, and a large bag of nuts.

Then we toured Cappadocia in the rain, taking turns to sing. Osman had a sharp, strong voice. Clare and I tried our best. Her graduate studies involved the history of death, and she chose the antique Scottish ballad "Barbara Allen": *O mother, mother, dig my grave / O make it long and narrow / Since my love died for me today / I'll die for him tomorrow.* In a burst of Canadian patriotism I launched into Gordon Lightfoot's "Did She Mention My Name?," which is more realistic though less riveting. Abdullah and Osman—and Clare too—may have wondered why it mattered if the landlord was a loser and the old folks still the same. One of the few pastimes the men and I shared was football, and I succeeded in reeling off the names of Liverpool's entire team. This seemed to impress them more than my singing. Clare and I performed a duet of an English Christmas carol, "Ding Dong Merrily on High." This did not impress the men at all.

When the rain lessened, Osman parked his car by an empty picnic spot in the Göreme Valley. Abdullah passed the wine and beer around with enthusiasm. I suspected that he drank alcohol only outside the home. Eventually Clare and I walked off in different directions to relieve our bladders. She came back to the car a little disturbed, telling me that Osman had followed her part of the way.

Abdullah recalled something in the area that he wanted us to see: a spectacular lookout, or a hidden valley, or another cave chapel. It meant climbing a hill beyond the picnic site. He tugged at Clare's arm, but she declined to go. He set off anyway, motioning me to join him, and I did. Somehow his eagerness and comradeship made me want to comply.

The path led over a ridge and into a grassy hollow. Abdullah stopped there to pick some yellow and purple wildflowers. We were high up the hill by the time we came in view of the car again and saw Clare, far below, crying and yelling.

In our absence Osman had groped her. She resisted, and he lunged at her. Clare had managed to fight him off and had run away from the car. But she'd been shouting in terror, her voice lost in the damp air, for several minutes.

We rode back to Nevşehir in a sombre mood. Osman apologized repeatedly—to me, not to Clare. We were engaged, or so he thought, and therefore he had insulted my honour. In his eyes she was only a woman; she belonged to me. His apologies did not make Clare feel any less offended, or alone.

Osman dropped us back at the hostel. An hour later Abdullah knocked on our door. He seemed profoundly contrite, but there was little we could understand of what he said, or could say in return.

Clare felt betrayed. She suspected he had lured me up the hill to leave Osman alone with her. I didn't want to believe this, but I also didn't want to provoke an argument. She was scared and angry enough already. Why had I abandoned her at the picnic site? "Eagerness and comradeship." What kind of answer was that?

Abdullah left a jar of wildflowers in our room.

EVER SINCE WE ARRIVED in Istanbul, Clare had been careful to dress modestly: long skirts and dresses, blouses and sweaters that covered her arms, never a bare shoulder. Unlike some Western travellers, she had not dressed in any way that might be seen as provocative. I had thought her restraint would serve as protection. We'd been happy to split up on occasion; in Ankara, while I was obtaining an Iranian visa, Clare was out looking at mosques. But the kindness so many Turks had shown us had led me to lower my guard. In the wake of Osman's assault, we would take no more risks.

The first consequence was that Clare would spend most of her waking hours in my company. She no longer set forth to see mosques or anything else on her own. As time passed, the strain would grow on both of us. She began to irritate me, and it was all too obvious I had the same effect on her. After Cappadocia my red notebooks changed in meaning: they became not just a record of events and sights but a psychological necessity. Clare liked to sleep longer than I did, and when she was in bed I occasionally seized the chance to go for a late or early walk on my own. More often, I would stay in our room and write my journal. The light bulbs were generally dim and the writing kept me sane.

A second consequence was suspicion. No longer would we assume that every offer of help was genuine. Saturday's disco drive and Sunday's attack had corroded our sense of trust. We grew more wary. We lost some of our willingness to accept friendship at face value.

THE SHORT RIDE FROM Nevşehir to the walled city of Kayseri — Caesarea, the Romans called it — took us across a plain unmarked by fences or walls. In the high, sloping meadows, great flocks of sheep remained unshorn, the ponderous wool allowing them to endure nights of wind and bitter frost. In Kayseri we saw, for the first time, large numbers of beggars on the streets. "Hope," a Turkish proverb says, "is the bread of the poor." A massive citadel — part Roman, part Byzantine, part Turkish — housed a market in which quail and young chickens, trapped in small cages, were crawling over each other. We visited two mosques and a mausoleum, all of them heavy with dark stone and broad arches, the youngest five hundred years old. The city is renowned for the making and selling of carpets, and in the absence of other foreigners several dealers harangued us in case we were richer than we looked.

"Hello, I am sorry," said a young man who had overheard one of the harangues. Unusually for the time and place, he wore not just a moustache but a beard.

"Do you live in Kayseri?" I asked.

"Yes, but I am a student at Istanbul University. Now it is closed because of demonstrations. So I came home. Are you liking Turkey?"

I assured him that we were, but something in Clare's expression led him to probe a little further. Soon he was apologizing not only for the persistence of carpet merchants but for the behaviour of Turkish men.

"Here," he explained, "until a man is married, you don't touch with a woman."

Given another hour or two, we could easily have made friends with Yusuf — the three of us were students, after all — assuming a friendship can blossom despite a serious imbalance of power. Yusuf could not afford to remain in Istanbul after his university shut down. His dreams lay at the mercy of political and economic forces far beyond his control. Clare and I could afford to ride long-distance buses through his homeland and deep into the east. The money we had at our disposal allowed us to purchase time. What would be the value for a Turkish student of three months without obligations, three months of absolute freedom? If our abundant fortune made our lives hard for Yusuf to imagine, we had equal trouble imagining his.

We left Kayseri at two in the afternoon. A generous splash of cologne at the bus station set us up for an overnight trip: through Malatya to Elazığ, changing buses after midnight and carrying on to Van in Turkey's craggy southeast. We were approaching Kurdish land — Kurds make up almost a fifth of the country's population; they form a majority in the southeast. Yet at the time of our visit, the government denied the very existence of Kurds, referring to them as "mountain Turks" and dismissing their language as a dialect of Farsi, the main language of Iran. Regimes have changed in Turkey, but the fear and the disparagement of Kurds remain constant. In 2018, the lead singer for a Kurdish band would be jailed for the crime of performing a song that features "Kurdistan" in its lyrics — Turkish law counts the very name as terrorist propaganda. The unflagging repression gives point to a Kurdish saying: whether in Turkey or Iran, Iraq or Syria, "We have no friends but the mountains."

A stork's nest balanced precariously on some telegraph wires. A distant minaret resembled a rocket on a launch pad. Before sunset, as the bus heaved its way up a forbidding pass, I noticed a red fire engine, alone and motionless on the roadside. Then twilight fell, lulling me into a restless half-sleep.

I jolted awake to the low, nervous voices of other passengers. The bus was plodding through a city — Malatya, it must be. But the road lay in darkness, and most of the houses showed no trace of light. We drew to a stop. Leaning into the aisle and peering ahead, I could see two men with rifles outlined in the headlights. Had we reached some kind of checkpoint? The passengers had fallen silent.

The bus jerked forward again, but now the road was muddled with broken glass. Windows were shuttered and boarded up. On a side street, clumps of paper and other debris fluttered in the air. Smoke curled above a roof. We were the only traffic.

We pulled into the bus station, and none of the passengers left their seats. The station was dim and empty. Three or four policemen strode to and fro on the pavement. The driver made a terse announcement — his tone of voice was clear, even if his words told us nothing — and within minutes the bus set off again. We had travelled a few hundred yards when a convoy rushed past, heading into Malatya: soldiers in seven truckloads. I glimpsed stars above the city's ripped backside. Only when the road was again a rural highway did the other passengers begin to speak at a normal volume. Somewhere in the darkness we crossed the Euphrates.

In the nearly deserted station at Elazığ, Clare and I had to wait a few hours for the next bus. A middle-aged man who was also waiting could manage a little English: "There was a bomb. In a letter. Four are dead." I was immediately full of questions. "Who did this?" was the first. The man raised his heavy eyebrows and turned away. We could tell from the headlines and pictures in the following day's newspapers that in Turkey, the events in Malatya were a front-page story. But we didn't, couldn't, understand what we'd seen.

The disturbances would last four days. On the first of them, a letter bomb had killed the city's mayor, Hamid Fendoğlu, and three of his relatives. No one claimed responsibility, but the mayor was a Kurd. The next day — hours before our arrival — twenty thousand people packed the streets of Malatya. Some were Kurds, outraged by the assassination, keen to take out their rage. Many others were Turks: proud boys and young men, pumped by a toxic mixture of resentment and prejudice. Though guns were rare, knives and hatchets, cudgels and metal chains were abundant. As protesters roamed through the city, their masked leaders dumped gasoline on buildings and set them on fire, chanting "Down with Communism!," "Killer Ecevit!," and "Muslim Turkey!" The mob ransacked offices, homes, and businesses owned by Alevis — a minority sect within Islam to which many Kurds belong — and also by socialists. Among the targets were newsagents and newspaper offices, printing houses and union halls, bars and shops that sold alcohol. Hundreds of Alevis were injured. At least eight died.

It's uncertain if the attackers included a twenty-year-old man whose name would soon become famous worldwide. Born in a small town north of the city, he grew up in a Malatya slum. A petty criminal from an early age, he attended a high school controlled by the Nationalist Action Party, which ran seminars in fascism aiming to make Turkey great again. The Grey Wolves were its youth wing. The clever, dark-eyed boy joined the movement and started to travel around the country, obeying the violent instructions of his masters. His whereabouts that week in April 1978 are a mystery. But in February 1979 he would assassinate Abdi İpekçi, a liberal journalist in Istanbul and a friend of the prime minister. Two years later, having made his way to Rome, Mehmet Ali Ağca would shoot the pope.

CLARE AND I CLIMBED wearily onto another bus and dozed through the rest of the night. To the south lay Nemrut Dagi, where colossal stone heads of kings and gods occupy a mountaintop, and the oil fields of Batman — no, really. It came as a relief to step off the bus into the cloudless sunlight of Van. The air felt thin in my nostrils: the city stands on a mile-high plateau beside Asia's tenth-largest lake. I was hoping to see one of the rare type of cats for which Lake Van is celebrated; Van cats are chalk-white animals, fond of swimming, perceiving the world through eyes of different colours. We fortified ourselves with tea in a noisy café where the waiter showed us his German textbook (in that faraway land of early risers, "Helga must be in school by eight o'clock"). Then, having found a cheap hotel on a kebab-scented street, we set out for the stone fortress in whose shadow the city lies. As we walked we were picked up by a Kurdish family in a van — no, really — and when they dropped us off, the driver's wife gave Clare some wildflowers she had been holding above the lap of her patterned tunic and her long bright dress.

The fortress, built on a massive hill, is at least 2,800 years old. Set in a rock face high above the ground, a niche contains a carved inscription in three ancient languages:

*A great god is Ahuramazda, the greatest of the gods, who created
this earth, who created the sky above, who created human beings,
created happiness for human beings, who made Xerxes king, one
king of many, one lord of many.*

Xerxes would acquire a dismal fame in the twenty-first
century as the pumped-up villain of a Hollywood action movie,
300. ("For God's sake," he bellows in English. "War!") *300* is
based—very loosely—on a Persian invasion of Greece. During
that conflict, Xerxes' soldiers burned Athens to the ground.

*I am Xerxes, the great king, king of kings, king of all kinds of
people, king on this earth far and wide, the son of Darius the
king...*

Maybe so, but this fortress had commanded the area long
before the birth of Xerxes or his royal father. Its builders were
a people known as the Urartu, the heartland of whose culture
lay beside Lake Van. In a museum in Ankara I'd seen a massive
bronze and copper cauldron made by Urartu craftsmen. The
cauldron did not exactly evoke sensitivity, but it suggested
immense strength. Heads of bulls poked out from near the top.

Clare wanted to explore every corner of the fortress and,
having learned our lesson in a Cappadocia parking lot, we had
no intention of splitting up. But my attention kept straying to
the sky. If only I'd stuffed a pair of binoculars into my backpack!
Eastern Turkey was in the thick of spring migration, and the
air quivered with raptors: sparrowhawks and harriers, buzzards
and eagles. Hoopoes billowed across the fields and budding
woods below the fortress. Closer at hand a bee-eater was chasing

winged food through the warm air, its plumage a harlequin mixture of blue and yellow, black and chestnut brown.

"I'm not going further east than Iran," said Bruce, a nurse from Seattle. Having formed a momentary friendship, as travellers so often did on the Hippie Trail, we were sharing a bag of Iranian pistachios near the top of the Urartu fortress while I looked up at the eagles, out at the salt lake, and down at the grape hyacinths growing wild around our feet.

"Why is that?" Clare asked.

Off to the southwest, near the highway that had brought us to Van, a rocky island glinted in the sun.

"The wrong kind of people want to go there," Bruce said. By "there" he meant Afghanistan and India: the destinations of choice for young Westerners thirsty for enlightenment, or oblivion. Many of them were convinced that the road of excess would lead to the palace of wisdom. "I'm happy to mosey around this part of the world at my own pace. I see…" — his intelligence was clear, yet he struggled to find the exact words — "I see things other people miss." Bruce was on the road, but for him, unlike a lot of Kerouac-besotted travellers, the road was not a be-all and an end-all. He liked to stop. He liked to think.

Clare and I eased our way down from the fortress and walked through the old city of Van, its mud-brick buildings deserted for sixty years. "There was an earthquake," a headscarfed employee had told us at the hotel. We entered the city through a towered gate. Walls and stone foundations had remained intact; most of the roofs had not. In the bare courtyard of a disused mosque, a man was on his knees in prayer. Rivulets and streams trickled through the ruins, soon to join the lake. When we stood still, a gurgle of running water made the only sound. I could imagine the apple trees and vegetable beds those streams must have nourished in times when laundry hung above the alleyways and voices rang through the narrow streets, calling, laughing, scolding. The ruins were a haven of peace.

Salt marshes divide Lake Van from the old city. It took longer to get there than we expected: the farther we walked, following a trail among the reedy marshes, the more the brilliant turquoise water seemed to recede into the distance. The breeze carried a magpie's rasping cry and a scent of wild sage. No cats of any colour were out for a swim. Having reached the shore at last, I left my shoes and socks in the dark sand and paddled for a minute—or less, for the water felt subarctic. It left a salt deposit on my skin. Clare surveyed the hills beyond the green-blue lake, shading her eyes for the clearest view of a tranquil, untroubled scene.

The island we'd observed from the high citadel is less than two miles from the nearest shore—temptingly close. One tale about Lake Van maintains that a lake monster or dragon inhabits the frigid depths; when he wasn't busy at politics, Bülent Ecevit wrote a poem about the creature. An equally unlikely story tells of a princess who lived on the island long ago and fell in love with a mainland boy. Every night she slipped down to the water's edge with a lamp and he swam across to her, finding his way by her light. But her father discovered what she was up to. One night he surprised the princess at the shore and extinguished her lamp. The boy lost his bearings in the darkness and drowned. This too became the topic of a well-known poem.

The island holds a tenth-century stone building. But the ferry never runs in April, or so we were told. No boat would take us over the frosty water. As we strolled back to the modern town of Van, a passing driver honked at us: the horn played "Glory, Glory, Hallelujah."

FROM VAN WE MOVED NORTH, then east toward a vast, dormant volcano looming nearly seventeen thousand feet above sea level. English speakers know it as Ararat: a holy place for Armenians, adorning the national coat of arms and inspiring countless works of literature, music, and art. The mountain's name comes from the ancient "Urartu," and the fortress-building ghosts of Urartu were very likely the ancestors of modern Armenians. Yet thanks to the convulsions of history and the military and political skills of Kemal Atatürk, the volcano now rises inside Turkey. Its official name is not Ararat but Ağri, the Turkish word for "pain."

The deep fault lines that cut this region are geological and cultural, geographical and religious, historical and linguistic. Breaks are manifest not just in the landscape but in the words that evoke that landscape—a name can speak volumes about what a person believes or has been told to believe. To situate these fractured hills and broad mountains on a map, they need to be identified as either Eastern Anatolia or the Armenian Highlands. Clare and I were on our way to the town of Ağri, known until 1946 as Karaköse: its renaming for a mountain of pain emphasized that Ararat had become Turkish property. Power grows from names.

The slopes were wordless and almost treeless. They hosted big flocks of brown sheep, their winter fur still shaggy, their ears floppy. Russian, Bulgarian, and Romanian trucks made a slow parade of traffic. A fenced-off military base stretched along the highway's edge: the frontiers of Iran and the Soviet Union lay close at hand.

We caught a bouncy minibus from Ağri to the border town of Doğubayazit. Absurd expeditions in quest of Noah's lifeboat have set off to Ararat from here. Doğubayazit smelled of drains. It felt to me like the setting of a yet unwritten novel by Graham Greene: both tense and sleepy; a lair of double agents. A blonde-haired girl from somewhere was retching by the side of a road.

"You understand this of course is a smuggling shop," said a tall German in front of us at a counter.

We were in line to purchase an excellent magnetic flashlight for what I thought was a very low price.

"Now they must pay to the police more money," he added. "The prices therefore are high."

In a second shop we bought halva, Turkish Delight, batteries for the flashlight, and a plastic water bottle in the shape of Donald Duck. A glass of tea in a dimly lit café cost less than two English pence. A Kurdish elder strode past the grimy window with a staff, a white beard, a fez, and ultra-fashionable sunglasses. Men rode horseback through the potholed streets, clasping their whips.

Next morning, hoping the fluid sloshing around Donald Duck had been safely boiled, we shared a ride from Doğubayazit to the border with a long-haired Afghan smuggler. To judge by his slangy, vivid turns of phrase and his quasi-Brooklyn accent, he'd picked up English from a New Yorker. He boasted that he was about to take a thousand dollars' worth of lapis lazuli, rings, and other jewellery into Iran. I wasn't sure if he was telling the truth, and I couldn't bring myself to care. My stomach felt queasy; my throat grated. Clare kept quiet. The Afghan looked at us as if we were tiresome children.

Dreams of Kathmandu and Delhi passed before my eyes: all they were was dust in the wind. A truck from somewhere in the Soviet bloc lay overturned in the ditch.

2.

Iran

"How many years you have
this job to be tourist?"

A minibus, a minibus, a minibus, a minibus, and finally we
reached Tabriz. Clare's smile had worked wonders at the border:
the crossing required just forty minutes and our backpacks were
left untouched. We moved our watches forward two hours and
found the Afghan and his jewels had vanished. To the north,
clouds smothered Ararat. We shared the first ride with a young
man who clutched a tiny green rucksack, hardly sufficient for
a change of clothes, and had no money except some Yugoslav
dinars. He carried a cardboard sign announcing *I want to go
Agvanistan by autostop*—but he did not speak English. As far as
we could tell, his only language was Serbo-Croat. The driver of
the first minibus allowed the man to travel for free. The driver
of the second refused to let him board.

Clare and I, like most foreign travellers in Iran, spoke no
Farsi. We could also read no Farsi—the language is written

in a graceful right-to-left alphabet based on the Arabic script. To us the road signs were unfathomable. Yet a red-and-white billboard by the highway conveyed a familiar meaning: Coca-Cola. I recognized the brand at once, as though by instinct, and wondered if the names and emblems of worldwide capitalism might become a sort of Esperanto in the future. No, too improbable a thought.

Power made itself visible fast: at a crossroads in a small town, a tall statue of the Shah atop a marble plinth. The northwestern corner of Iran has long been contested land; most of its residents speak Azeri, not Farsi, as a mother tongue. Late in 1945, a breakaway socialist regime, propped up by the Soviet Union, had seized control here under the cumbersome name "Azerbaijan People's Government." The United States, in an early bout of the Cold War, persuaded the Soviets to back down. Soon the Shah's army marched into Tabriz and dismantled the mini-state. His soldiers looted, tortured, raped.

On the final bus, as I was idly looking at a small flock of camels grazing on a hill, I realized that a black-eyed girl of nine or ten was watching us from across the aisle. The bus sped past the camels and the girl kept staring. At last I looked directly back at her. She pulled up the hood of her robe to cover her neck, ears, and hair, and turned away.

We scrambled out of the fourth minibus hoping it had stopped near the centre of the straggling city. It had not. Somehow a strap of Clare's backpack had broken in one of the vehicles, heightening the difficulty of walking any distance. My eyes fought to adjust to the intensity of the dry light. We were standing outside the bus station, feeling lost and clueless, when a young man rolled down the window of his Mazda.

"Are you needing help?" he asked.

A minute later we were perched uncomfortably on the back seat, gripping our backpacks as the car zipped through traffic.

"What would you like to do in Tabriz?"

"Go to the bazaar," Clare said.

The city was rumoured to hold the largest covered market in the world. Seven hundred years earlier Marco Polo praised it as a place where "travelling merchants make great profits." He added, "The inhabitants are a mixed lot and good for very little."

The driver kept silent, even though his car was facing a red light.

"It is closed tomorrow," he finally said. "People are not good with the Shah—but we don't like to talk about that."

There is a Persian proverb that predates the Shah, let alone the Islamic clergy who now run the nation: "Walls have mice, and mice have ears."

The man found us a small hotel near the ancient centre of Tabriz; it was full. He insisted on driving us to a second; it was not. We said goodbye without ever knowing his name. I would have thanked him profusely and repeatedly for lighting on a hotel where lilac bushes flowered in an inner courtyard and, for the first time since Venice, a shower produced hot water. I washed some clothes and doctored my sore throat with a harsh Turkish cough syrup; the taste of turpentine lingered on my gums as we ate a small meal. Then we ventured out into the streets.

WHAT SOUNDS DO FOREIGN travellers hear? In Tabriz, speaking
neither Farsi nor Azeri, Clare and I were oblivious to everything
except the wordless noises of a modern city: engines firing and
backfiring, horns, the odd siren; doors opening, doors closing; the yawps and cackles of hundreds of starlings roosting
on high branches along a boulevard. Cassettes and transistor
radios played music we did not recognize. Cries and whispers
made use of languages we did not know. Little wonder that
English-speaking tourists go out sightseeing, not soundhearing.

And what sights do foreign travellers see and recall? To
wander through a land where not just the food, the religion,
the buildings, and the climate but also the national alphabet is
foreign—all this can deliver a burst of what Arthur Rimbaud
believed every poet needed to experience: "a long, boundless,
systematic derangement of the senses." The notes I made in
Tabriz have a visual clarity about them, along with an almost
complete lack of context and history.

Many of the shops in the bazaar had defied the call to close,
and in one that remained open, we saw a white Persian cat lying
asleep on a cushion; a samovar stood between the dormant
cat and an oval tray bearing an image of the Mona Lisa. We
touched and admired the ceramic lid of a beehive, elegantly
glazed in blue, purple, and black, in a small antique shop that
also sold copperware, clocks, and carpets of an intricate geomet-
rical design. Near the bazaar we passed a grocery store with the
words CANADA DRY on its open door, and a young woman in a
black chador standing inside, looking out. Ginger ale was part
of her life; I was not.

In search of some context, even a little history, I bought a
copy of the *Tehran Journal,* a national English-language paper,

and tried to decipher it: not the language, which was standard
English, but the meanings behind the words. What struck me as
the day's most urgent news—France's detonation of a neutron
bomb—merited less space than a humdrum address by an
Iranian cabinet minister. The point of the article, I suppose,
lay in the reassuring blandness of the minister's prose. The
newspaper's reporting seemed forthright on some issues: land
speculation, smuggling, profiteering, even education (a journalist noted that only 44 percent of Iran's school-age children
were actually in school). But the paper offered no direct criticism of the regime—and nowhere did it mention the violent
unrest in Tabriz.

What Clare and I saw in the city's streets, we did not understand. Was it on government orders that two mosques we tried
to visit were shut? A crowd had gathered outside a third mosque.
The men spoke in low voices if they spoke at all. Squads of riot
police, their rifles prominent, waited on open trucks. More
policemen—or were they soldiers?—stood ready down a side
street. Walls and street lamps were smeared with photocopies
showing the bearded faces of young men: students, killed here
in February during protests against the Shah's regime. In their
blurred eyes I read a tale of hope and defiance. Death had trans-
figured the students into martyrs. But were they martyrs for a
shared vision of the future, or was the Shah's overthrow their
only common aim? In my journal I wrote, "I wish the rebels
every success." I did not know who the rebels were.

One of the articles in the *Tehran Journal* detailed a state visit
to Iran by the president of West Germany. The visit was political. The meetings involved trade, not culture. Yet the reporter,
leaving oil and steel negotiations aside, proudly noted that

Persian poetry has been translated into German since the eighteenth century. It was as if the poems created an indelible bond between the two nations. "Persians take poetry seriously," the scholar Omid Safi has observed. "For many, it is their singular contribution to world civilisation: What the Greeks are to philosophy, Persians are to poetry." In Iran, poems that date from six, seven, eight hundred years ago are still in imaginative currency, and their authors continue to be household names. As a poet, at least an aspiring poet, I had arrived in the perfect country.

An official tourist brochure for Tabriz described a mausoleum as "the resting place of poems like Khaqani the great." (Khaqani had died eight centuries earlier; I had no idea that one of his most celebrated works is a long autobiographical travelogue.) The brochure extolled the beauties of "this pretty town which has given numerous brave men." A few brave men were now memorialized in makeshift black and white, not in a mausoleum but on the city's doors and walls. The murky, insurgent photographs hinted at the depth of hostility to the Shah's regime and the extent to which resistance might go. Yet Clare and I never suspected that in less than nine months the Shah would flee into exile, his secular kingdom razed and recast as an Islamic republic in an ayatollah's grip.

Foreign travel in Iran would promptly become much harder. Soon the Hippie Trail would fade to a dream, an insubstantial pageant of the past.

ONCE A GLOSSY INTER-CITY bus had dropped us in Tehran, we hastened to the central post office. There, passport in hand, heart beating a little quicker than usual, I joined a line of unkempt foreigners and asked a clean-shaven man behind a screen if any mail was being held for me. He walked off to look. When he came back, he handed me a thin blue airletter with the crowned head of Queen Elizabeth at the top and the simplest of addresses: "Poste Restante, Tehran, Iran."

All the news and wishes in Annie's letter moved me less than her first two words: *My love…* Clare had lined up too, and a sweet letter from her boyfriend was awaiting her. *I'm missing you*, Annie wrote. *Hugs and kisses… Look after yourselves…* These tangible reminders of love we had left behind made the next couple of days tense.

We scrutinized Iran's crown jewels, kept under guard in the basement of a bank, and argued whether the viewing had been worth the price of admission. We spent a happier couple of hours — happier for me, at least — in a museum of Persian miniatures, and argued whether the oldest paintings were the best. After nearly being run over by a boy on a Vespa, we chanced on an English-language bookshop: I thought Clare might not share my desire to read Sufi poetry. Her opinion of me fell further when I failed to close the lid of a Dettol bottle, spilling antiseptic over the green headscarf Pinar had given her in Cappadocia (Clare had prudently worn the scarf in the streets of Tabriz).

"If the journey's good for anything," I wrote in my journal, "it must be good for dealing with worries, problems, crises. I need to become more resilient. I let things get under my skin too easily. It's not that I can't cope — I need to learn to cope in an unflustered way, and to believe in my own ability to cope."

Clare and I had a room in the Amir Kabir, a grubby hotel and car repair shop that catered to foreign youth. Built partly in ramshackle circles, it looked like the remnants of a poorly funded effort to construct an urban spaceship. But it was a favourite stopover for India-bound travellers who had boarded the Magic Bus in London or Amsterdam. In the men's toilet, among an array of profane, lustful, and badly spelled inscriptions, one piece of graffiti stood out for its eloquent simplicity: *Tragic Bus.* An Australian man wandered around the courtyard, a mullah's turban over his long red hair. We overheard him talking to a pair of American girls about to fly home to Denver.

"If you got the money to do that," he said, "why are you staying in a dump like this?"

The girls giggled.

None of my conversations in the Amir Kabir had to do with Iranian culture or history. They focused on practical matters: where to exchange travellers' cheques at the best rate, where to sleep cheaply yet safely in Delhi and Lahore, where to buy food in Tehran at the lowest cost. I listened to other exchanges about the price of illicit drugs and the risk of arrest: "I know this place in the bazaar that sells hash, but you gotta be careful. They'll ask way too much..."

There was an irony in all this. Whether we had taken to the road in quest of escape or adventure, wisdom or bliss, most of the backpackers in the hotel meant to thumb our noses at our wealthy, complacent elders. We liked to see ourselves as immune to the virus of materialism. But stinginess rewarded us: it could buy us more time; it could delay our return home. In a continent of rampant poverty, Western travellers would hold lengthy conversations on ways of spending as little money as we could.

I don't recall any overlanders, including me, suggesting that our presence in the country might be harmful to the people of Iran. Foreign oilmen and local mullahs be damned—we saw ourselves as harbingers of a future more carefree and more just. Lots of women and girls in Tehran sported lipstick, makeup, and chic Western clothes; they allowed their hair to flow loose and their legs to go bare. We took their glamour as a sign of progress, both desirable and inevitable, as if freedom's just another word for less and less to wear. Surely the future would sidle up in halter tops, not chadors. Surely religious extremism was an ailment of the past.

One night in the Amir Kabir an Irishman with a guitar sang Graham Nash's "Chicago." For days to come its hopeful lyrics echoed through my head. Could we change the world, rearrange the world? Somehow, as the old order spluttered and choked, people would at last be free. History was on our side. Or so we thought.

Even the dream of enlightenment depended on the right papers, so Clare and I spent two long mornings in the Afghan Embassy. Kabul, we discovered, went by the nickname "the Paris of central Asia." I looked forward to its arch of triumph, its red windmill, its Elysian fields. The city even boasted side-walk cafés. By the end of the second morning, my passport held a pair of visa stamps. One of them, a blue circle, bore the name "Section Consulaire de l'Ambassade de la République d'Afghanistan." The other, a black square, said "Afghan Embassy Tehran" at the top. An official had crossed out the words *entry* and *transit,* leaving only *tourism.* I knew from a succinct article in the *Tehran Journal* that a political leader had just been assassinated in Kabul, provoking unrest on the streets. Did this explain why the date of issue inside the black square was three weeks in the future?

We would need to remain in Iran longer than expected. The reason was a mystery: we didn't even notice the stamped date until we'd left the embassy. But rather than continue east toward the Afghan border, we headed south to Isfahan and beyond.

MY SORE THROAT HAD WORSENED, and now my head felt congested too. On the luxurious coach ride to Isfahan — each passenger received a free bottle of Coke — a little girl of five or six kept coming up the aisle to inspect us. Her smile revealed that her front teeth were missing. Soon she brought Clare an orange. The coach pushed through a desert of sand devils and mirages: shimmering trees, expanses of shining water. Rocks that looked cool and violet in the shade of a high cloud would turn a bright red-brown, like rare roast beef, when the cloud moved on. By some fearless contortions, the driver and conductor changed places without stopping the vehicle: this was no mirage. We passed the holy city of Qom, glimpsing the domes and spear-thin minarets of a huge mosque and shrine. Until his arrest and exile in 1964, the Ayatollah Khomeini had taught, preached, fulminated, and written poetry in Qom. On his return to Iran fifteen years later, he would bend the nation to his will and set out to rearrange the world. Smaller towns along the way crouched lower to the earth, their flat roofs of baked clay punctuated by a mosque's blue dome.

When my eyes grew tired of sand I browsed *The Conference of the Birds*, a book-length poem from the twelfth century. Its author, Farid ud-din Attar, was a Sufi, a herbalist, and an avid traveller. Long before Chaucer wrote "Parliament of Fowls" for an audience in medieval England, Attar imagined a gathering of birds in quest of wisdom and divine truth, and evoked the arduous journey they undertake. And long before Saint-Exupéry invented a little prince hopelessly in love with a rose, Attar described a nightingale in the same predicament. The leader of the expedition is not an eagle, as you might expect, but a hoopoe: a plump bird with a dramatic crest, a black-and-white back, and an orange-pink head and neck. Its colour scheme makes the bird look as if some blunder of evolution has juxtaposed tinned salmon with baby zebra. The images and stories that Attar placed in the hoopoe's long, downcurved beak are cryptic, surprising, and wonderfully fresh: "He who travels on the path of self-striving must regard his heart only as shish kebab. The man with the watering pot does not wait for the rain to fall."

The man with the burning throat does not wait for the doctor to appear: on our first afternoon in Isfahan, I found a pharmacy and bought eight doses of over-the-counter penicillin. A glass of melon juice, newly blended by a fruitseller at a street corner, gave some faster solace. "Hello, how's life?" said a young man with a grin. Then, not waiting for an answer, he broke into Farsi.

Except for my throat and chest, life was terrific. How had I not known what a fabulous city Isfahan is? In the late sixteenth century—judging by the Christian calendar—a brilliant and despotic ruler had made it the capital of the Safavid dynasty, which ruled Persia and a bevy of neighbouring lands. Shah Abbas I reigned for forty-two years, time enough to endow the city with some of the most spectacular buildings and urban spaces anywhere. "Isfahan is half the world": the boast became a familiar saying throughout Persia.

The heart of Isfahan is a square—rectangle, rather—laid out for Shah Abbas beginning in 1598 and named in his honour. After Ayatollah Khomeini assumed power, it would be renamed Naqsh-e-Jahan: "Image of the World." Armies would gather there in Abbas's day and horsemen would play polo; phallic stone goalposts remain in place at either end. The square is seven times larger than the Piazza San Marco in Venice, which lingered in my mind as a quintessential public space. Around the edges are the royal bazaar, a pair of mosques, and a palace graced by a long spiral staircase and a music room with walls like a plastered honeycomb. I marvelled at the colours and symmetries of the Shah Mosque, built around a courtyard with a rectangular pool at its centre. (Water is nowhere more sacred than in a desert.) The glazed blue tilework extends from the dome and minarets all the way down to floors on which, whenever we visited, men had bowed their bodies in prayer. Off to one side, a smaller courtyard held a rose bush in flower. A pair of hooded crows flapped across the pool, cawing sharply at each other.

One of the shrewdest decisions Shah Abbas made was to relocate hundreds of thousands of people from the Caucasus— Armenians, Circassians, Georgians—who would owe their loyalty to him alone. By doing so, he bypassed the nagging feuds within the Safavid regime—members of his family showed an alarming willingness to murder each other, even as tensions churned among competing tribes, regions, and strains of Islam. The new immigrants had no choice: Abbas refused to tolerate dissent. In Isfahan he created an Armenian district, New Julfa, confident that the international trade of its merchants and silk dealers would enrich the whole city. Armenians from Isfahan would establish a few of the earliest cafés in Paris: a telling example of what the West owes to the East.

Clare and I walked to New Julfa across an arched stone bridge that spanned a river clouded by waterweeds. In a park on the far side, the trees wore numbers on their trunks. Six or eight thousand Armenians still lived in New Julfa, but within half an hour we passed enough churches, convents, and monasteries to serve a population many times that size. Bored-looking Americans on a guided tour were brandishing cameras. Keen to stay out of the picture, we ventured into a museum. There Clare examined the tiles and sacred vessels; I pored over the manuscripts and seventeenth-century printed books. Both of us gazed at an item in the final case: a biblical verse written on a human hair, readable only with a microscope. It astonished me, though not as much as a stark fact we learned elsewhere in the museum: the ruined city we'd explored in eastern Turkey is a testament to genocide.

THAT RED STONE BUILDING on an island rising above the turquoise waters of Lake Van? It was an Armenian cathedral, looted and abandoned in 1915. That poem about a princess and a drowning boy? It was composed in the Armenian language; a palace existed on the island only briefly, but Armenian monks lived there for the best part of eight hundred years. Most of the forsaken buildings in the old city of Van were inhabited by Armenians; most of the voices that echoed through its knotted streets would have spoken Armenian. Clare and I had ambled through the placid ruins unaware that their devastation was not, as we'd been told, the product of an earthquake. Warfare and genocide had left all of Van's Armenians dead, exiled, or converted to Islam at the point of a gun or the blade of a sword.

Van in this life, heaven in the next. The proverb reflected the fertility and beauty of a land at the very core of Armenia. It adopted Christianity a decade before Rome. For long stretches of time, however, Armenia was a nation without a state. True, it could boast an ancient strongman, Tigranes the Great, who styled himself "king of kings." But he was a belligerent exception — Armenians mostly lived under foreign empires. They became, like Jews in Europe, admired and resented for skill at commerce. Their relationship with Turks, often fraught, never simple, decayed in the late nineteenth century. Armenians were massacred on the orders of the Sultan's regime, many of the atrocities being carried out by the Ottoman Empire's downtrodden Kurds. Armenians hit back, attempting to murder the Sultan. They did so at a moment when Turks felt outrage at the killings of Muslims in eastern regions of Europe where Christians now held sway.

Then came the First World War. The reformist "Young Turks" who had plucked power from the enfeebled Sultan pushed the Ottoman Empire to enter the conflict as a German ally. The empire took up arms against Russia, where many Armenians sought a perilous embrace. And early in 1915, faced by the prospect of foreign invasion, the Ottoman rulers decided to eradicate the Armenian people from lands that had been theirs for millennia.

The date usually given for the start of the catastrophe is the 24th of April. That evening, a few hundred Armenian physicians, artists, scholars, writers, lawyers, priests, and community leaders were arrested in Istanbul. As the war intensified, most of the Armenians in the country would be killed, imprisoned, or driven in starving, pathetic convoys into the desolate wastes of northern Syria. Numbers, like so much else, are disputed; but in all, as many as 1.2 million Armenians would die.

In truth the genocide began weeks before April 24 — in the culturally diverse province of Van. Armenian villages were ransacked, Armenian farms and orchards burned; refugees poured into the city. Even though the Ottoman army rained fire on Van from the heights of the ancient Urartu fortress, the Armenians would not give in. Hand-to-hand battles raged in the mud-brick streets. After weeks of intense fighting, the Armenians were on the point of surrender — when Russian troops arrived in Van and the Turkish soldiers fled. Over the following months, in spite of the devastation, other Armenians found refuge in what remained of the city. *Van in this life, heaven in the next*…

The Russians left and the Turks regained control. The Turks left and the Russians regained control. And then, in the wake of the Bolshevik Revolution, the Russians withdrew for good. In 1918, surviving Armenians vacated the homes, churches, and gardens of their broken city and moved north into a fragment of the Caucasus: it would become the Soviet republic of Armenia and eventually, at last, a small independent state.

The last Armenians in the province of Van, rounded up by the Turks, were deported or killed.

It's an immense tragedy. Small wonder the restaurant owners, hoteliers, and shopkeepers in the new city of Van preferred to keep it quiet. When Clare and I travelled through Turkey, the genocide could still be denied with a straight face. Since then, archival discoveries—notably in Germany—have proved the Young Turks planned the murders and the ethnic cleansing. Dissent on the ground was forbidden. Djemal Pasha—one of the triumvirate running the Ottoman Empire—decreed: "Every Muslim who tries to protect Armenians will be hanged in front of his house, and his house will be burned down." He and the other Young Turks despised the multinational nature of the Ottoman Empire: they saw its diversity as proof of weakness. They aspired to build a new nation that would be ethnically, culturally, and religiously pure.

At the war's end, its treasury bankrupted, its leaders disgraced, the floundering Ottoman government set up a military tribunal with the power to try the masterminds of genocide. The tribunal issued a bill of indictment, stating: "The massacre and destruction of the Armenians were the result of the decision-making by the Central Committee." But Kemal Atatürk seized control, adopting a policy of silence and a goal of amnesia. His new regime denied the truth. And Turkish governments ever since have pursued Atatürk's lead, suppressing the archival records and claiming that any pain experienced by Armenians was matched by equal or greater pain among Turks.

What does constant denial do to a people? The inquiry is often directed at Armenians, who have spent a century trying to persuade foreign states to acknowledge the genocide. But perhaps the question needs to be asked not of the victims but of the perpetrators. In recent years, some brave and dissident voices — Turkish writers, artists, scholars — have dared to attempt an answer.

THAT DAY IN NEW JULFA, Clare and I visited three Armenian Orthodox churches, all of them, like mosques, with domed roofs and carpeted floors — yet their inner walls and ceilings, unlike those of mosques, teem with human figures. In two of the churches, those figures are in extreme pain. The frescoes show the butchery of the faithful departed: saints being twisted, mutilated, beheaded, drawn and quartered. It was as if admission to heaven required endurance of hell on earth. A tape of sacred Armenian music, austere and serene, was playing in the cathedral as we gazed on the graphic martyrdoms. I tried to reconcile what I saw with what I heard.

History and politics keep on proving the frescoes' point. The original Julfa, located just inside the present-day nation of Azerbaijan, contains only a few thousand residents. None of them are Armenian. Every church in the area has been wrecked. And in 2005 Azerbaijani soldiers marched into war against Julfa's unique cemetery. Equipped with axes and sledgehammers, the soldiers demolished thousands of medieval tombstones, each one intricately carved. They tossed the rubble into the river that flows between Azerbaijan and Iran. Having destroyed all evidence of Armenian churches, graveyards, and works of art, Azerbaijan could rewrite its history. The absence of living Armenians was not enough; the dead also needed to be erased.

Beside the cathedral in New Julfa, Clare and I saw a stone memorial bedecked with fresh-cut flowers. It paid homage to the victims of the 1915 genocide. Similar memorials now exist in many countries, not including Turkey or Azerbaijan.

THAT EVENING IN ISFAHAN, I had a large bowl of chicken soup; Clare ordered fish with dill. Everything else we ate and drank was the same. But in the night, I awoke to find her stricken by food poisoning. She was repeatedly, violently sick. Penicillin must have saved me, or chicken soup. I spent most of the next day looking after her as best I could — breakfast was a glass of watermelon juice and an expired Mars bar — and writing my journal when she managed to sleep.

WE STAYED ON, and Clare recovered. From the stone remnants of a Tower of Silence on a hill west of the city, we could look down at Isfahan: a vast, cypress-filled oasis in a parched land. Over many centuries, Zoroastrians left corpses on the tower for vultures to consume. Theirs was the faith of the ancient Persian emperors — the creator god, Ahura Mazda, incarnated fire and light. A bee-eater darted across our path, its blue and copper feathers glinting in the noon sun like butterfly wings. In a sidewalk café at the base of the hill, we talked with a New Zealand couple slowly travelling to England — for them the Hippie Trail was a westbound route, overlying part of the ancient Silk Road.

"Watch out when you get to Afghanistan," the young woman said. "Pakistan too. They don't like us there."

A rooster strutted beside my chair. But it wasn't the rooster who came up with a soundtrack to the ruins above our heads; it was a local radio station, blasting out the opening fanfare of *Also sprach Zarathustra.*

I wouldn't have believed it — would anyone have believed it? — if I'd been told that a year later, all forms of music would be banned from Iranian radio and TV. The silencing must have extended to "Isfahan," a lush, dreamy number by the Duke Ellington Orchestra. (The Duke's musicians had played a concert here while on a world tour financed by the U.S. State Department.) Ayatollah Khomeini, echoing what Karl Marx once said about religion, declared that music is "no different from opium" because it "stupefies persons listening to it, and makes their brains inactive and frivolous." A less intrusive president would relax the ban two decades later, and today Iran even has some rappers, yet music remains controversial. The supreme leader, Ayatollah Ali Khameini, warned in 2010 that "promoting and teaching music are not compatible with the highest values of the sacred regime of the Islamic Republic."

Soon after taking power the clergy briefly prohibited chess-playing too, saying it encouraged people to gamble and discouraged them from attending to their five daily prayers. The irony is that chess is one of Iran's great exports to the world. Persians adapted an ancient Indian pastime into a near forerunner of the game we know today — the Indian chariot piece, for example, became a Persian *rukh* — and Arabs then carried it into medieval Europe. The English word "checkmate" comes from the Farsi phrase *shah mat:* "the king is helpless."

Back in the city, we passed a theatre showing a Japanese action movie, *Which Is Stronger, Karate or Tiger?* Men congregated outside other theatres too, but the titles of those films appeared in Farsi alone, and the meaning of the words was lost on us. When we stopped at a newsstand, I found that apart from selling lottery tickets and images of "scenic Isfahan," it also stocked 3-D postcards displaying the uncovered heads, necks, and shoulders of young women. Depending on my angle of vision, the women would languorously wink or smile. Less expensive postcards featured the luxurious bar of the Shah Abbas Hotel.

Young men and teenage boys — and a few girls too — paced back and forth in the city's squares and parks, clutching a book, sometimes reciting to themselves. Many were studying English. A boy approached me and said, "Your name is Abbas!" An older man gestured at Clare and asked me, "Friend or woman?" However little our presence impinged on the lives of most people in Iran, there was at least one task we could perform: answer questions about the English language.

On occasion our answers differed. "You should say," Clare told a boy with the fuzz of a new moustache, "'Have you a map?'"

I shook my head: "No, that's wrong. You should say, 'Do you have a map?'"

Clare unleashed a chilly glare.

Inquiries could pop up at unlikely moments. We were gazing at the Sheikh Lotfollah Mosque, built for worshippers in the ample harem of Shah Abbas — how did it contrive to pull the luminous sky to earth, or lift the honey-coloured ground into the heavens? — when a young man dashed out from the entranceway to greet us, textbook in hand. Like many Isfahanis, he wore crisp, immaculate jeans. The man showed us a page and jabbed a finger at *societies*. "How do you say this word?" he asked.

The duty of response began to grate on me. I'd come to Asia to see, not teach, and I felt no particular desire to help the people who were helping me. After being asked "How are you?" for the tenth or twelfth time, I joked to Clare that the next time I heard the question, I would reply "Fucking good, man." I didn't lower my voice enough, for a man walking nearby looked at us and calmly said, "Everybody wants to know how are you."

Reproved, indeed shamed, I strolled with Clare to the royal bazaar—another magnificent building from the days of Shah Abbas. Above the main entrance, a pair of turquoise centaurs frolicked in tile. They were archers—Sagittarius images, in fact—whose lower bodies resembled those of elephants as much as horses. The scampering figures looked not quite familiar, not quite alien. Metalworkers were hammering inside the bazaar, its long aisles redolent of leather and wax, spices and sweat. Small courtyards held teashops and goldfish-filled ponds. Men were busy at dominoes. Thick wooden doors felt like portals to who knows where? We certainly didn't.

"I lived in Paris," an antique dealer told us with a sigh. We may have looked quizzical, for he added, "in 1929." Had we travelled here from England? "Ah, if I could see the Persian miniatures again in the British Museum. The Victoria and Albert also. The finest anywhere."

I was, at the time, delighted to hear this.

He offered us a dish of pistachios and almonds before

pointing to a sombre portrait of Ali, "lion of God," the tragic, black-bearded hero of Shia Islam: a saint with a sword.

"No good," the man said. "Ali was always killing. Jesus Christ never was killing."

Was he a Christian—an Armenian, perhaps? Or was he Jewish? I noticed several menorahs on his shelves, but I was too shy to ask. Whatever the answer, we lingered in the shop long enough for me to overcome my qualms about behaving like a tourist and to bargain my way into a purchase: an illustrated page from a nineteenth-century copy of Persia's national epic, the *Shahnameh*, or Book of Kings. Its author spent more than thirty years writing the gigantic poem. Iranians revere Ferdowsi not just for his mastery of Farsi but for his critical role in saving their language in an era when Persia was divided and Arabic exerted a heavy weight.

"Do not show it at customs," said the man as he wrapped the page in tissue paper, then with filigreed cardboard that had once covered a boxful of nougat. "Keep it in your valise." Out of politeness he added, "Do you have many children?"

Clare and I had come to the conclusion that in Iran we should pretend to be married.

"No," she said, "not yet."

The *Shahnameh*, which is even older than *The Conference of the Birds*, comprises tales from Persia's mythical past. Siavash, the son of a king, is spurned by his father and beheaded on the orders of his father-in-law. A second prince, Esfandiyar, dies in battle because he believed a promise his father had falsely made. Zal, a hero with a happier fate, is brought up by a sacred bird, his father having rejected him at birth. The most celebrated story in the entire epic, Sohrab and Rostam, tells of a king who stabs his long-lost son to death. The *Shahnameh* is a beautiful monument to terrible parenting.

"I wish you many children," the antique dealer said.

A *COUP D'ÉTAT* HAD taken place in Kabul. We learned this from the latest *Tehran Journal.* Following the unrest of previous days and the dissolution of the old regime, Afghanistan's borders were closed. The new rulers were Communists.

I didn't stop to ask what the turmoil might mean for the people of Afghanistan. Coups come and go, I thought; Paraguay had suffered fifteen of them in half a century. What I cared about was my own disappointment at not seeing the immense sandstone Buddhas carved into the cliffs near Bamiyan, not contemplating the garden tomb of the first Mughal emperor, not exploring the Paris of central Asia. Worst of all— *I'm missing you already... Lots of love*—I might never collect the letters awaiting me in a box or pigeonhole at Poste Restante, Kabul.

Clare and I tried to remain optimistic. Perhaps the borders would reopen soon. Afghanistan stood at the heart of the Hippie Trail; it had been at peace, more or less, for the past thirty years. Why should serious trouble arise now?

ON OUR LAST EVENING in Isfahan, the smell of fresh-baked bread pervading the streets, we walked back to the darkening central square and sat there until night fell. The great buildings were illuminated subtly, their domes awash in a pale half-light. A few puddles near the polo goalposts mirrored snippets of the Shah Mosque. When the fountain in the central pool splashed to a halt, the image of the Sheikh Lotfollah Mosque across the square disappeared. Gradually the water settled and the image redefined itself. The reflection of a lamppost, inconspicuous by day, loomed high in the wet sky below. We stood up and began to walk on, stopping before a floodlit dome. An old man, holding a single rose, paused to look up too. He gave us a careful greeting, inquired after our health, and said in formal tones: "I welcome you to my country."

Then we made our way to the bus station for an overnight trip to Shiraz.

We arrived, exhausted, on the first morning of May. Shiraz is a city renowned for poetry, gardens, and wine—grapes have been cultivated in the area for five thousand years or longer. But my heart was back in Oxford where, as dawn broke, Annie and some of my other friends would be standing in a crowd outside Magdalen College, listening to choirboys sing madrigals high up a Tudor tower, then watching groups of Morris dancers swarm the car-free streets. The rivers would be alive with pleasure craft; the aroma of bacon and sausages would be drifting out of restaurants and pubs. Nostalgia heightened my irritation when we knocked on the doors of five hotels and found that none of them admitted to a vacancy. The scent of flowers was everywhere in Shiraz, and I felt stupidly annoyed these were not the fragrances of an English spring: hawthorn, elderflower, lily of the valley.

Eventually, when we'd found a place to stay and drunk glasses of fresh lime juice from a corner stand, common sense returned to me. Iran returned to me. I began to notice life again: the nomadic Qashqai women dressed in crimson and purple robes, some of them with red, henna-dyed hair, many carrying bundles on their scarved heads to keep their arms free; the schoolchildren racing around the bare courtyard of a mosque built more than a thousand years ago; the uncomplaining donkeys whose flanks served as living stalls, balancing baskets of eggplants, cucumbers, pomegranates, walnuts, and other produce. We discovered the pleasure of cold *paloodeh*—a starchy sorbet, flavoured with rose essence and lemon juice—in the daytime heat. After lunch Clare rested in the hotel and I went off to find the marble tomb of Hafez—the most popular, within Iran, of all its great poets. Like Rumi and Attar, he was a Sufi, and the copper dome above Hafez's tomb has the stylized shape of a dervish's hat. A young Iranian couple knelt down and placed their hands, side by side, on the gravestone. The gardens around the tomb were a blaze of marigolds and orange trees, rose bushes and pansies blooming in every imaginable colour.

I made my way back to the hotel. I watched the motorcade of the white-clad Shah. And after the hotel manager taught us the Persian way to sip tea, he asked a question: "Have you seen the tomb of the poet Hafez?"

"I have indeed," I said.

"Very good. Have you seen the tomb of the poet Saadi?"

It began to dawn on me that in Iran, mausoleums of poets serve more than one purpose. The trees and flowers surrounding them keep the breath of nature alive in a city. The paths and open spaces enable people to talk in relative privacy. Most of all, the tombs allow Iranians to celebrate those whose only power lay in the words they used—people who had no authority to imprison, torture, kill.

HIS IMPERIAL MAJESTY Mohammed Reza Shah Pahlavi, Vice-Regent of God and Centre of the Universe, Shadow of the Almighty, Light of the Aryans, Shah of Shahs, Commander-in-Chief of the Iranian Armed Forces, Sovereign of the Order of the Pleiades, Sovereign of the Order of the Lion and the Sun, Sovereign of the Order of Splendour, Sovereign of the Order of Gratitude, Sovereign of the Medal of Effort, Sovereign of the Decoration of Sorrow, Sovereign Recipient of the National Uprising Medal, Grand Cross of the Order of Propitious Clouds (Taiwan), Member of the Most Glorious Order of Bright Kinsmen of the King (Nepal), Knight Grand Cordon with Collar of the Supreme Order of the Chrysanthemum (Japan), Collar of the Royal Order of Seraphim (Sweden), Knight of the Pontifical Order of the Golden Spur (Vatican City), Chief Commander of the Order of Merit (United States), Grand Cross with Collar of the Order of the White Lion (Czechoslovakia), Grand Cordon of the National Order of the Leopard (Democratic Republic of Congo), came from modest stock.

The full quantity of the Shah's titles exceeds the ninety-nine names of Allah. Yet his grandfather was a professional soldier, his grandmother an immigrant from Georgia. His father, Reza Shah Pahlavi, began his career as a private and scampered up the ranks—brigadier general of the Persian Cossack Brigade, minister of war, prime minister—until finally, in 1925, he had himself crowned the first king of the Pahlavi dynasty. Reza Shah changed the country's name from Persia to Iran ("Land of Aryans"). He modelled his rule on that of Kemal Atatürk, and like his Turkish contemporary he encouraged free mixing of the sexes and insisted that men appear in Western clothing. He went even further than Atatürk in issuing an outright ban on the hijab and chador. These reforms had an unforeseen effect: many husbands compelled their wives to stay home, and some women chose to remain there.

Reza Shah seized power after the British had put an abrupt end to the previous regime; they mistrusted the influence of the new Soviet Union in a feeble and divided Persia. He lost power during the Second World War when the British, now allied with the Soviets, invaded Iran and shipped Reza Shah off to a distant exile; they suspected him of nurturing German sympathies and wanted control over Iran's oil reserves. To replace him on the throne, the British installed his son — the Shah we saw in a Cadillac — in 1941.

Twelve years later the British were at it again, this time as junior partners of the United States, when the CIA overthrew a democratically elected prime minister, Mohammad Mossadegh, while the second king of the Pahlavi dynasty hid in Rome. (Mossadegh had nationalized the holdings of a British company that produced most of Iran's oil and paid almost no royalties.) Once the dirty work was done, the Shah flew home with the CIA director and gave out National Uprising Medals to the perpetrators of the coup, himself included. No prime minister would challenge his power again. Being a king was not enough for the Shah; in 1967 he declared himself an emperor.

In Iran today, many young people look back fondly on an emperor they never endured. They do so out of frustration with life in the Islamic Republic. It's an ironic echo of what Clare and I saw in Iran, where young people — including Marxist students in Tabriz and Tehran — were turning to the mullahs as the fiercest, best-organized enemies of a tyrant. The Shah promised to foster a "Great Civilization" and under his rule, the economy blossomed: "I could not stop building supermarkets," he bragged in his memoirs. Highways and airports sprouted as never before. But at what cost? To make sure the system worked with the smoothness of premium firearm grease, the Shah relied on American weapons, corporations, and military advisors. "We used to run this country," said an American diplomat as he fled Iran in February 1979, just after the monarchy had fallen. "Now we don't even run our own embassy."

The Shah also relied on a secret police force whose full-time agents sifted and weighed the news they received from many thousands of part-time informants. Iranians came to believe that if you placed unthinking trust in your neighbour, your cousin, your employer, your teacher, your friend, you were a fool. *Walls have mice, and mice have ears.*

WALLS IN PERSEPOLIS HAVE mice and graffiti. The ruins stand on a huge stone platform where the Zagros Mountains begin to unfurl from the edge of Iran's southwestern plain. Darius founded the city in 515 B.C., and his son Xerxes — the king whose boastfulness we'd glimpsed above Lake Van — completed the work. Persepolis was a capital built for ceremony, for ostentation, for shock and awe. Its purpose was imperial. Yet in the grand sweep of Persian history, its glory days were brief: in 330 B.C., Alexander the Great (as he's called in Europe) trampled the Persian Empire. His soldiers looted, tortured, raped. They also burned Persepolis to the ground.

Or at least, the flammable portions burned down: the cedar roofs and beams; the palaces with their tapestries, silks and parchments, their frankincense and myrrh. But the massive stone staircase at the entrance remained intact, and does so still. Likewise an imposing array of columns, arches, and sculpted walls — Clare and I looked on them in wonder. The columns stretch toward the sky like broken fingers imploring mercy from Ahura Mazda or relief from the desert wind. After the vandalism of Alexander's troops, Persia would recover its strength. But Persepolis would never be rebuilt.

The ruins have resisted collapse and erosion, though not the knives of foreigners. When British and European visitors reached the site, many of them recorded the fact by carving names and dates on a convenient tomb or column, or the stone flesh of a lion. Henry Stanley did this a year before he sailed to Africa in search of Livingstone. In 1911, the British Indian Army dispatched a squadron to protect the "rights" of British traders in Persia, and a slabful of engraved graffiti at Persepolis still proclaims the arrival of the Central India Horse.

The words that struck me most verged on a limestone haiku: *John Foster Fraser. / Cycling round the world. / 1897.* Fraser was a Scottish journalist keen to make his reputation — two years later he would publish a bestselling book about his travels, *Round the World on a Wheel.* The insolence of the man! Outside the cities of Persia and several other countries, he and his two companions rode the first bicycles local people may ever have seen. Did they regard the freewheeling young men as invaders? Or centaurs? Or potential sources of income? In his book, Fraser was dismissive about Persepolis (the columns "looked like a lot of battered ninepins on the top of a shaky table") and often scornful of Persians ("A limping-hoofed, cringing old sinner wanted to act as guide"). Even so, he betrayed a trace of unease about what he and his friends had done: "All is lordly and forlorn, and no misty, sorrowful-countenanced, ghostly monarch disturbed our barbarian act as we scribbled our names on the marble slabs."

Fraser had the power to behave in this manner, and Persepolis was always about power. On ruined wall after ruined wall, we saw a commander kill a rearing lion by stabbing it in the breast. When a sculptor carved into a long sweep of rock the figures of nine abject Babylonians subservient before their Persian conqueror, he was revelling in the might of his own empire. Fraser recognized the impulse. He met the grandeur of Persepolis with casual arrogance. As the American writer John Leonard once observed, "The ego of the tourist is imperial." The words that Fraser left behind are befitting for a Scottish avatar of an empire at its height, an empire whose soldiers, agents, spies, and administrators swaggered through Asia and Africa in much the same spirit of entitlement that Xerxes and Alexander had displayed so long ago. We saw next to no graffiti at Persepolis in the Farsi script.

Fraser and his companions travelled with guns, but guns were not their only weapon. Their most potent missile was the English language, which even the stones of Persepolis could not repel. The words that told Fraser's story also fuelled his sense of command. Everywhere he went, he felt equipped to give orders. People who spoke a different mother tongue listened and obeyed. Then he inscribed his accomplishments in print.

In my day, even more than his, English has become an empire of the word—a mother tongue, or stepmother tongue, wielded by women and men around the world. The *language* of the tourist can also be imperial. "Do you have a map?" "How do you say this word?" For all my doubts and qualms, was I following in Fraser's tracks?

I KNEW, EVEN AT THE TIME, that Persepolis inspired and obsessed the Shah. He had spent tens of millions of dollars to celebrate the 2,500th anniversary of the Persian Empire and to claim political descent from its founder, Cyrus the Great. Much of the money went on a three-day party held at Persepolis in October 1971. The regime imported eighteen tons of food for an event at which Haile Selassie rubbed shoulders with Imelda Marcos, Marshal Tito with Princess Grace, the President of the Soviet Union with the Vice-President of the United States. Guests at the Shah's grand banquet washed down their caviar-stuffed quails' eggs with champagne bottled in 1911, cognac in 1860. Princess Anne is said to have remarked, "I'll never eat another peacock." In case the troupes of dancing girls failed to amuse the visitors, fifty thousand caged songbirds were flown in from Paris. Exiled in Iraq, Ayatollah Khomeini warned: "It is the duty of the Muslim people of Iran to refrain from partici-pation in this illegitimate festival, to engage in passive struggle against it, to remain indoors during the days of the festival, and to express by any means possible their disgust and aversion for anyone who contributed to it. Let the festival organizers know they are despised by the Islamic community."

The Shah didn't care.

The Shah had no interest in forging a spiritual link to Islamic dynasties of the past. Instead he wanted to embed himself in the heroic, pre-Muslim lineage of Cyrus, Darius, and Xerxes. Oil wealth made it all seem plausible. So what if Iran had to pay for twenty-three miles of silk to house the Shah's guests in air-conditioned tents? So what if thousands of bottles of premium Scotch were smashed and discarded in the desert? So what if the French songbirds couldn't cope with the travel or the extremes in temperature—intense heat by day, near frost at night—and almost all of them died before the party began? *Shah mat:* the king was helpless. He delivered his main speech, assuring Cyrus the Great he could finally rest in peace, while a sandstorm raged. To mark the occasion in ribbon and metal, he created two prizes and bestowed them on himself: a Persepolis Medal and a Commemorative Medal of the 2,500 Year Celebration of the Persian Empire.

Dignitaries and despots were only some of the people his regime drew to Shiraz and Persepolis. An annual festival pulled in Bhutanese dancers, Rwandan drummers, Ravi Shankar, and some of the leading avant-garde artists of Europe and America: Karlheinz Stockhausen, Jerzy Grotowski, the Merce Cunningham Dance Company, the Open Theater... The perceived damage to Iran's cultural integrity led to the coining of a Farsi word, *gharbzadegi*—two of the English translations are "Westoxification" and "occidentosis." (Even Santa Claus had become familiar in Iran, under the name "Baba Noel.") The oddest recipient of the Shah's largesse was *Orghast,* a nocturnal play mounted in 1971 by the English director Peter Brook from a text by the poet Ted Hughes. Most of the text was incomprehensible—Hughes wrote it in a guttural language of his own invention—but tactlessly he based the plot on Prometheus: a hero who stole the gods' fire and gave it to the Greeks, the arsonists of Persepolis. The cast featured actors from eight foreign countries; a few Iranians had minor roles. Following months of work and vast expense, *Orghast* was performed twice on the ramparts of Persepolis and the royal burial site of Naqsh-e Rostam. The small audience for the second event included the Shah's wife; she waited for hours in a bus until the play began at midnight, a fireball lighting up a tomb.

After the empress had watched the play, the festival cancelled a third performance. It said the Kraków Philharmonic needed time to rehearse a concert amid the columns and the stone lions.

The ruins of Naqsh-e Rostam are four miles away from Persepolis. We had set out to walk there when three young Iranians stopped to pick us up; they drove out of their way to practise their English and take us to the site. A spectacular array of rock faces, Naqsh-e Rostam holds four royal tombs and some stunning bas-reliefs cut into the cliffs. One of them shows Valerian, a captured Roman emperor, paying homage to King Shapur of Persia while a second sorry Roman leans forward to clutch an outstretched hoof of Shapur's horse. (Nearly eighteen years of schooling, three of them at Oxford, yet I was shocked to discover that Persia had humiliated Rome in battle and taken its emperor captive.) We saw a roller hurtling through the air, the colour of the sky on its head and wings, the colour of the desert on its back. A few fat lizards lurked on the crags. A pair of kestrels did their best to emulate the imperial falcons of old.

On the return journey we were even luckier: a chemical engineer, his wife, and their small son offered us a ride back to Shiraz. The ride entailed stopping for a picnic: cucumbers, salted nuts, oranges, sweet green cherries, and a very sour apple. No cognac; no peacock. If I'd owned a car in England or Canada, would I have given an hour-long ride to a pair of young Iranians travelling through my homeland, and would I have shared my meal with them? I was troubled by the answer in my heart.

IN THE ICONOGRAPHY OF the Shah, a lion reigned supreme: on the Iranian flag, on banknotes and coins, on plates and cups, above the entrances to public buildings, on trashy souvenirs. The state flag and coat of arms showed a lion brandishing a curved sword in front of the rising sun. The armed lion symbolized the Pahlavi dynasty and others before it. After the Islamic revolution, the animal would be replaced on the flag by the stylized name of God.

Lions once roamed the Zagros Mountains, west of Shiraz and Isfahan. The last one, it's believed, died in the opening years of the Shah's reign, shortly before the death of the last Caspian tiger. But everywhere in the country we saw cats—they far outnumbered dogs. In the desert city of Yazd, we shared a hotel room with a mother cat and her two kittens, one more assertive than the other. Clare and I called the kittens Bruiser and Dubious, and their grey mother Lady Jane. We were formally introduced to the cats by the mother of the young manager: a widow, we assumed. In the morning she banged angrily on the window when she peered in and saw me reading on a bed while wearing my shoes. Lady Jane had been standoffish until midnight. She then leaped onto my bed and pushed me farther and farther toward the edge as the night wore on.

The smaller the city in Iran, we found, the more likely that women would be veiled. Reza Shah's decree against hijabs and chadors had never been popular outside Tehran, and as the decades passed it was largely ignored; in southern and central Iran we saw few women dressed in anything else. We visited a shrine in Yazd to which Clare alone gained admission — she borrowed a black chador to wear over her headscarf, long-sleeved blouse, and ankle-length skirt. Both of us won approval to see another shrine, whose interior shone in the jangled light of chandeliers and silver mirrors. The mirrors surrounded a saint's tomb, draped in green velvet, imprisoned in a mesh cage; pilgrims could reach through the mesh and toss money onto the tomb. I felt like an intruder in the midst of their piety. The reflections cut everything in the shrine, myself included, into jagged fragments.

The sinuous, camel-coloured streets of Yazd — broad enough for bicycles and motorbikes but not for cars — reminded me of medieval cities in Europe. Setting out along a passageway, we found it impossible to tell if it would lead to a courtyard with pink azaleas, a further thin alley, or a dead end. What looked like the elaborate gateway to a mosque opened into a small bazaar. A large, conical structure with no obvious purpose left us baffled. Later we discovered the cone was a windcatcher: part of a traditional system of refrigeration, involving pits, tunnels, and hidden canals, that furnished local people with cold water even in summer's militant heat.

The windcatchers of Yazd, the gardens of Shiraz, the mosques of Isfahan: these are all products of a sophisticated urban culture, one that depends on the presence of water. But deserts make up roughly a third of Iran's territory. The trans-formation of the country's landscape since the Second World War — a change that began under the Shah and intensified under the ayatollahs—suggests the devastating cost of ignoring ancient lessons. For water is disappearing from Iran.

The country's second-largest body of water was Lake Bakhtegan, east of Shiraz. A stream we saw near Naqsh-e Rostam joined the Kor River, which fed the lake. But the Kor and other rivers have been dammed, mostly for irrigation, and the lake has vanished. It has become a dustbowl, where salt flats turn into temporary marshes after a rare storm. The Zayandeh Rud ("giver of birth")—the wide river we crossed in Isfahan—has also gone dry. People used to toss coins from an arched bridge into the running water, wishing for luck; now any coins would settle in clumps of earth and mud. Thousands of illegal wells dug in and around Tehran, combined with the impact of climate change and the mass migration of families from rural areas, have left Iran's capital suffering a permanent water crisis. More than fifteen million people now live in the Tehran area; it ranks among the most congested, polluted cities on Earth. What was once the biggest lake in the Middle East—Lake Urmia, west of Tabriz—had shrunk by 2017 to a tenth of its former self. Thanks to determined efforts to replenish what's left of the lake and the rivers that nourish it, Urmia has lately recovered some of its size. It remains fragile.

It's not as if Iran can plead ignorance. To the north, the fate of the Aral Sea in the former Soviet Union stands as an object lesson in the dangers of treating nature with contempt. Beginning in the 1960s, the authorities, first in Moscow, later in a newly independent Uzbekistan, decided to maximize cotton production at the expense of all other crops. Accordingly, two great rivers were diverted into a network of shoddy canals. The canals equipped vast fields of cotton, which then received massive and repeated blasts of pesticide. Deprived of fresh water, the gardens, orchards, and farms in the river valleys failed; towns and villages succumbed; fish and birds died out. Almost the entire Aral Sea dwindled to a contaminated, salt-encrusted wasteland. Today the skeletons of fishing boats ride waves of toxic sand. The Aral Sea has become the Aralkum Desert: an invention of humans. Penguins in Antarctica have its windblown dust in their blood.

Iran badly needs water because of its rapid population growth. A census taken in 1976, not long before Clare and I travelled there, showed the nation had less than thirty-four million people. During their first years in power, the Islamic clergy promoted large families, informing women of their duty to bear "soldiers for Islam." The policy was then reversed as the regime encouraged birth control, and in rural areas the number of children per family saw a dramatic fall—but more recently the directives changed again. By 2022, Iran's population had topped eighty-six million and "Two is enough," a slogan on billboards, had given way to new catchphrases like "More children, a happier life."

Whether or not that sentiment rings true, the country's air, lands, and waters are now under acute pressure. The head of its environment agency, Issa Kalantari, dared to tell Iran's highest leaders, "Stop repeating the shibboleth and saying our country is great. Our resources are limited...If the level of our water consumption is not reduced, Iran's eight-thousand-year-old civilization will be destroyed." His message went unheeded. In 2020, eight members of the Persian Wildlife Heritage Foundation were jailed for up to a decade, their crime being "collaborating with the enemy state of the U.S.A." A ninth

person — Kavous Seyed-Emami, one of the group's founders —
died in prison while awaiting trial, supposedly by suicide.

MONSIEUR TAVAKOLI WAS THE first person we'd met in Iran
who gave us his family name when he introduced himself. We
never did learn his first name. He called us over to his car as we
were trudging toward the central square in the city of Kerman,
having failed to obtain a room in the first hotels we passed, and
he invited us to his home. A bald, plump, middle-aged man
with a dark moustache, Monsieur Tavakoli spoke French but
not well enough for us to be sure that we understood him. His
home was larger than two or three hotels where we'd stayed: built
around a courtyard with flowering shrubs and an ornamental
pool, it contained both a formal sitting room and a television
room. He said he had no children, but could the small boy who
served us lunch as we sat cross-legged on the carpeted floor really
have been his *frère*? We assumed he was a nephew or cousin.
Lunch consisted of sliced lamb with yogurt and a pale flatbread.
While we ate, we watched TV: a *Tarzan* cartoon. The villains
had African features. Monsieur Tavakoli phoned a friend who
he said spoke English, and the man hurried over.

"Do you want *no*?" he asked. "*No* do you want?"

This appeared to be the extent of his English.

Monsieur Tavakoli told us he was "married twice," but there
was no sign of a woman in the house, and Clare was becoming
uneasy. When he said his house was ours, he mentioned not
just *manger* but *coucher*. Was he asking us to sleep there? Or
was he merely inviting us to rest after the long coach ride from
Yazd? For the moment, Monsieur Tavakoli seemed to expect us

to go nowhere. He phoned a second friend, an English teacher at a local high school, and we told the man that we meant to find somewhere else to stay. The teacher relayed this news to Monsieur Tavakoli, who nodded and smiled — but insisted we leave our backpacks in his house while we searched for a hotel.

As we were marching back toward the centre of Kerman, a high-school student came up to us — a pupil, it might be, of Monsieur Tavakoli's second friend. His name was Farhad, and he proudly showed us a mosque where a venerable sundial stood in the courtyard. "It is sandwich," I heard him say. No: "It is sun watch." The sundial still had its uses, for the mosque's clock was ninety minutes slow. Farhad understood English well until I asked a question about Islam; then he went blank. Soon he recovered enough to ask, "How many years you have this job to be tourist?" The boy led us from the mosque to a guest-house; it was full. He found a second and a third hotel, which advertised their presence only in Farsi; those hotels were also full, or else they did not accept Westerners. Farhad looked chagrined and told us that Kerman had just one other hotel, far from the centre. He gave us the address, wished us luck, and said a quick goodbye.

Farhad was right: the next hotel was remote indeed. We walked and walked and eventually hailed a taxi. The hotel appeared shiny and expensive — but regardless of the location and the price, it had no empty rooms. Or so the clerk said. The afternoon was waning and we still had nowhere to stay. Why had someone in Kerman inscribed English phrases — LOVER AVE. and LOVE IS FUNNY — on a grey wall? I began to feel a long, boundless derangement of the senses. Or maybe it was just anxiety. Clare and I debated our next step.

A young man named Reza approached us and saved us. A student of electrical engineering at a Kerman university, he had worked with Americans in oil refineries, and he spoke English with colloquial flair. We explained our predicament, and he drove us down a main road and a few side streets to a hotel that welcomed visitors in both Farsi and English. A letter *E* was missing from its sign, which read ALI BABA GUST HOUSE. This hotel was neither shiny nor expensive.

With immense relief we checked in. But Reza didn't abandon us there. He walked with us to the cafeteria of a recently built hospital. "We can get a drink here," he said, "that we can't get anywhere else."

He meant good coffee. The nurses in the cafeteria sported white uniforms similar to those worn by nurses in Europe and North America; they were the first women we'd seen in Kerman not wearing chadors. Reza came from Mashhad, a large city in northeastern Iran, and he told us he disliked Kerman—although he would not explain why. Perhaps he feared the multitude of soldiers in the streets. He drove us back to Monsieur Tavakoli's to pick up our backpacks.

"Who is this guy?" Reza said as we reached the spacious house. "Winston Churchill?"

In the evening Clare and I strolled around Kerman on our own. The city appeared much newer than Yazd or Shiraz— I had no clue why. Somehow I'd left a jacket on the floor at Monsieur Tavakoli's, but we didn't want to go there a third time on the same day. We visited an old bathhouse, now a museum with life-size wax models in its tiled passageways and, on the edge of a bathtub, the carved head of a cat. The bazaar, long and elegant, held a garden in which fading pink blossoms clung to

Judas trees. I did a double take at the sight of a robed woman smoking a water pipe in a teashop. We were waiting in line at a kebab stall when a man handed us a meat-filled skewer from the shish kebab he had just bought. Again the kindness of people in Iran astounded us.

"You are" — a schoolboy seemed to be addressing me — "you are English, madam?"

"Yes, I am."

"Goodbye."

"Salaam."

"How are you?"

"Very well!"

End of conversation. Again I wished I knew more than a few words of Farsi. Clare and I walked back to the hotel.

It was in Kerman that I began to appreciate the size of Iran's insects. From Isfahan onward I had noticed the ants: fat-bodied, bigger than a thumbnail, eager to bite. But only in Kerman did I see a praying mantis, longer than an entire thumb, swivelling its scarlet head. And only in Kerman did I find green centipedes. I would have examined them with interest in most circumstances, but not in a shit-reeking toilet. Cockroaches were present there too, in modest numbers. The numbers inside our room were beyond all modesty. When we opened the door and switched on the meagre light bulb, forty or more cockroaches scuttled for cover. In the Ali Baba Gust House, they took the place of thieves. Most of them, judging by their bulk, were on steroids.

Clare and I shuddered, recoiled, slammed the door shut, went back into the scruffy courtyard, and stared at each other helplessly. But she came up with a plan. We marched around the hotel, inside and out, looking for the four largest buckets, bowls, or watermelon shells we could find. We half-filled them with water. Then we tugged the large double bed into the middle of the room, away from every wall, and lifted each of the four bed legs into a watery receptacle. Having double-checked the mattress and the sheet, murdering a pair of cockroaches in the process, we crawled into our sleeping bags, zipped them up to the top, and slept with eyes half-open. If cockroaches chose to attack us by falling from the ceiling, there was nothing we could do about it. But come morning, we remained unbitten.

This was a kind of enlightenment I had not expected to gain before the journey began.

KERMAN HAS A LONG and remarkable history, full of Sufis and Zoroastrians, and Jews once lived here in enough numbers to develop a separate Farsi dialect, Judeo-Kermani—but in 1794 the city, the people, the history crashed headlong. Its residents gave shelter to a youthful king of Persia named Lotf Ali Khan. He belonged to the Zand dynasty, which had ruined itself by infighting—Lotf Ali was the eighth shah in a decade. In Shiraz, the Zand capital, Lotf Ali may still be remembered fondly, but he never had much chance to enjoy the beauty of its gardens, mosques, and mausoleums. He spent nearly all his short reign battling the forces of Agha Mohammed Khan, a eunuch from the north who had been castrated as a boy by the warlord of another clan.

By 1794, Agha Mohammed controlled most of Persia. But Lotf Ali and his faithful troops held part of the nation from their walled stronghold in Kerman. The northerners besieged the city: it took four months before they broke through. Lotf Ali fled southeast to the desert citadel of Bam. Few Kermanis accompanied the king: this ancient city was their home, their sanctuary in a perilous world. Here they rose and prayed at the rising of the sun; here they looked on the faces of friends and loved ones; here they watched the moon and stars roam the unclouded heavens. Here, before the siege began, the market-place had teemed with fruit: musk melons and pomegranates, dates and figs.

Agha Mohammed, furious at Lotf Ali's escape, took revenge on the city. He decreed that all the boys and surviving men in Kerman should have their eyes gouged out, and he demanded proof that his orders had been obeyed. Soldiers brought baskets of eyeballs and dumped them on the floor in front of their commander: twenty thousand eyeballs in a pile. Agha Mohammed told his troops to rape and enslave the city's women and girls. Then, leaving only the occasional mosque, the soldiers razed Kerman to the ground.

Flush with triumph, Agha Mohammed led his army up to the Caucasus, where he brutally... But no, why go on? He moved the nation's capital to Tehran; he founded a dynasty that lasted until Reza Shah and the British dismantled it in the 1920s. For years, thousands of blind Kermani boys wandered the roads of Persia, holding out begging bowls.

WE TOOK A LOCAL bus to the small town of Mahan, home to the shrine of a fourteenth-century Sufi saint and poet, Shah Nematollah Vali. Iran was forcing me to ask how so many saints could be poets and, more vexingly, how so many poets could be saints. To enter the shrine, Clare had to don a chador; the one she was handed came with polka dots. Candles burned to one side of the tomb, on which a few books stood. I saw a man rise from prayer, his hand on his heart. He lifted a book and kissed it, then put it back on the tomb.

Cypresses touched the sky above a garden where roses grew in sweet-scented profusion: red, white, pink, in great spreading bushfuls. We sat there, glancing from time to time at the minarets and the turquoise dome, eating oranges and perusing a three-day-old paper. Our isolation blurred the news: the folk-singer Sandy Denny had died at thirty-one; the new regime in Kabul was executing its enemies; "Martin Luther wrote the words to the *Easter Cantata* in a martial vein, but Bach sitting in a trance at the organ was moved to compose music in lighter vein." I hoped Afghanistan would soon calm down and wondered if the *Tehran Journal* needed a new music critic.

Who knows where the time goes? A long street in Mahan followed the course of a stream. Women were rinsing clothes in the bright water; children ran to and fro beside it. The air had grown hot in the remorseless sun, but mulberry and plane trees offered some cooling shade. A hoopoe flew down from somewhere, prodding the soil with its long bill in search of underground insects. We had been nowhere more quiet since the shore of Lake Van.

Back in Kerman we went round once more to Monsieur Tavakoli's to retrieve my jacket. Now his house was full: Madame Tavakoli, three other women, a couple of men. One of the men spoke enough English to say he wrote books about the stars, but not enough for us to know if he meant astronomy or astrology. Monsieur Tavakoli was in his element: an elegant, gold-coloured house robe shielded his shirt and trousers. I couldn't tell if we were on display for his friends, or if they were on display for us. Or could the pageant be mutual? All the women wore chadors, but now a bout of folk dancing filled the TV screen, and the lower legs of the female dancers were exposed to public view. This thought would never have occurred to me before I arrived in Iran.

Clare and I were treated to a sugary feast: shortbreads, candies, meringues flavoured with rose essence, freshly baked cakes, cardamom tea. Again the Persian culture of showing hospitality to strangers gave me a jolt. I felt uneasy, even guilty, at being so constantly and generously *served.* Leaning too far back on a cushion, I almost spilled tea on the carpet. Perhaps, after all, Monsieur Tavakoli had wanted us to be overnight guests in his home. Perhaps we had transgressed a code of subtle courtesy beyond our grasp.

"You must tell me," he said in French, "why do you stay at the Ali Baba?"

We did not have a compelling answer.

Next morning we got up early—even at dawn, the hotel clerk had his head deep in a math textbook—and walked with our backpacks to the bus station. The man who sold us our tickets wasn't sure of my name. "I'll show you," I said, pointing at a page in my passport. As a result I appeared on an official form as Mr. ISHOYU.

Two young soldiers sat opposite us in the cramped waiting room, saying nothing. We had decided to traverse Iran's eastern desert and cross the border into southwestern Pakistan—if we made it to Afghanistan, it would not be along an expected route. The next stop would be the city of Bam, and the first few minutes of the journey were enlivened by a loud-voiced man who stood by the open door until Kerman had given way to sand. Whenever the vehicle slowed, he shouted "Bam, Bam! Bam!" The bus jerked to a halt three or four times for new passengers to jump aboard. They slipped some cash to the driver without receiving a ticket. "Bam! Bam, Bam, Bam!" Far from imitating the baby in *The Flintstones*, the men were running a vibrant business.

We passed Mahan and then, for more than two hours, saw almost no trace of human settlement. The newly paved highway was devoid of traffic. Only here and there did clumps of grey-green tamarisk bushes disturb the monotony of sand. We were skirting the interior of the Lut Desert, one of the most arid and exacting on the planet. A surface temperature just above seventy degrees Celsius has been recorded here, and an air temperature above sixty-one (in some artificially provided shade, that is). Parts of the Lut — "the plains of emptiness" in Farsi — have an ecosystem based not on plant life but on migrant birds falling out of the sky, snagged in a sandstorm or exhausted by the heat. Insects eat the carcasses of birds; lizards feed on birds and insects; sand foxes devour the lizards, the insects, and the birds.

Black volcanic hills on the horizon. Jagged rocks amid the dust. A train of five camels, moving at a scriptural pace. As we approached Bam, a stream pushed through the sand; shrubs and a stunted tree fought to grow by the water's edge.

TWO BAMS EXIST: the old and the new. Palm trees abounded in the new city, where we checked into a hotel whose manager, an affable man with a severe curvature of the spine, brought us some unforeseen luxury: a tray of Lipton's tea, two small pots, a pair of porcelain cups. Our wallpapered ceiling overlooked a silent efficient fan and a framed photograph of the Shah, waving. Thanks to Iran's oil wealth, goods from all over awaited purchase even in this remote place. In a little store with a big Pepsi sign, I noticed Panamanian bananas, Taiwanese pineapples, Italian blenders, and portable stoves made in China.

"You must go to the citadel," the hotel manager said, but he did not elaborate. (We followed his advice rather than that of Rumi: "The entrance door to the castle is inside you.") As we strolled through the afternoon heat to the old city, we were unaware of its origins, its architecture, its abandonment. Nor did we realize that Lotf Ali Khan, having survived the long siege of Kerman, was captured here by Agha Mohammed Khan's soldiers. The grotesque tortures he suffered...But no, why go on? There are tales of cruelty so extreme, it serves no purpose to repeat them. Such tales exist almost everywhere: the republic of Venice, for example, was renowned for its beauty, wealth, and tolerance—and notorious for its imaginative techniques of torture. Besides, I knew nothing then about the history of Canada's "Indian residential schools." If Iran seemed a little unusual in the recurrent viciousness of its rulers, it struck me as even more unusual in the constant graciousness of its people.

Bam's citadel was made of adobe—sun-cured clay and straw—and was the largest such building in the world. The cobbled road to the inner stronghold curled and twisted, and what promised to afford a slender way up might lead only to a dead end, a trap into which arrows could be shot or burning oil poured from the walls and towers overhead. The ancient city stretched over fifteen hundred acres. Many of its vacant homes were in livable condition. A mosque seemed ready for worship at a moment's notice, if only the absent believers would respond to a muezzin's call. These were not sun-bleached ruins, I thought, so much as honey-brown dwellings and empty shops waiting, silent, patient, for the rebirth of life. I found it impossible to tell if a house or a bathhouse, a school or a bazaar, was two hundred years old, or five hundred, or a thousand. Far below the turreted citadel, a pair of trucks and a bicycle inched along a highway through the sand. Somehow the desolation heightened the city's beauty.

It began as a village in the era of Cyrus the Great, more than 2,500 years ago. Bam was the only settlement in a vast region, and a welcome halt on the Silk Road. It could draw on enough water to nourish citrus orchards and date palms, sustaining life for thousands of people. By the time of Shah Abbas I, the fortified city had a proud nickname: Emerald of the Desert. A haven for traders, it also thrived on the weaving of silk and cotton. Bam became an army town during the reign of Agha Mohammed Khan and his heirs, as the barracks and stables of a military garrison displaced the silkworm breeders. Civilians moved to the new town nearby, planting trees for food and shade. The soldiers lingered on until in Reza Shah's reign they too left for newer quarters, relinquishing the citadel to the desert sun. Time appeared to stop.

Time did not stop. On December 26, 2003, a hidden faultline below the citadel gave way and a sudden, massive earthquake destroyed old and new Bam, killing nearly thirty thousand people and leaving three times as many homeless. The mud-brick houses and shops in the modern city, like those of its predecessor, had no support beams; but unlike the citadel, the new buildings came with cement roofs and steel slabs. They collapsed, killing or grievously wounding residents entombed at home. Date palms alone remained upright in the debris.

When the earthquake hit, the ancient city disintegrated. Photographs taken in the following days show what had been the citadel of Bam and its adjacent structures: sunlit chaos; a mess of rubble; blond dust. Over the centuries the fortress had been built, developed, replenished, extended, conquered, and forsaken. Now it lay in ruins, a wasteland of powder.

Much of it has since been rebuilt. Immense care and large sums of money have gone into making sure today's citadel looks old enough to please and deceive tomorrow's visitors. The economic catalyst of Bam's future lies in its broken past.

CONFUSION ON THE BUS TO ZAHEDAN: a man asked us to stay with his family. Clare and I weren't sure how to respond. On the Hippie Trail, no amount of preparedness could replace the skill to improvise. In a cloudless evening sky, colour dwindled from a faraway peak, tempering it to a bluish silhouette. The man resolved our doubt when the bus arrived at the terminal, saying "Goodbye, everybody!" Only part of the highway from Bam had been paved, and we were glad to disembark. The terminal stood on the edge of a dusty frontier town: twenty-five miles to the north, Iran, Pakistan, and Afghanistan collide at a single point. We set out into Zahedan on foot.

The driver of a pickup truck picked us up and dropped us near the centre of town. As usual, the first hotel we tried had no vacancies, but a curly haired, round-eyed young man named Rais introduced himself and led us down a side road to the Hotel Asia. A large room with a cold shower was not all it had to offer; the staff had lugged some metal beds onto the hotel's flat roof. We could keep our backpacks safe in the locked room and spend a couple of nights in sleeping bags under the desert stars. *I saw the green farmland of heaven*, wrote Hafez, *and the sickle of the new moon; / I was reminded of what I myself had sown...*

After breakfast, we walked to the railway station. A train into Pakistan was scheduled to depart the following morning.

"This is correct," the clerk said. "The train will leave at half past seven."

We asked to buy two tickets.

"This is not possible. The train may be cancelled."

What? It might not set off?

"Yes, the train will not be cancelled."

Call me the king of the mad, Hafez also wrote, *For my colossal ignorance exceeds all.*

Back in our hotel room — ticketless, perplexed — we rested for a while. If the train was a fact, not just a guidebook rumour, it would be a thirty-six-hour test of our endurance. Then we decided to explore Zahedan. I was standing in the corridor, waiting for Clare to finish writing a letter, when a soldier knocked on the door of the room opposite ours. He spoke briefly to the occupant — rumpled, T-shirted, middle-aged — and saluted.

A few hours later we met Rais again by chance in a park, books under his arm. He was studying at a Zahedan college with the aim of becoming a teacher. "I am *very* clever," he said with a grin. "I know everything!" But his own words betrayed him, even if he had read Hemingway and morsels of Shakespeare. "Can you tell me," he asked, "about a book named *One Thousand Nine Hundred and Eighty-Four*? I have heard it is about Iran."

Rais was a Baloch, from a village of four hundred people. As a mother tongue he spoke Balochi, a language that has a rich oral literature but little in written form. His people, like the Kurds, suffer the perpetual misfortune of national borders that sever their homeland: Baloch territory is divided among Pakistan, Iran, and Afghanistan, and nowhere does the language enjoy official status. In all three countries, Baloch people have engaged in small-scale wars and hopeless insurgencies of the sort that abound in the poorer regions of the planet, seldom earning more than a paragraph in the international press.

Three of Rais's friends joined us in the park before he had to leave for class. Their skin was noticeably darker than that of Iranians elsewhere. One of them, a fresh-faced boy named Saeed, insisted on guiding us to the post office and on buying the stamps for Clare's letter when we got there. He told us he was eighteen, although he looked younger. His English had a whiff of old-fashioned formality. "God forbid," he said as we left the post office, "a policeman!"

Saeed and his friends were unwilling to say goodbye. Indeed, they invited us back to their home. Clare and I accepted at once: Zahedan was hardly blessed with historic mosques or attractions of any sort. It had been a village in the 1930s when Reza Shah made it a provincial capital. Zoroastrians were once the only outsiders keen to visit the region — they believed Lake Hamun, on Iran's Afghan border, held the seed of the prophet Zoroaster, and the lake would play a crucial role in the final salvation of the world. Alas, Lake Hamun has disappeared. Like the Aral Sea, it is now a dustbowl. A series of dams in Afghanistan captured and terminated the Helmand River, preventing fresh water from flowing into southeastern Iran and transforming a fertile basin into a wasteland of salt flats.

Assailed by a sandy wind, we walked toward the outskirts of Zahedan. We passed a pair of liquor stores, both run by Sikhs. Saeed told us not to be concerned about the soldiers — "but if we are stopped by a policeman, please say we are taking you to the railway station." The police, he warned us, keep a close watch on Baloch students.

Home proved to be a pair of clean but dingy rooms shared by Saeed, Rais, and four other boys studying at school or college. The landlord, a bearded man with grey-green eyes and a white headscarf, was also Baloch. After Rais arrived back from his class, the boys asked us to share their dinner — rice, flatbread, spiced chicken, Coke — and withdrew to the other room while we ate. I had a sad suspicion that because of us, their own meals would not include chicken.

After eating, we looked through their English textbooks. One volume, published by the University of London Press, contained an article on the joys of student life in Oxford. What could that provoke, other than puzzled envy, in the mind of a Baloch teenager from a desert village in Iran? I was relieved that none of the students had read that chapter, exempting us from the need to interpret the privileged intricacies of what felt like another world. A second textbook, published in Tehran, had a chapter on women's rights. The author noted that, as of 1976, tens of thousands of women were enrolled in Iran's universities. Yet Baloch girls, Saeed told us, do not attend school. In a few months, after gaining his college diploma, he would marry a young girl, sight unseen. "Young girl" is an accurate phrase. To our disconcerted surprise, one of Saeed's friends explained that Baloch parents like to arrange weddings a few years in advance, when a son is fifteen years old, a daughter seven or eight.

This practice survived the ayatollahs' revolution: girls today continue to be forced into marriage. In November 2020, a Kurdish scholar was sentenced to nine years in prison after carrying out research into female genital mutilation and child marriage in Iran. A girl as young as nine can, if her father consents, legally be married; the practice is most common in rural areas. "It can be said," the judge declared in handing down his verdict, "that increasing the age of marriage for children is one of the enemy's strategies for weakening and ruining the family system." It could also be said, as George Orwell warned in *1984*, that war is peace and ignorance is strength.

Night fell quickly in Zahedan, and after we said goodbye to his friends, Rais walked us back to the Hotel Asia. Had we heard of *Hamlet*? Yes, we had heard of *Hamlet*. Had we heard of *Julius Caesar*? Yes, we had heard of *Julius Caesar*. We had also consumed some of his dinner. Had we given him anything in return?

Over the following years I would often wonder what became of Rais, Saeed, and all the other people who helped and befriended us in Iran. So much tumult, so many mutations: the monarchy became a republic; the billboards that incited spendthrift consumption were supplanted by murals of mullahs;

decades of peace were ruptured by a long and terrible war with Iraq. But the habits of torture would persist, and the unspoken or whispered fear of the Shah's secret police would quickly become a whispered or unspoken fear of the Revolutionary Guards. Somehow, people must be freed... "They are all the same here," realizes the newly imprisoned hero of Dalia Sofer's novel *The Septembers of Shiraz*, "the remnants of the shah's entourage and the powerful businessmen and the communist rebels and the bakers and bazaar vendors and watchmakers. In this room, stripped of their ornaments and belongings, they are nothing more than bodies, each as likely as the next to face a firing squad or to go home."

It is so easy—and not just in Iran—for armies and governments to instill fear in a people. It's much harder to nourish hope. Maybe that's what poets are for.

WE DECIDED TO TAKE our leave before sunrise the next morning. In my backpack, safe inside its wrapping of tissue paper and cardboard, lay the page of the *Shahnameh* I would be smuggling out of Iran—not a valuable antique, nothing that belonged in a library or museum, but still an elegant fragment of the national epic, a leaf torn from a flourishing culture with deep roots in the written word. *John Foster Fraser, cycling round the world...*

Sleeping fitfully on the hotel roof, nervous of any possible mishap at the train station, I woke near midnight, the sky tar-black, the stars dazzling in their brightness and abundance. Was Jupiter aligned with Mars? Only in my dreams. "Hello, how's life?" My head was both clear and spinning. *"No* do you want?" Cats were brawling in a street below. "How many years you have this job to be tourist?"

A rotund employee of the Hotel Asia silently patrolled the bagfuls of sleeping travellers. I raised myself on an elbow and grinned at him. He reached out a hand and tousled my hair.

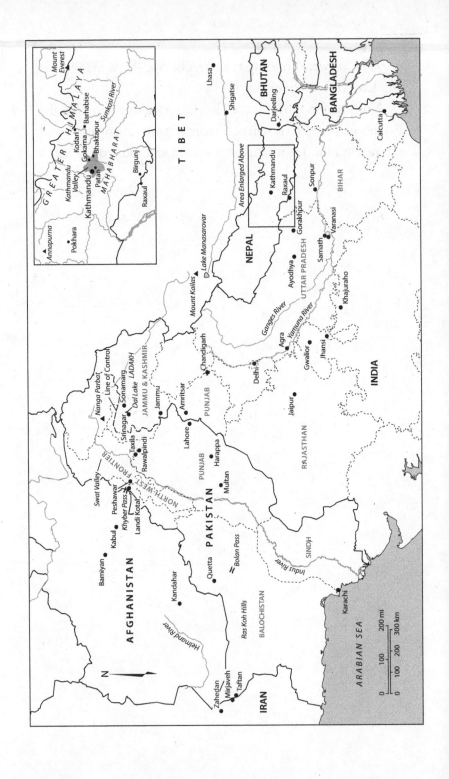

3.

Pakistan

"How do you feel about this life?"

Clare and I clambered aboard the smugglers' train. Its departure was a weekly ritual; why had we feared it might be cancelled? In the arid brilliance of a Zahedan dawn, we bought first-class tickets to travel second-class: the official second-class was the real third-class, and the real first-class went by the name *first-class deluxe*. There was no mystery, no pretence about the purpose of the train; the engine driver, the police, the railway inspectors, and the customs officers were all in on the deal.

We shared the carriage with a couple of dozen Baloch men and several Westerners. An hour before departure the men were already busy packing small items into spaces behind the seats, niches in the ceiling, nooks in the walls: wrenches, screwdrivers, pliers; boxes of Tide; bottles of liquor. Heavier and more valuable items remained in bundles or protruded from bags: coffee grinders, blenders, and other kitchen equipment; crates of Styrofoam in which more dangerous or furtive cargo may have been stashed. We saw no Baloch women on the train, and the only Baloch man who might not have been a smuggler was a grey-bearded elder with a white headscarf and a recurrent smile. Perhaps he merely wanted to visit relatives in Quetta, 450 miles away.

The train took three hours to reach the Iranian border post of Mirjaveh. Two motionless hours elapsed before we crossed over. I began to realize the full hardness of wooden seats. The work by the Shah's men was perfunctory: I didn't need to worry about the *Shahnameh,* and the Baloch men didn't need to worry about their tools, bottles, and appliances. Clare and I talked to a smuggling manager—a man who issued instructions that others obeyed, and who never divulged his name. With his squarish face, wide smile, and receding hair, he bore a startling resemblance to Jack Nicholson. The Pakistani customs officers, he said, would demand five thousand rupees in bribes: close to three hundred pounds.

The train lurched forward. It halted at a second border post where we had to buy new tickets for Pakistan. A further spell of languid movement, and we stopped in the little settlement of Taftan, this time for several hours. Once we felt confident the train was going nowhere fast, Clare and I walked a short way into town and bought some food at a stall in the marketplace. The signboards looked as if nobody had touched them for a decade. Flies zigzagged above the frying pans, buzzing, and the brave ones descended. A dog howled when a boot hit its flank. In the smoky heat, the smell of cooking oil mingled with the odour of shit. But the daal and chapatis tasted delicious.

I wasn't sure where the smugglers had gone. Just before we reached Taftan, the train had slowed to a crawl and most of them had jumped off, holding their bags or carrying bundles on their backs. Jack Nicholson stayed in the carriage, no doubt to pay the required fee. Hours later, the other men trickled back to the train with their assorted wares.

And then a fight broke out. A young American named Greg and a couple of his fellow travellers were relaxing in their first-class deluxe sleeper when a Baloch man walked in, hoping to retrieve or replace an item he had stowed in their private toilet.

"Get out!" Greg shouted.

The man refused. I wasn't sure which of them first shoved the other, but the corridor turned chaotic. Greg began shouting for the police. One of his companions pushed a Baloch teenager into a wall. A Baloch man in a long shirt and baggy trousers intervened. Soon the two of them were clutching each other by the throat. I and a few other people helped restore a semblance of order.

"It's so stupid," Greg said. He was quivering with anger. "I can't figure out why the Pakistanis would let a train get fucked up like this."

Some Baloch men disembarked and sat on the bare earth outside the window of the first-class deluxe sleeper. Jack Nicholson gripped a small knife in one hand, a mock noose in the other. He held them both up toward the window. The sliver of rope dangled in the air like a question mark.

Greg laughed at the men. He didn't care about their sense of honour. He was on his way to an ashram in India.

The Baloch men cleaned their faces and hands with sand, as the Quran advises travellers to do when water is unavailable. A Dutchman began to draw mandalas in the dust. I was puzzled by the clothes he wore in the late afternoon heat: a towel on

his head, a parka on his torso. A policeman arrived from somewhere, spoke briefly to a few people, and left.

"You have to remember," a woman heading slowly home to
New Zealand said to no one in particular, "they're just children."

The sun dropped before the train budged. On the floor of
our carriage, the Baloch men recited prayers. Sitting silently
beside the window, looking at nothing, I endured hours of
intense and miserable boredom — the carriage had no lights,
making it impossible to read or write, but I couldn't sleep.
I gripped *Anna Karenina*, a comfort blanket in thick paperback
form. Through a cold night I remained uncomfortably in my
seat while Clare shared an upper bunk, or ledge, with a girl
from Switzerland.

In the morning we stopped for an hour at a Pakistani army
post. Afghanistan lay a few miles to the north — for much of
the journey, we were skirting its closed-off border. As the train
approached the army post, the Baloch men again leaped off,
cargo in their arms and on their backs, and vanished into the
hills. Soldiers walked through a succession of almost empty
carriages. Once the engine had started up, the train pushed
ahead into the beginnings of a mountain pass before the driver
applied the brakes. But we didn't stay in place for long — maybe
other soldiers would appear, unwilling to turn a blind eye to
smuggling, or maybe the driver feared insurgents or bandits.
The Baloch men emerged from cover and ran hard to rejoin
us — I reached through the window to haul in three or four
bundles. A man of fifty or sixty didn't make it. The driver pulled
away leaving him a few yards shy of the open door, clutching
a boxful of blenders, alone on a bare slope.

Because of the help I briefly offered, and because of Clare's modest attire and friendly manner, one of the Baloch men assured us we were "good tourists." Jack Nicholson presented us with some chapatis and fresh-brewed tea.

"On the way back to Iran," he said, "we take oranges."

I didn't ask what else they might carry. A Swiss guy in our carriage must have been an even better tourist than we were: a smuggler gave him a small cake of hash.

For much of the day I immersed myself in Czarist Russia: elegant young ladies in fur-lined satin coats were travelling through Moscow's chilly streets, their wagon pulled by a horse... The land beyond these dusty windows seemed impossibly distant from the intrigues of the big world, yet two decades later the Ras Koh Hills, south of the tracks, would provide the setting for Pakistan's first test of a nuclear weapon, and rumours would circulate that Osama bin Laden was hiding out in the crumpled, roadless mountains along the Afghan frontier.

Twilight was greying a village near Quetta when the train stopped for some unannounced reason—perhaps the engine driver wanted to delay our arrival so that once we reached the city, the smugglers could melt into the darkness. Again most of the Baloch men stepped down onto the tracks. Now they left their bundles on the train and stood outside, talking and smoking. An old blind man appeared, hauling himself along the other line of rails. Was he a beggar? His clothes were ragged, his eyelids closed over. One of the younger smugglers put the blind man on his back and piggybacked him to the village station a hundred yards away.

Thirty-seven hours had passed since the train left the glare of a Zahedan sunrise and arrived in the blackness of a Quetta night.

PEOPLE WHO SET OUT on the Hippie Trail, or the Ashram Trail, were unlikely to give Pakistan much thought. Nearly all of us craved a mind-altering experience of Afghanistan or India. Some of us hoped to make it as far east as the snow peaks of Nepal, while others meant to venture south to the jungles and beaches of Sri Lanka. But Pakistan? A few Westerners headed up to the northern mountains where, in former princely state-lets, hundreds of tons of opium were grown. Such travellers were a small minority. Not many of us intended to linger in a country with little of the romance and none of the exotic wisdom that, in our Orientalist fantasies, other nations pos-sessed. Pakistan—in Urdu, the national language, the name means "land of abundant purity"—lacked glamour. Pakistan was an interlude, a stopover to be endured.

I should have read *The Conference of the Birds* more closely. When the birds begin to falter on their long journey, the hoopoe turns a famous Arab tale of undying, star-crossed love into a parable about the search for enlightenment: "A man who loved God saw Majnun sifting the earth of the road and said: 'Majnun, what are you looking for?' 'I am looking for Laila,' he said. The man asked: 'Do you hope to find Laila there?' 'I look for her everywhere,' said Majnun, 'in the hope of finding her somewhere.'"

There was much I could find in Pakistan, as long as I was willing to sift the earth of the road.

WHEN WE'D LEFT THE station forecourt, I stopped to check our directions. My senses were already reeling: the closeness of the stars in a clear sky; the scent of spices, drains, and nighttime flowers; the profusion of rickshaws and horse-drawn carts in a wide, potholed street. Most of the taxis had but a single head-light. Two men promptly befriended us, one of them a civil servant from Lahore dispatched to Quetta for a year to work on pensions. On their second attempt they found a hotel with a free room, but it recoiled from Westerners—too high a risk of illicit drugs and inquisitive police. On the fifth try, the men succeeded. Our room came with a diligent fan, a private toilet, and only a single visible cockroach.

Clare and I were hungry. Since our street-market daal the previous afternoon, we had survived on a few biscuits, chapatis, and oranges. The manager, Mr. Kalmati, suggested an unassuming restaurant that stayed open late, and when we'd set off into the darkness, he hurried after us with a loan of twenty rupees. I'd told him we had little cash on hand. The chicken curry was intense—fiercer than an Oxford vinda-loo—and sweet hot milk infused the cupfuls of tea. After all the glasses of clear tea we had sipped in Turkey and Iran, chai came as a shock. It served as a reminder that the prov-ince of Balochistan, indeed all of Pakistan, had belonged to the British Raj—or, you could also say, had been an integral part of India.

A few years after our journey, Quetta would be evoked on the opening page of Salman Rushdie's novel *Shame* as a remote town that looks, from the air, like "an ill-proportioned dumb-bell." It had about two hundred thousand residents when Clare and I were there. Today the population is several times higher, swollen by an influx of refugees from the unending conflicts in Afghanistan. Many of them are Hazaras, a minority people who suffer persecution no matter who reigns in Kabul. Between

2001 and 2021, Quetta would also serve as a stronghold of the Afghan Taliban's exiled leadership.

I knew nothing about the place, and the *Quetta Times*, which I read over breakfast, did little to enlighten me. It included a rambling feature on mythology and literature, and another article, equally lengthy, exploring the work of Baron Heinrich Friedrich Karl Reichsfreiherr vom und zum Stein, the architect of Prussia's reforms in the early nineteenth century. Neither Prometheus nor Baron Heinrich could explain why, as a much shorter article stated, the editor of a rival Quetta newspaper had been stabbed in broad daylight. The attack seemed particularly shocking because, for the past ten months, Pakistan had been under martial law. But far-off cities also had their troubles: Tehran, for one, was facing serious unrest.

After Clare dragged me away from an empty cup and the *Quetta Times*, we exchanged money in a cavernous bank. Fenceposts near the hotel were adorned with scraps of tinsel. Then, having repaid Mr. Kalmati, we tramped back to the railway station to arrange the next leg of the journey.

And what a station! It boasted a Railway Magistrate's Office, a Watch and Ward Inspector's Office, a Lamp Room, a Latrine for (Ladies), a Latrine for (Gents), and a Chief Confidential Stenographer's Office. It also contained a sombre memorial to railway staff: they had died in an earthquake that devastated Quetta in 1935, killing tens of thousands of people. A stall held some nonfiction books on Pakistan, the American bestseller *Love Story*, and, to my astonishment, *The Sensuous Man*. In the dim and capacious Office of the District Superintendent, it took us half an hour to obtain tickets at a student rate. But with the discount came a request from the ticket-selling clerk: "Please, will you buy some liquor? It is for my friend and myself."

The 1977 coup that had placed Pakistan under martial law — "Operation Fairplay," it was called — deposed the left-leaning, secular government of Zulfikar Ali Bhutto. In a futile attempt to forestall the coup, Bhutto had banned the sale of alcohol to Muslims. ("Yes, I drink," he admitted at a rally of supporters, "but I do not drink the people's blood!") Now a conservative military regime ran the country, led by General Zia-ul-Haq, a man who allowed for no distinction between a sin and a crime. A leading Pakistani writer, Mohammed Hanif, would sum him up as "a mullah with the instincts of a corrupt tax inspector." Members of minority faiths — Hindus, Christians, Sikhs, Parsis — could still purchase alcohol, although only at a government-run store that kept a register of names and addresses. Foreigners enjoyed the right to buy liquor for their own use.

We didn't think about the possible consequences when we agreed to help the clerk. He must have been ready for us — ready, I mean, for anyone willing to help out — because five minutes after issuing our tickets in the District Superintendent's Office, he led us to a car waiting outside the station. Clare and I climbed into the back. The clerk took the front passenger's seat on the left-hand side of the vehicle (in Pakistan, unlike Turkey and Iran, people drive on the left). His friend steered along some half-paved roads and stopped the car a minute's walk away from a dingy, unmarked building. The men handed over four large banknotes and several smaller ones. As we made our way to the liquor store, I could feel their eyes on the back of my head. We had our instructions.

Only one person stood in line ahead of us: a white-haired Hindu man, born in Delhi, who greeted us with amiable courtesy.

"I worked in Persia for the British," he said. "My family? Thank you for asking. They are living now in Australia, in England, in Canada."

We never found out why fate had stranded him in Quetta, for his turn at the counter arrived.

Our turn involved much filling out of forms and a close examination of our passports. No, our names do not appear on the local register. Yes, these drinks will be for our own consumption. Yes, we are devout Christians (out of the corner of my eye, I saw Clare stifle a grin). Do you really need to know my father's middle name? Very well. It dawned on me at last that we were about to commit a small crime—foreigners were prohibited by law from buying alcohol for Muslims. On one of the forms I went down as "Mr. Chaupman," a misspelling of my own middle name. The vendor asked a question for the second time: Did Clare and I intend to drink these thirty-two pints of beer, these two small bottles of brandy, and these two large bottles of Quetta Vodka? *Yes, of course. Pakistan is a very hot country in May, and we are good tourists. Thirsty tourists, I mean.* All these bottles would cost a total of 446 rupees. Did we have that much money on hand? *Why yes, here it is, already counted out.*

Our new acquaintances were delighted to see us—or rather, to see what we held in our arms. For once on the journey, we had been of service to others. Months later, General Zia would impose a new penalty on any Muslim caught drinking alcohol: a flogging of eighty lashes.

LEAVING QUETTA, I showed just how good a tourist I was.

Two middle-aged men began a conversation with us as we waited for a train that would thread a line through the Bolan Pass, across a scrubby desert, and down into the Indus Valley. Rameez was on his way home; he had failed to reach Mecca without a passport. Arrested by guards at the Iraqi border, he'd spent seventeen days in an Iranian jail before being sent back to Pakistan. He withstood two weeks in prison in Quetta before, somehow, obtaining the three hundred rupees he needed for his release. Yet he didn't want to describe these recent adventures in detail. Having worked in a Birmingham factory for four years in the 1960s, he wanted to talk about England. Rameez had tried to fly back to London in 1971 after his father died there, but Britain had refused to admit him. Not reaching his destination seemed to be a theme of his life.

Now he was repeating the names of Birmingham streets and London neighbourhoods — "Do you know *Ilford*? Do you know *Wanstead*?" — as though to fix them in our minds as well as his own, establishing a vital connection with a country he would never see again. We nodded, listened, and sipped the sweet chai that his friend Bashir bought for us all. Bashir took a sip, cleared his throat, and began to express his anger at Britain's citizenship laws and immigration policies.

"Will you agree, English treatment of Pakistanis is shameful?"

Clare and I nodded some more.

"Do you know *Walthamstow*?"

The train pulled into the station, absolving us of the need to remember the tangled geography of outer London. I wished the men well and turned away. Passengers-in-waiting had filled the platform.

"Be sure to find seats," the vodka-drinking clerk had told us. "This is the important thing only." The train was very long, but it had just a few first-class carriages—not counting the air-conditioned deluxe sleepers. I jumped into the nearest one, followed by Clare, a Swiss couple, and three German youths.

"Isn't this a Ladies Only compartment?" Clare asked as we heaved our backpacks into the luggage space and lowered ourselves onto seats that were, mercifully, softer than those on the smugglers' train.

"It doesn't say so anywhere."

"I thought I saw it chalked up outside."

She was right. But by then we had our seats. Forty minutes after we boarded, a railway guard asked us to move elsewhere. We said no. He marched away and came back accompanied by another guard, then by an employee who worked in one of the station's many offices. They instructed us to pick up our belongings and switch carriages. The Germans and I looked at each other.

"You have to find us other seats," we said. "We'll leave if you do that."

This may have been true in theory, but we knew the train was packed. The guards walked off and eventually returned with a pair of policemen. One of them wagged his finger and said in a loud voice, "You are preventing Pakistani ladies from boarding!"

The Swiss woman began to weep and said she could not be separated, under any circumstances, from her beloved fiancé.

"We were shown this compartment by a station clerk," I lied.

The guards, the policemen, and the railway official hemmed and hawed, then asked us one more time to leave. Instead of answering, I lowered my eyes into the final chapters of *Anna Karenina* (soon the passionate heroine would throw herself under the wheels of a train). Our train whistled, hissed, and rumbled away from Quetta at last; we had caused a delay of half an hour.

"I do feel some qualms," I wrote in my journal. "We are abusing the nation's customs, even their laws. If we weren't foreigners, we'd have been thrown off physically. It does sour things, and after the last train trip I want to keep things sweet! But if it weren't for this, we'd be in great discomfort."

That's the young man I was in May 1978, and although I know the following month would find us squashed on a train in greater discomfort than I imagined possible, it stings to read the entry today. I had become a prime specimen of what the Antiguan-American novelist Jamaica Kincaid has called "people from rich countries in the process of experiencing the world as spectacle." Her words are an unsettling summary of the entire Hippie Trail.

From the comfortable solitude of a mostly vacant carriage, Clare and I looked out on the bare peaks and spectacular gravel gorges of the Bolan Pass. Ridges jutted out from the mountains like giant skeletal ribs. A sign beside the tracks warned: STOP DEAD. A riverbed, dry for most of the route, acquired a trickle of water before the train plunged down and down. It passed through a set of tunnels, one of them as dark as Kaymakli. Sandstone tablelands and serrated hills gave way to a desert with sparse vegetation, a lizard on the run, a hot wind that bruised our faces through the window slats. I peered out and saw a man sitting alone on a flat-topped rock, no house or vehicle or animal in sight. At sunset camels appeared on a highway that ran beside the tracks: groups of four or six or twelve, marching in single file, each impossibly long neck a letter *U* on the move. Some of the smaller camels were so pale as to be almost white. Then darkness took hold.

We woke at dawn to the sight of the Indus River, split into several languid branches. In one of them, small boys were swimming naked. The sandy-coloured earth sustained crops and tall-treed woodland. Domestic animals seemed to be everywhere: oxen, horses, water buffalo. Men sowed the fields by hand and plowed them by ox. Tractors were rare. Clare and I were in the Punjab now, the wealthiest province of the country and the most populous, thanks to the life-giving waters of the Indus. Strategic, fertile, densely populated, the whole Punjab region has long been disputed territory among empires, kingdoms, republics, and religions.

We passed through the city of Multan, got off in Sahiwal, and, leaving our backpacks at the station, caught a local bus the twelve miles to Harappa, one of the oldest settlements on Earth. It emerged nearly five thousand years ago, at the core of what archaeologists call the Indus Valley civilization. In the remote past the river, which springs to life in Tibet and now flows almost entirely through Pakistan, gave its name to a country: India. Until the political cataclysm of 1947 that severed India and created Pakistan, the richly fertile lands of the Indus Valley had been integral to the whole idea and meaning of India. The river also named a language (Hindi) and a religion (Hinduism), neither of which play any significant role in Pakistani life.

At noon, as we arrived in Harappa, the museum, resthouse, and "archaeological bungalow" were all closing for lunch. We strolled to the nearby modern village chaperoned by a pair of friendly students, one of them a Hunza boy from the snow peaks of the north. The heat we had experienced in Iran was nothing to the heat here: more than forty degrees Celsius in the shade. What shade? Some villagers were lugging water in stone jars, others had bundles on their heads—how much, I wondered blearily, had changed in five thousand years? A striped squirrel darted through a garden that smelled like a tropical greenhouse back home. What home?

The students who had led us into the village stayed as we drank mango juice after mango juice. (Water after water would have been a risky pleasure.) They went elsewhere when we plodded back to the archaeological site, but two others took their place. Their desire to be helpful was undermined by their erratic English. A bony horse appeared on a path, its front legs shackled together, and one of the boys exclaimed "A zebra!"

We laughed, of course. But Clare and I did not know the word for *horse, zebra, squirrel,* or any other animal in either Urdu or Punjabi, the main language of the province. I thought nothing of this at the time: it seemed only natural that people in Pakistan would address us in English, sometimes bruising it in the process. In Iran I'd made a modest effort to learn about Farsi poetic traditions, yet in Pakistan I had no idea that Urdu is also a language rich in poetry. The British Empire had died, and its heart still beat faintly inside me: I had internalized a right to power.

A city made of bricks...organized in a grid...boasting a citadel...ingenious drains...I was interested in Harappa, truly, but the heat defeated me. My sunstruck imagination failed me. In the absence of air conditioning, even the gaming pieces, toys, and animal figurines in the museum held little allure. Clare and I drifted outside again and stood for a minute, grateful for the dense shade of a thorn tree (the people of the Indus Valley civilization are thought to have worshipped trees). The ruins exposed in the distance had welcomed life for more than a millennium, until Harappans became too successful for their own good; their domestic animals and crops exhausted the land, leaving them at the mercy of drought and climate change.

Beyond the blistering urban remnants stood some high mounds—not all the area had yet been excavated. The whole site suffered irreversible damage in the nineteenth century when the British constructed a railway between Multan and Lahore. They wanted bricks to serve as ballast for the tracks, and Harappa had bricks in plenty. By dismantling the ancient houses and digging beside the mounds, the railway builders destroyed much of the city.

Fortified by hot tea and a chilled Coke, we took the bus back to Sahiwal and a stopping train on to Lahore. The wheels rolled for a hundred miles above the crushed debris of Harappa.

THE PAKISTAN OF 1978 was a nation steaming with pressure and brimming with grievances. Its citizens were still coming to terms with the loss, seven years earlier, of the eastern half of the country. Modern India (a source of perpetual grievance) had humiliated Pakistan in a war that saw the birth of a new nation, Bangladesh—and the world's sympathies were not with Pakistan, whose soldiers had raped and murdered thousands of Bengali women. A lack of American aid in the war induced an extra layer of grievance—most Pakistanis had imagined Washington to be a close ally. Britain gave further cause for anger, and not just because of its immigration policy. In 1947, as its self-righteous and often brutal empire staggered to a close, it had imposed a sudden border that severed families and communities, causing immeasurable grief and pain. The partition left India controlling much of Kashmir; many Pakistanis felt betrayed, as the vast majority of Kashmiris were and are Muslim. And so on. The nation's shoulders were scarcely wide enough to bear the weight of all its chips.

Every commentator on Pakistan during those years (and many since) fumed at the corruption, the violence, the crippling failures of government. But there was no agreement on who to blame: the military, the Bhutto socialists, the feudal landowners, the Muslim clerics, the police, the quarrelsome provinces... Was this so different, though, from England? Complaints were rife there too, whether the source of annoyance was the current government, the previous government, the coal miners, the press, the Irish, the French, the Arabs, or any number of other groups. Unless the British mood were to improve, these complaints risked attaining the level of rage that many Pakistanis already felt. Clare and I had left a grumbling England to arrive in a tinderbox nation where anyone might be clutching a match.

At the time, Zulfikar Ali Bhutto was lying in solitary confinement in a tiny cell of a Lahore prison riddled with mosquitoes, flies, and other insects. He had lost forty pounds since his arrest and was vomiting blood. Bhutto had been sentenced to death in March, eight months after the coup that ejected him from power. Most of his large and talented family displayed extreme arrogance—it was among the traits that brought him down. (His daughter Benazir, a student at Oxford, had stood on Annie's hand at a garden party while wearing high heels, and she had not apologized.) While in office, Bhutto had treated General Zia with open disdain, calling him "my monkey general" and shouting "Come here, monkey!" Zia enjoyed the sugar-high of righteous revenge. He made sure the courts would show Bhutto no mercy. The general cut a much less suave figure than his predecessor: with his plump belly, awkward moustache, and centrally parted hair, he needed his medal-heavy uniform to resemble a leader. Bhutto had the image of a modernizer. But it was Zia, with his insistence on Sharia law, imposing prison terms for blasphemy and the death penalty for adultery, who wrenched his country into the future.

Clare and I understood little of this. We knew only that in the Pakistani newspapers we bought, the name "Bhutto" was continually absent. As we discovered when we crossed the border into India, those newspapers also kept silent about the flogging of Pakistani journalists who dissented from the government line.

THE TRAIN TO LAHORE was a slow one. It didn't reach the station until 9 p.m. A ponytailed North American tried to pick me up: "Are you of the Family?" he asked three times. He meant the Family of Love—a California-based cult, previously known as the Children of God, soon to become notorious for various sorts of sexual misconduct. When the recruiter had moved along to the next carriage, a young Pakistani man began to chat with us. Amin came from a rich, well-connected family. He had spent a year in Woolwich, he told us, on the south bank of the Thames, but now he was a student at Lahore's University of Engineering and Technology. Indeed, he and his aunt lived in a house by the campus—would we like to stay the night? Mention of an aunt reassured Clare (men, unlike those in Iran, had pestered her over the past few days). We accepted the offer.

In the dark the train chugged through a suburb of Lahore. "Mr. Bhutto," Amin said softly, "is being kept in the prison here."

The taxi that whisked us through the city suffered a flat tire after a sudden high-speed manoeuvre. Tehran's traffic had been tame by comparison. At the house, we found ourselves in the thick of a family dispute. Amin had a request for us: "Do not tell the army man anything!" The army man was a retired officer who lived with Amin's aunt—his mother and father, after a divorce, had found new partners elsewhere. Neither the officer nor the aunt looked happy to see Amin, or us. After a difficult period of silence, Amin's imagination began to run wild. One of his uncles, he informed us, was the president of Pakistan, or had been. His father's current girlfriend was the daughter of the Egyptian president Anwar Sadat—Clare and I traded frowning glances—but, five minutes later, she worked as a secretary in the Turkish Embassy.

I played three games of chess with Amin that evening, although the rules were not quite the ones I knew: his white queen, for instance, faced my black king. (That's how the board was arranged in India long ago, before Persians, Arabs, and Europeans borrowed and adapted the game.) The result was happily inconclusive: a win for each of us, and a draw.

"The wrong type of people go from Pakistan to Britain," Amin said as the night wore on. "Illiterate people. Uneducated people from the villages."

He seemed desperate to make sure we didn't see him that way.

"They asked me about you on the train," he confided. "The CIA."

I assumed this must be a delirious invention. And maybe it was. I didn't realize, however, that Pakistan's Central Investigation Agency has the same initials as America's spy service.

Finally Clare and I crawled into our sleeping bags on the floor. The aunt was equally terse in the morning and the retired officer kept to his bedroom, making it easy for us to tell him nothing. Amin suggested we travel with him from Lahore down to Karachi, the largest city in the country, or head up to Rawalpindi, where he said his family had another house. Instead we decamped to a hotel near the railway station, whose tall brick turrets looked like a hybrid of English clock towers and Asian minarets.

We spent a couple of scalding days in one of the great cities of the Indian subcontinent—also, by common consent, the birthplace of Pakistan. The inner heart of Lahore has ancient walls, and even in the forty-two-degree heat it was easy for us to walk to a fort, a museum, two elaborate mosques, the tomb of the Mughal emperor Jahangir, and a pair of elegant gardens that echoed with the inelegant squawks of parakeets and the bubbling cries of mynas. Fountains in the Shalimar Gardens had slackened to a dribble. Flimsy wooden scaffolding rested against the walls of the Wazir Khan Mosque, built with lavish grandeur in the 1630s, and nobody appeared to mind that in its shade, some men were lying down. Shade, anywhere, was a blessing.

"There are two social classes in Pakistan," a sardonic professor remarks in Mohsin Hamid's novel *Moth Smoke*. "The first group, large and sweaty, contains those referred to as the masses." The much smaller second group—the elite—are those with air conditioning. "You see, the elite have managed to re-create for themselves the living standards of, say, Sweden, without leaving the dusty plains of the subcontinent. They're a mixed lot—Punjabis and Pathans, Sindhis and Baluch, smugglers, mullahs, soldiers, industrialists—united by their residence in an artificially cooled world." The elite are more numerous today than when Clare and I travelled through Pakistan, but so are the great uncooled. Pakistan's population has tripled since 1978, a year when Lahore had fewer than three million residents. By 2022, over thirteen million people lived there.

This was Kim's home city, and the huge cannon that Rudyard Kipling's novel had made famous decades earlier still guarded the Lahore Museum. I had read *Kim* in a high-school English class. It's a proof of lingering colonial influence that in the era of Pierre Trudeau, a Canadian province would oblige its students to plow through a lengthy novel exalting the British Empire of the late nineteenth century. *Kim* meant almost nothing to teenagers in Saskatchewan: with all its *khandas* and *kuttars*, its *chumars* and *bunnias*, the richness of its Indian-inflected language was deeply obscure to us. By the 1970s the novel's assumptions about empire, army, race, and masculinity were hopelessly outdated. Yet it would have been inconceivable then for any Canadian school board to assign a compulsory text by a living author from India or Pakistan.

I wish I could say that I celebrated my twenty-third birthday by purchasing a novel by a Pakistani writer. But no. That day we wandered through the Old Anarkali Bazaar, named for a prostitute who fell in love with the crown prince—the future Jahangir—only to be executed by his emperor father. Or so the story goes. Merchants in the bazaar tendered fruits and boots, textiles and tea, jewellery and leatherwork, and I shunned them all in favour of the booksellers. One of the shops promised "Latest Books for all sexes and all tastes." In the scruffy, unruly swagger of the Ideal Book House, I bought a hardcover copy of *Jubilate Agno* by the eighteenth-century poet and madman Christopher Smart. No poet before or since has delivered such beautiful praise to a cat, nor asked the dawn to rejoice with the frigatebird upon the coasts of India. And besides: *For there is a traveling for the glory of God without going to Italy or France.*

The glory of God can be a troublesome concept. That morning, in the *Pakistan Times,* a government frontman had declared: "Pakistan is an ideological state with ideological frontiers." The nation has a single reason for existence: Islam. But how do you confirm the borders of an ideological state, and how do you guard them from invasion?

The Punjab festered with competing religious angers: Muslim, Hindu, Sikh. When Clare and I tried to visit a prominent Sikh temple, the Gurdwara Dehra Sahib, we found its doors were locked. I did not realize—and the tourist brochures did not say—that Lahore holds immense significance for Sikhs as well as Muslims. Dehra Sahib may well stand on the exact spot where a leader of the faith, Guru Arjan, was murdered at the behest of a Mughal emperor in 1606. The city contains other Sikh temples built where adherents of the young faith endured torture, incarceration, or death; at least one of those temples now functions as a mosque. In the early nineteenth century,

Lahore would become the capital of a Sikh empire ruled by Ranjit Singh, "Lion of Punjab," a gifted military leader with twenty wives, dozens more concubines, and a serious weakness for alcohol. Forces loyal to the Raj put an end to the Sikh regime. Yet in 1946, just before independence put an end to the Raj, two million Sikhs lived in the regions of British India that would soon become Pakistan. Partition sundered their lives. By 1978, no more than twenty thousand Sikhs made Pakistan their home.

The newspapers we read in Pakistan bulged with stories about Operation Dragon King, a purge of Rohingya Muslims in Burma. That year hundreds of thousands fled across a porous border into Bangladesh, escaping malice and oppression in a country run by Buddhists. In Burma, as in so many other places, faith had become identity, and identity had turned to rage. Was there a single organized religion, I asked myself, whose leaders had *not* incited hatred of people who worshipped in a different manner? I began to wonder if every God-shaped emptiness should, on moral grounds, remain unfilled.

AT STRAY MOMENTS ON the trip, I tried to revise old poems — between Isfahan and Quetta I tinkered feverishly with a lyric about death and snow — and compose new ones. Most of these attempts were abject failures. The noise, heat, and commotion of Pakistan brought out the worst in my pen. On a steam train going north from Lahore, I began a poem by writing: "The ice cream cone you eat will soon be part of you." No: no, no, no. I was straddling a low box in the aisle, having boarded too late to grab a seat. A lick of ice cream would have been a joy.

We were heading northwest to the ruins of Taxila, a wide valley in which cities have risen and fallen for millennia. Among them are the remains of an early Buddhist culture, one that inspired extraordinary works of art. I was keen to explore Taxila partly because of a sculpture we'd seen in the Lahore Museum: the *Fasting Siddhartha*. A brilliant, shocking work carved deeply into stone, it shows a man of skin and ribs. The expression on his face suggests torment, not serenity—a figure whose body is primed for death but whose mind refuses to follow. The man is a hunger artist, a maestro of atrophy. Sitting in a meditative pose, he seems all action, all nervous energy. His stomach is an indrawn hollow; his arms are rods, his eyes small bowls of darkness. The sculpture serves as a graphic reminder that for Siddhartha to become the enlightened Buddha, he had to renounce renunciation. Hermann Hesse made use of the tale in *Siddhartha*, one of the most popular novels among travellers on the Hippie Trail.

The *Fasting Siddhartha* was unearthed in the Swat Valley north of Taxila. Throughout the entire region, over several centuries, Indian and Greek culture had fused in graceful, unexpected ways. "Beware," warned a sign outside the Taxila museum gate. "Fake sculptures and coins are sold in plenty around here." Indeed, we were offered many, not just by freelance hawkers but by an official guide. One of the coins purported to show Alexander the Great, who dismounted here with his troops three years after they ravaged Persepolis. The intellectual quality of Taxila surprised him: it was a haven of philosophers and gurus, even (by some accounts) a university town. Instead of ransacking the place, Alexander made a useful deal with the local ruler: he traded Persian tapestries and

Greek vases in exchange for hundreds of horsemen, thousands of sheep, and thirty elephants.

Twenty-three hundred years later, we had to sidestep animal droppings along the uneven paths of Taxila. A black-tailed godwit flaunted its orange throat near a stream cut by stepping stones. We saw the remnants of three Buddhist monasteries, all of them akin to their Christian counterparts in faraway realms: chapels, a central quadrangle, a shrine for images, a manuscript room, sleeping cells, and a communal kitchen. Are there unrecognized threads, I wondered, that tie Buddhism and early Christianity together? Could Buddhist sites like these have influenced monastic life far to the west? I mistrusted, and still mistrust, the standard academic reluctance to consider the idea.

In the museum, near a display case of stone heads, we came upon a piece of marble with a fragmentary inscription. It records the words of Ashoka, an emperor who governed most of the Indian subcontinent and who played a critical role in transforming Buddhism into a powerful, wide-reaching faith. Ashoka, like Xerxes and Darius before him, deployed rock slabs to broadcast his authority. Unlike them, he had other news to share. His edicts urged people to refrain from killing or mistreating animals. He called for the planting of forests, the love of morality, the avoidance of useless ceremonies, and the proper instruction of elephant trainers. I was amazed to learn that the marble chunk unearthed here in Taxila had Aramaic wording—two and a half centuries later, Aramaic would be the daily language of Jesus. Ashoka dispatched Buddhist envoys into Greek-speaking territories far beyond India: the traffic of art and knowledge between East and West has always flowed in more than one direction. In 1958, before Afghanistan began to tumble into its many circles of hell, excavators working near the city of Kandahar unearthed a rock edict with a bilingual text in Aramaic and Greek. There Ashoka announced that he and many other men had given up fishing and hunting, and said that "Everything thrives throughout the whole world."

Clare and I stayed in the Taxila Youth Hostel. We arrived there in a two-wheeled horse-drawn cart driven by a silent boy who took evident pleasure in whipping his horse. Ashoka would have shared our dismay. The caretaker, a tall, slender, meticulous gentleman, looked startled to see us. Halfway through May, we were only his second couple of the month. He showed us to a private room complete with toilet, shower, and lizard. Having been ill for days with a recurrent fever — malaria, I suspected — the caretaker had a haggard appearance and moved with ponderous care. He prepared a potato curry for our evening meal, a curry so ferocious that after a single mouthful, Clare burst into tears. I recalled the glum advice about Pakistani food in *Student Guide to Asia*: "On the trains it is very bad, and even in the good hotels it is not much better." But we needed to eat. Luckily Clare had the bright idea of retrieving our medical kit and stirring some glucose tablets into our bowls. This made the curry taste both sweet and weird, the culinary equivalent of "Disco Duck."

The caretaker's halcyon days had come and gone. Sydney, Tokyo, Manila: he had visited them all, he said, as centre-half on the field hockey team of an undivided India. In 1936, at Hitler's Olympics, India had triumphed, defeating Germany 8–1 to win the gold medal. But the caretaker wasn't in Berlin to play hockey. He was there to compete in the high jump where, he told us, he won the silver medal by leaping six feet and seven inches. After returning home he gave up his athlete's uniform for military gear and fought the Japanese, being awarded two stars for valour in the British Indian Army. But now, he said, "My life is finished."

There was, of course, no Google in those days. No easy way for me to check the records of the 1936 Olympics and to learn that a Black student from Alabama had won the silver medal in the high jump. No athlete from India competed in the event.

I'm glad I didn't know this at the time. The caretaker looked as if we should be serving him, but instead he served us. We had, at the very least, an obligation to listen. He complained repeatedly about his scanty pension and pulled down a portion of his upper garment to show us the scars on his back. They came, he said, from wounds inflicted in Borneo or Malaya. Aside from praying five times a day, he devoted what little energy he had to maintaining this obscure and modest hostel in the midst of spectacular ruins. Before we left he tried, unsuccessfully, to stop us catching a bus from Taxila to Peshawar in the North-West Frontier Province. "The train," he attempted to explain, "is very like you."

Maybe so, but the bus was efficient. I'd never seen a vehicle dripping with such a psychedelic shower of images: flowers and diamonds, eyes and hearts, centaurs and airplanes. On a smaller scale, the rickshaws of Peshawar displayed the same aesthetic. Pathan tribesmen, wearing bullets around their necks, crowded the city's streets and bazaars. A clamorous district near our hotel contained at least forty "Chemist and Druggist" shops. Another store boasted the name "Quite Cool Refrigeration." I exchanged some money in a prominent bank; the transaction was entirely unofficial, completed without a receipt, a signature, or the usual filling out of several forms.

We made a final attempt at Afghanistan. A man in the tourist office scrutinized our passports and visas and gave us a tentative go-ahead. But a clerk at the Peshawar bus station disagreed. He said we needed to buy new transit visas, ones that would allow us to enter Afghanistan via the Khyber Pass and the Kabul Gorge. Those visas would also require us to leave the newly Marxist country within four days, using a different exit point far to the west or south. Clare and I decided, with regret, that the pale blue airmail letters awaiting us at Poste Restante, Kabul, would forever go unread. Nor would either of us ever see the Buddhas of Bamiyan.

That evening, over a pulao of rice and lamb, or perhaps rice and mutton, or conceivably rice and goat, we talked to an English youth. Hugo had graduated from a private school in London and would begin his philosophy studies at Cambridge later in the year. He was the son of an Anglican priest. Having hitchhiked to Tehran, he was now paying his way, as cheaply as he could, to Kathmandu. Hugo had a mild, fresh-faced look, but he struck me as someone with a lot of inner toughness. He told us a story, impossible to verify, about his time in northeastern Iran.

"I met a Frenchman in Mashhad—he was painting the hotel where I was staying, and we became friends. He took me out to a cave in the desert where he's been living for the last three years. It was beside a wide, dry river. He simply meditates all day, lying on his back, staring at the sun. The thing is, he's developed these psychic powers. He can understand what's in your head, and he wants to control it."

Hugo spooned some more pulao into his mouth. I think my mouth was hanging open.

"On the fifth day I was there, he gave me some acid, and then I felt his mind inside my own. It was like his consciousness was working away at me from within, destroying all my own awareness of things. I couldn't tell where my identity began or stopped. It was like you could see a room in four dimensions, not just three, and then you *had* to see it that way."

"But you're here now," Clare said.

"Yes. I struggled to get away from him."

Then Hugo rose to gather his belongings and catch a night train to Lahore, leaving Clare and me to wonder about psychic powers. I had read some classic writings in the mystical tradition, and Hugo's story fascinated me. Hadn't the desert monks of Christian Egypt also performed feats of strange endurance in a barren wilderness? Didn't hermit monks in Tibet do the same?

Clare was skeptical. "I think," she said, "what Mother Teresa does is much more amazing than some guy ruining his eyesight by staring at the desert sun."

Neither of us remarked that if Hugo's story was true, the Frenchman had abused whatever gifts he'd developed by trying to seize control of someone else's mind. Maybe there were visionaries strung along the Hippie Trail. There were certainly charlatans.

THE HIPPIE TRAIL MAY have had its greatest influence not in the vastness of India, where all of us were headed, but in smaller, more vulnerable countries: Afghanistan, Nepal, even Iran and Pakistan. In the 1970s, these nations were in the throes of massive cultural change. Young travellers from the West supplied a constant warning, or promise, of what liberal values might entail. By our clothes and hairstyles, our language and music, our sexual and social freedom, our whole sense of what was normal and appropriate, we unwittingly tested and provoked the societies we travelled through.

Lives changed course as a result of our presence, although—unlike the colonial masters of the previous century—we set the changes in motion with no conscious intent. We had a minimal, erratic feel for Asian histories and cultures: How many Western travellers in Pakistan knew that apart from the national language of Urdu, each of the four provinces has a dominant language of its own? (I certainly didn't.) Many of us hoped to imbibe or inhale some tranquility; we didn't intend to proselytize for Western beliefs. Missionaries, whether for the Family of Love or any other cause, were few and far between. But as Clare and I had found on the smugglers' train to Quetta, close contact between local people and foreign tourists could easily produce friction. Only now, with the flight of time, is it clear how cross-cultural pressures in the 1970s affected some of what has happened in the region since.

The Asia-hungry travellers of the age—whether or not we self-identified as freaks—were nearly all in some kind in revolt. We rebelled against the suburbs. We rebelled against the authority of scripture and the dictates of mainstream religion. We rebelled, at least in theory, against doctrines and practices that subjugated women. We rebelled against the burdensome weight of government and big business. We rebelled against puritan views of sex. In short, we aimed to stick it to the Man. But in Asia we had little sense of who, or what, "the Man" could be.

We failed to grasp that our style of revolt would pose a challenge to cultures and nations far beyond the West.

For many of us, rebellion could blur into affectation. Some of the longest-haired and scruffiest-dressed travellers were actually on a Grand Tour no more political and no less privileged than the cross-Europe journeys made by pampered aristocrats in the eighteenth century. Privilege underwrote our dissent: we required time and money to travel so far. Privilege allowed us to ignore the daily lives of the local people we noticed along the way, as if in a side mirror. But when they looked at us, did they perceive idealistic rebels bent on achieving world peace and personal enlightenment?

Not likely. We were, I imagine, just part of a barrage of influences that included mass media, pop culture, new technology, unfamiliar foods and drinks—all of the shining and skin-deep appeal encapsulated in the name "America." If we were mimicked—in a friendly way, that is—we thought it was cool. Young Pakistani men began to grow their hair and sideburns: a minor change in its own right, and a symbol of much else. The arrival of cassette tapes had brought American and British pop music into South Asian homes for the first time: the fusion sounds of Indipop would soon follow. But if Western guests were easy for Asian hosts to observe and imitate, we also provoked mistrust. Even in the absence of paisley shirts and halter tops, even without dreadlocks and ponytails, Clare and I had been turned away from many half-empty hotels in Iran and Pakistan.

Western travellers, seen through reproachful eyes, took some dangerous liberties; our morality was dubious and our wealth, scattered so casually, underscored the poverty of others. Rich, innocent, dishevelled, many of us lacked dignity. (We could also arouse indignity in others.) We embodied the shock of the new. Our unexpected presence was but one of the many changes underway in South Asia, changes that promised—or threatened—to undermine the power of tradition. "The cultural makeover," observed the Indian writer Pankaj Mishra in *Age of Anger: A History of the Present*, "forced upon socially conservative masses aggravated a widely felt sense of exclusion and injury. The radical disruptions left a large majority of the unprivileged to stew in resentment against the top-down modernizers and Westernizers." Zulfikar Ali Bhutto, like the Shah of Iran, would discover the strength of that bitter resentment. It has continued to eat away at public life in Pakistan, a frail democracy haunted by the memory of military rule.

The early years of the decade were known in Pakistan as the Swinging Seventies. And the tensions of the period were on full display in the movie *Miss Hippy*, a musical released in 1974. Its title character, who goes by the surprising name of Bubbly, is the daughter of a nightclub-loving businessman. She takes to alcohol at a precocious age and runs away to join a cult of hash-smoking freaks led by an unscrupulous guru. The guru, also known as "comrade," presides over a drug binge that doubles as a group communion. He and most of the other characters speak Urdu, although the opening credits and occasional lines are in English.

"What country are you from?" a Pakistani man asks one of the guru's foreign disciples.

"Italy," replies a blonde girl with a British accent.

When an undercover cop infiltrates the cult, he learns that the guru, aided by some evil hippies, is smuggling large quantities of hash from the West into Pakistan. (The plot would have been more realistic if the drugs had moved in the reverse direction.) The hippies intend to corrupt the nation not just with hash but with orgies. Just in time, Bubbly sees the error of her ways. She helps the police restore order. In her last big speech, she asks why the government of Pakistan allows hippies to penetrate the country and argues they should be banned from entry. Just as Hollywood movies have often depicted zealous Muslims as a menace to the values of America, *Miss Hippy* showed decadent young Westerners as a peril to the virtues and traditions of Pakistan.

There's more to the film, however, than its righteous plot. Its box-office success in Pakistan belies the moralizing in its last half-hour, for what *Miss Hippy* preached is not what *Miss Hippy* evoked. With her big sunglasses, funky jewellery, bell-bottomed jeans, and long, free-flowing hair, the heroine symbolized Western glamour. To Pakistani men huddled in the cinemas of Karachi and Lahore, Bubbly was an enticing, unsettling object of desire. *Miss Hippy* personified cultural makeover in the guise of an erotic nightmare.

I HAD NO FAMILY connection to this part of the world. But Clare did. During the Second World War her uncle, a major in the Royal Artillery, had a grand piano hauled up the Khyber Pass to entertain British troops on the Afghan frontier. He also brought along an Italian piano tuner, to make sure the instrument would sound its best when the soldiers heard it played. Clare wanted to experience the route her uncle and his unit had taken. So did I.

And I got my wish. It would be wrong, though, to say that the experience was pleasant, or that on the journey from Peshawar up to the small, gun-laden town of Landi Kotal, I even *saw* the Khyber Pass. Clare and I were sitting near the back of a crowded bus that took almost two hours to crawl out of the Peshawar basin and climb more than a thousand metres through the Safed Koh mountains. Both of us had suffered some digestive issues throughout our days in Pakistan, and I thought mine had been resolved. I was mistaken. After half an hour on the bus, I began to feel the need to shit. After forty-five minutes, I felt an urgent need to shit. After an hour, I felt an overwhelming need to shit. The bus was guzzling fuel with infinite slowness through dry, treeless mountains, but I had little awareness of the rolling world outside: my entire will and energy were focused on my own body. I pulled my thighs together and pressed my buttocks down hard onto the seat. *Breathe...squeeze...breathe...squeeze...* How much longer could I last?

The bus creaked to a stop near the summit of the pass. Some of the Pathan tribesmen on board were evidently in spasms of the same distress as me. Two, three, four of them left the bus and walked a few yards to the roadside ditch. *Breathe... squeeze...* From the window, semi-hallucinating, I could see a white headscarf but not the man below it. Somehow I managed to stand up. Still pressing my thighs together, I staggered up the aisle to the front—the effort felt superhuman. Oblivious to the noises of warning or encouragement from other passengers, I heaved myself off the bus. In the ditch, in full view of God knows who, I lowered my pants and squatted to obtain instant, blessed, semi-liquid relief.

This is one way to gain enlightenment: How much pain can your body withstand? How much embarrassment can you endure? I don't recommend it for a moment.

The bus arrived in Landi Kotal and many of the passengers vanished, perhaps to buy guns—the town was and still is renowned for its weapons bazaar. Over the final few miles between the settlement and the Afghan border, Clare and I rode in the back of an open pickup truck with twenty other people. I kept my balance by clutching a chain along the starboard side. We outraced a small convoy of donkeys bent low beneath heavy packs. The checkpoint was a drowsy outpost—in the aftermath of the Kabul coup, the number of crossings had fallen sharply. Sand hung in the air. Dust clouds drifted up when a vehicle passed.

Soon the tense peace beyond the Afghan frontier would disintegrate. The Soviet invasion in 1979, a vicious civil war, the medieval brutality of the Taliban, the American-led invasion in 2001, flagrant corruption and further acts of terror, the Taliban's unsparing resurgence in 2021... How does a nation begin to recover? One or two suicide bombers even chose to blow themselves up on Chicken Street in Kabul, where bargain-hunting travellers had revelled in the lapis lazuli, leather bags, leopard skins, and other merchandise. The country has been devoid of tourists for decades. Yet in Europe and North America half a century ago, the prevailing cliché about Afghanistan was not a *mujahideen* with a rifle or a Talib with a bomb but a Volkswagen bus with a fragrant aroma. (Some of the trippy overlanders on the bus would have draped themselves in Afghan sheepskins.) Travellers once basked in the easy hospitality and the cheap drugs that local people offered them. The dollars greased the country's sputtering economy. No one stopped to think about the impact of so many foreigners with such alien dreams and beliefs.

How alien? Well, in 1968 an English psych-folk band then known as Tyrannosaurus Rex released a song with the title "Afghan Woman." It plays havoc with financial reality: the Afghan woman inhabits a palace, while her penniless English admirer somehow lives under a well. He imagines her bedecked with jewels and likens her to both a gazelle and a thoroughbred horse. Even so, he hopes that his youthly face will "quench" her. But was there ever an Afghan woman who longed to be quenched by the face of a foreign pauper, youthly or otherwise? In the late 1970s, an Anglo-Australian bus company filmed a documentary that showed pictures of a Kabul market accompanied by the voiceover remark: "Afghanistan typifies the real overland: that is, being able to view people in their natural habitat." David Attenborough might have said the same about camels.

Before I left England I met someone who admitted he nearly provoked a riot in Afghanistan by taking photographs of tribal women. The women were fully and ornately clothed, but their men demanded he remove the roll of film from his camera and pulled out their guns when he refused. Some Western travellers dressed skimpily; swimming in Afghan lakes, watched by Afghan men, they stripped down to underpants and bikinis. The writer Bruce Chatwin, who loved Afghanistan, blamed the behaviour of young overlanders for kickstarting the country's long downfall—he thought educated Afghans had become so angry or bemused, they turned to Communism in protest. Freaks pursued an innocent form of hedonism, or so it appeared, yet it had consequences.

Amid the decaying watchtowers of Landi Kotal we found the bus again, guarded by two men with guns and cartridge belts hung ostentatiously over their shoulders. A long, low fort made of orange and pink bricks marked the headquarters of the Khyber Rifles regiment. On the return trip to Peshawar, I saw the mountains and the switchbacking pass for what felt like the first time. So *this* was the route by which, in 326 B.C., the soldiers and horses of Alexander the Great had invaded India — Clare and I passed lines of roped horses on the road and underwent two police checks — the same route by which, in 1524, Babur's army had streamed out of Afghanistan to conquer northern India and create the Mughal Empire... The rapid, insistent swirls of Pathan music saturated the bus: earlier, during the intensity of my troubles, I'd been unaware a radio was even playing. The grey and khaki mountainsides looked too bare to sustain life. That night, venturing no farther than the hotel café, I consumed a traditional Asian meal of egg and chips.

Throughout the journey Clare and I liked to pick up a used book from a shelf in our hotel or hostel, leaving one behind for future travellers. I had abandoned *Anna Karenina* in Taxila and replaced it with *The Way of the Sufi* — an anthology of writings that included, among much else, a tale about Nasreddin, the offbeat mullah, and poems by Rumi, Saadi, and Hafez. Next morning in Peshawar, packing sluggishly, still thinking about the Khyber Pass, I came upon the briefest of parables: "A man once asked a camel whether he preferred going uphill or downhill." Looking across the room at Clare, I quoted the camel's riposte: "What is important to me is not the uphill or the downhill. It is the load."

"That's all very well," Clare said briskly, hoisting her backpack onto her shoulders, "but Sufis don't have trains to catch."

We set out just in time for a train back to Lahore—the main border crossing between Pakistan and India lies near the edge of the great city. To find our carriage at Peshawar station we obeyed a large sign: "Entry for Upper Class." The steam engine that powered the train seemed even smokier and noisier than usual.

"How do you feel about this life?"

A Pakistani man across the aisle was looking in my direction.

"Very good, and you?"

"Not good. Everyone has no money."

"Ah."

Then the man began to complain about the young Westerners staying in the Peshawar hotel he'd just left. They had smoked hash. They had talked loudly for much of the night. They had shown no respect for other guests. Clare and I apologized on their behalf—we liked to see ourselves as good tourists. Besides, it cost us nothing to express regret.

The train was full when it rumbled off, and it grew fuller after stopping in Rawalpindi, the fourth largest city in Pakistan. A lawyer from Multan joined the carriage there; standing in the aisle beside us, he began to talk. Before long he was formally inviting us to visit Multan.

"I'm afraid we don't have the time," I replied.

Having already told other passengers that we would not be travelling down to Karachi nor visiting the Murree hill station, we were accustomed to such offers. But the lawyer wouldn't let the matter drop. After informing us about a mosque, a cricket stadium, a striped mausoleum, and some other attractions of his home city, he expounded on the quality of Multan mangoes, plump and juicy, bursting with flavour: "the finest in the country."

"But this is not the mango season," said a gaunt old man sitting nearby.

The lawyer did not reply. He abruptly changed topics: "Have you embraced Islam?"

Clare and I glanced at each other.

"We are studying it," I said. This was not entirely a lie, as Clare had bought an English-language translation of the Quran and had delved into it more often than I had.

"I hope you will act on it."

"When we get back to England."

The train stopped at another station and the lawyer found an empty seat behind us. He began to chat to the old man in Urdu (or was it Punjabi?). A minute later, I heard one of the speakers resort to English: "But why should I bother foreigners?" The answer came in Urdu (or Punjabi).

The journey took eleven hours. Between Peshawar and Rawalpindi several beggars made their way down the aisle: a blind man, a child with Down syndrome, a couple of people on crutches. After Rawalpindi their number grew. A girl with a spinal or brain impediment moved with the utmost care. A woman in a torn shawl held out a bowl with her only arm. For me the most distressing sight was a tall, middle-aged man with half a face. The right side of his face looked normal: an eye allowed him to see. But the man had no left eye or ear — he appeared to have only half a nose and mouth — and huge swaths of skin hung in folds down the left side of his head almost to shoulder level.

"He must have been born like that," Clare said in a low voice.

I felt sad and sick at heart. The man made his rounds more slowly than any of the other beggars, even the blind: he knew his looks commanded attention. *He's turned deformity into an asset*, I thought, and immediately felt ashamed of myself. He stopped beside us. For the first time on the trip, I yearned to be back in England, or Canada, or anywhere. I did not want to see the man. I did not want to imagine his life. I gave him a few coins and tried to stop thinking about him.

IN HER MEMOIR *Songs of Blood and Sword*, Fatima Bhutto — a granddaughter of Zulfikar Ali — recounts a statement by her father, Mir Murtaza Bhutto. "There is supposed to be no poverty in Pakistan," he told a reporter. "When I speak of the poor, of the shirtless, the homeless and the hungry; of the need for clean water, rural dispensaries, schools; of the crying need to eradicate corruption, rape, drugs and so on, I am supposed to be living in the past. The presumption being that these are not the urgent tasks facing us as a nation..." In 1996, two years after making these remarks, Mir Murtaza Bhutto was assassinated.

On our last day in Pakistan I rose at 5 a.m. The hotel room resembled a furnace even in the small hours. It was a relief to step outside: until the heat became excruciating, I could wander through Lahore and not feel that my flesh was a well-greased frying pan. When would the monsoon arrive? Oxen, goats, and buffalo ambled along the placid streets, all of them seemingly confident about where they needed to go. Men and boys stretched across makeshift beds on the pavement. Others huddled motionless, without beds, on the pavement.

All around me, as I passed the Roshnai Gate, the Palace of Mirrors, the enormous Badshahi Mosque, I saw the poor and the shirtless. Some of them showed the clear effects of heroin addiction. Clare and I had bought chlorine tablets to purify our drinks, but the homeless and the hungry, unable to afford such luxuries, had no safe drinking water. Their children would not attend school that morning or any morning. Injured, excluded, forsaken, they would be intimate with sickness and well-acquainted with death.

The sun rose in the direction of India, and the city began to stir. Another scorching day lay ahead, a diesel-fumed, horn-blasting, sweat-spilling day in which nothing would come easy for many of the citizens of Lahore. Not that they would abandon their dignity. Not that they would surrender before the absurdities of fate. Full-faced or otherwise, old or young, in good health or ill, morning after morning they would rub their eyes, clear their throats, gather phlegm, and spit into the dust. I was free to go. I would soon be gone.

4.

India

"Looking is free"

I saw a temple but not a garden. I spent a night beside the temple. I didn't know the garden existed.

Clare and I had strolled across the border and climbed aboard a local bus to Amritsar. The name means "pool of nectar" in Punjabi, and at the heart of the city stands the Golden Temple, an exuberant structure of marble, copper, and gold leaf almost entirely surrounded by water. The religion it upholds was born in India—like Hinduism, like Jainism, like Buddhism. Whereas the origin of those faiths is lost in time, Sikhism arose a mere five centuries ago. For the devout, Amritsar is holy ground.

We stayed in the Guru Ram Das Serai, a guesthouse in the temple complex. The Sikh authorities asked no payment for the hospitality or the vegetarian meals. But to shield the pious from dubious pipes, needles, and morals, unbelievers were restricted to three sweltering rooms on the ground floor.

Instead of crowding in with other perspiring overlanders, Clare and I hauled two guesthouse mattresses and our own sleeping bags up to the roof and spent a night under the stars and the full moon.

Faith, wrote the Indian poet Rabindranath Tagore, *is the bird that feels the light / And sings when the dawn is still dark.* By the half-light of 5:30 a.m., many pilgrims were up and about. "You are most welcome here," said a man with a voluminous beard. Clare and I — grateful and surprised at the Sikhs' acceptance of doubting or scoffing travellers — followed his lead.

A constant flow of adults and children were already walking over a causeway to the site of worship. The sky lightened by the moment. Catching the new sun, the blueness of the vast pool and the shimmering gold of the temple roof grew more intense. I rinsed my feet in the hallowed water. Early morning was rush hour: the pilgrims swept us up in a pedestrian jam, and I felt no embarrassment or awkwardness about joining a procession over the Steps of God. My senses sharpened. I noticed the coolness of the marble floor against my bare feet; the scents of food and flowers offered by the faithful; the cascading rhythms of the music played on sitar and tabla to accompany the chanting of hymns in the gem-studded inner sanctum. These hymns would be voiced, unbroken, through the day and into the night. Sikh practices took shape under the guidance of ten successive Gurus, and the scriptures are revered as a Guru's living, permanent embodiment.

The day's heat magnified. Sweating mightily, Clare and I climbed to the sixth-floor viewing platform of an ivory-coloured tower and looked out over Amritsar. Bicycle rickshaws swerved through the clotted streets of the walled city. Other gurdwaras, or places of Sikh worship, were visible in all directions. We found a museum of Sikh history that presented an array of images no less blood-soaked than those in the Armenian churches of Isfahan. The tenets of the faith speak of justice and humanity, but its history is violent. Paintings showed Sikhs beheaded, boiled in oil, crushed by a train, chopped vertically in two... The newest martyr had met a hero's death in 1971 fighting in the Indian Army against Pakistan. In the temple, hours earlier, we had passed memorials to Sikhs killed in previous wars and skirmishes. I discovered from the pages of "The Sikh Religion: An Outline of its Doctrines," a blue pamphlet offered to all temple visitors, that for a pure-hearted Sikh, "wherever he stands, he will stand as a garrison," and that "life is like a cavalry march."

Perhaps the figures of speech work better in Punjabi. Of all the world's major languages, it may be the least familiar to outsiders. In 1978, more than sixty million people in Pakistan and India spoke it as a mother tongue, as well as millions more in the South Asian diaspora. But as if to underscore the painful divide between neighbouring countries and faiths, it can be written in two scripts, one of them ("from the king's mouth," right to left) dominant in Pakistan, the other ("from the guru's mouth," left to right) dominant in India. Punjabi is only one of the vessels for the Sikh scriptures; they incorporate texts in Hindi, Sanskrit, Farsi, Arabic, and several other languages. It's as if no single tongue could possibly be adequate to convey the grandeur and scale of the divine. For Sikhs, multilingualism is not just convenient; it is sacred.

The words of the scriptures inspired the sacred buildings and outlasted some of them. Over the centuries Sikh gurdwaras have been repeatedly damaged and desecrated. Mughal and Afghan rulers, hostile to the new religion and its warrior adherents, defiled the Golden Temple: it was used as a dancehall, its sacred pool was polluted with excrement and the entrails of cows, and finally it was blasted to pieces with gunpowder. Again and again, Sikhs repaired and rebuilt. By the early twentieth century, Muslims, Hindus, and Sikhs shared Amritsar more or less amicably, united by a common wish to see their British overlords gone.

I must have peered down on Jallianwala Bagh from the sixth floor of the pale tower, but I was ignorant of the history of my parents' and grandparents' empire: I had no idea what I was seeing. The place is a garden now, with a well at its centre. In 1919, it was a dusty, rundown recreation ground, a short walk from the Golden Temple. On a warm Sunday in April, about fifteen thousand people gathered there, most of them for a peaceful demonstration against the arrest of two political activists. Emotions were fraught, and Sir Michael O'Dwyer, the lieutenant-general of Punjab, had outlawed such meetings. He feared chaos. He feared rebellion. In the early evening British-led troops marched through the single entrance to Jallianwala Bagh and, giving no warning, opened fire on the crowd. By the time they stopped shooting, they had killed several hundred Indians, all of them unarmed, and had wounded more than a thousand. The Amritsar massacre would become a galvanizing symbol in the campaign for India's independence.

The officer who gave the command to shoot died eight years later of a stroke, beset by doubts about what he had done. O'Dwyer, who had ordered the troops into Amritsar, showed no remorse. He was assassinated in London in 1940 by a Sikh insurgent who, after years of trying, had managed to track him down. The insurgent went to the gallows. "Despite the concerted British effort to bury Udham Singh's name and legacy," the British-Indian writer Anita Anand observed in *The Patient Assassin*, "somehow his story managed to live on...Punjab had never stopped being proud of the avenger of Jallianwala Bagh, but in the decades following independence, his reputation grew throughout the nation. In the 1970s an Indian mass movement demanded the return of Udham Singh. Eventually it got its wish." When India received his body in 1974, the prime minister, Indira Gandhi, laid a wreath on the coffin. Udham Singh's remains were cremated in his Punjab birthplace, and his childhood home became a pilgrimage site.

So did Jallianwala Bagh. Some of Udham Singh's ashes were eventually reburied there. A statue just outside the garden, unveiled in 2017, shows him looking to the future with an outstretched arm, his hand grasping a clump of metal soil.

THE FRACTIOUS NEWSPAPERS of India revealed far more than did their pallid, censored English-language counterparts in Pakistan and Iran. Apart from delivering more news, the prose had more blood and muscle in it. Much more astrology too. The day after we arrived in Amritsar, the *Sunday Tribune* in the state capital of Chandigarh ran a forthright notice:

O, MONGOL
I, Rustam-e-Zaman DARA SINGH, accept your challenge!
MONGOL, As Long AS I have the confidence of millions
of my brothers.

NO FOREIGNER can ever escape from me on this holy
land, of PUNJAB!!!
I shall not spare you this time!
Historical Free style wrestling at Chandigarh.

I may never know who the "Mongol" was. Dara Singh
is another matter. He had bestowed the title of Rustam-e-
Zaman — "champion of the age" — on himself. Born into a
Sikh farming family in 1928, he moved to Singapore and Hong
Kong as a young man and made his name as a professional
wrestler. From there he switched his talents to Bollywood action
movies. Soon he was a thick-chested celebrity, juggling dual
careers on the mat and the screen, famous both for trouncing
a rival wrestler named King Kong and for playing the monkey
god Hanuman on Indian TV. He would go on to become a
producer and a politician. "It felt good to be the first macho
actor," he once recalled, "as my colleagues at that time were very
thin and lanky. No one had a body like mine."

The *Sunday Tribune* articles on sport, movies, and politics
were financed in good measure by its matrimonial ads. Only
a few described men. Most of the ads we saw were along these
lines: "Verma Khatri match for a graduate homely girl, 22,
165 cms. Beautiful good-looking. Respectable middle-class
family." Or, more ambitiously: "Match for Commerce Graduate
1.66 m., girl 21, Canadian University. Jat Sikh medicos prefd.
Other professionals could be considered. Well-established
families with boy intending to settle in Canada/USA correspond
Box 3445B." The names Jat and Verma Khatri refer to particular
subcastes in India's ancient, intricate, and immensely durable
system — in his later years Dara Singh served as chairman of the

Jat Mahasabha, a nationwide group that promotes the interests of Jats.

A handful of the matrimonial notices had a twinge of desperation: a 32-year-old "hunchback" looking for a wife, "caste no barrier"; a 38-year-old Brahmin virgin in search of a "moral marriage." As if to expiate its sins or its ads, that day's *Sunday Tribune* ran a news feature about abuses in the Indian marriage system, especially those committed by the parents of young men who demand larger and larger dowries from a bride's helpless family.

Unmarried and casteless, Clare and I caught a bus to Jammu. She was battling a cold and a bad cough. Perhaps she was longing for her boyfriend too. Yelling silently in my journal, I wrote "I need to hear from you, Annie!" putting the entire sentence in capital letters. Public-service messages abounded on billboards along the highway: Drink milk. Fight malaria. Drive safely. Don't drink alcohol. Fight smallpox. Smallpox? Sikh farmers were winnowing chaff by tossing spadefuls of grain into the air. Water, when it came, if it came, would be a blessing. In the absence of rain, we'd read in the *Sunday Tribune*, the heat wave afflicting much of India had killed dozens of people.

The northbound bus from Jammu took more than ten hours to reach the Kashmir Valley. But the journey through an outstretched limb of the Himalaya allowed me to forget time. The land kept on hiding the sky. The driver stopped twice at village cafés — tea shacks, really — and once at a waterfall by a small Hindu shrine: a bell rang as passengers informed Vishnu of their presence, the sound echoing down a canyon to a river a thousand feet below. The air smelled delicious: mingled scents of cedars, pines, and alpine flowers in the precipitous green meadows. A big, grey-furred monkey strutted on all fours above the road. The reminders about milk, malaria, and smallpox had given way to an inventive series of notices that promoted safe driving: "Better be late than the late"; "Divorce speed if married"; "This is not a race or a rally. Take your time and enjoy the valley." As we climbed painstakingly toward a long tunnel that led into the valley, dozens of military trucks passed us. Turbaned Sikh men made up roughly half the troops on board. The Pakistani border—officially a Line of Control, no permanent boundary in Kashmir having been accepted by either side—was less than twenty miles from Jammu.

Once the bus barrelled down from the heights—wet rice fields flanking the road, snow-crowned peaks resplendent in three directions—it was easy to believe the marketing jargon: "Welcome to Happy Valley!" Or, as a billboard announced just beyond the tunnel's exit: "You're in Paradise now." In the late 1970s, it often seemed, I and everyone else were trying to get to the bar. But the name of the bar? As David Byrne knew, the bar was called Heaven.

IN KASHMIR WE TURNED into tourists. In truth we'd been tourists ever since leaving Oxford, but for much of the trip Clare and I had been able to tell ourselves, or delude ourselves, that we were sophisticated travellers on a journey of artistic and intellectual discovery. Foreign tourists seldom showed up in Kerman, or Quetta, or even Taxila. The Hippie Trail bypassed such places. It did not bypass Kashmir. And for decades Kashmiris had earned a living by satisfying the desires of tourists, both foreign and domestic. People went there to enjoy themselves, people from Bangalore just as often as Boston or Berlin. In Kashmir the simplest enlightenment I could gain would be the self-awareness that even high-minded aspiring poets like to have a good time—while paying as little as possible for the privilege.

Like most other tourists, hippie or otherwise, we stayed on a houseboat near the shores of Dal Lake in the watery city of Srinagar, the summer capital of what was then an Indian state named Jammu and Kashmir. In winter, when snow plunging down from the mountains might close the highway for days on end, the state's business would be conducted from Jammu. Clare and I didn't need to find a boat upon arrival; the boat found us. Wahid, the eldest son of the manager of Houseboat Miami, was a passenger on the Jammu bus, and over cinnamon-spiced tea at one of the roadside stalls he quoted us an excellent price (or so we thought) for a week, breakfasts and dinners included. It wasn't Wahid's fault that we reached the Miami coated in dust. As the bus chugged into Srinagar, workmen were dynamiting the side of a hill. A cloud of gritty powder hung over the city and brushed us when we disembarked.

Next morning the cloud was gone, the light pure, and the houseboat an otherworldly contrast to run-of-the-mill hostels and fleabag hotels. It boasted a sun roof, a hot shower, a dining room, and a sitting room with four vases of fresh flowers and gold-curtained windows overlooking Heaven Canal. We shared all this with only one other guest. The owner, Hakeem, was an entrepreneur as well as a hotelier—I disappointed him by my ignorance of the price of gold in Iran. Wahid was one of his eight children. Most of the others also worked for their father. When the electricity flickered and failed in a thunderstorm, a

girl of about ten presented us with an oil lamp. Sheet lightning illuminated her face for a second; then she was gone. Her
slightly older brother fetched and carried throughout the day;
he could hear but he could not or would not speak. When we
asked why, Hakeem shrugged his shoulders.

Clare and I had arrived in Srinagar neither to discover our
souls nor to see great architecture. We would have liked to visit
the Hazratbal Shrine, a cream-coloured mosque that contains,
or so it's said, a hair of the Prophet Muhammad's beard — but
the mosque was closed for repair. (When the hair was stolen
from the shrine in 1963 and briefly disappeared, riots ensued
not just in Kashmir but in Bengal far to the east.) One morning
we paddled around in a *shikara* — a long, slim cedarwood
boat — going in circles, banging into an assortment of hulls
and gunwales, and giving local children some scornful laughs.

The next day a professional boatman rowed us along Heaven
Canal and through Dal Lake. Clare and I reclined on plush
seats below the canopy of an ornate *shikara*, feeling decadent
and guilty and relaxed. We passed the Shalimar Bagh, designed
by the emperor Jahangir in 1619 as a gift for Nur Jahan, his
twentieth wife; with their plane trees and terraces full of snap-
dragons and roses, the gardens sweep down to the water's edge.
I loved the contrast between the strict Mughal pattern and
the lake's informal floating gardens of lotuses and water lilies.
Our boat was the *Naya Zamana* (Hindi for "new era"). Other
tourist *shikaras* had English names: *Free Love, Dream Boat,
Green Rocket, Horse of the Lake*. Local people manoeuvred their
floating shops along the canals and the lakeshore, visiting each
houseboat in turn. From their *shikaras*, they sold fruit, cold
drinks, and cauliflowers; baskets, jewellery, and knives; shawls,

rugs, and much else. The shawls were finespun goat wool: cashmere, as the word is spelled outside Kashmir.

Srinagar, like Venice, had become a city addicted to tourism. Its liquid splendour came with undercurrents. The boatman of the *Naya Zamana* paddled us swiftly past a boy on a smaller vessel who shouted, "*Salaam, sahib, baksheesh?*" It's a testament to the influence of Asia on the English language that we understood him instantly—not that I wanted to be called "sahib." When we'd left the boat and were exploring the shabby streets of the old quarter, small boys threw stones at us and ran off laughing. Many Srinagar adults, I imagine, also nurtured some resentment of tourists, but their livelihood depended on charm. Children had the liberty to pester.

We did hear a few Kashmiris express resentment—though not against people from abroad.

"I would like Kashmir independent," Hakeem told us one day. "A country of our own."

In saying this, he kept his eyes down. Then, signalling his unwillingness to expand on the topic, he shook his head. A sparrow flew into the sitting room and perched on the sofa; Wahid chased it out.

Wahid had obeyed his father in approaching Westerners on the bus ride from Jammu: Hakeem didn't like to rent his houseboat to Indians. At least, that's what he told us. Perhaps he meant to imply that he didn't like to rent the property to Hindus. Most of the people in Kashmir are Muslims; as a mother tongue they speak Kashmiri, not the national language of Hindi; they have a culture of their own. Both women and men wore long tunics or *pherans*, men with a conical or cylindrical cap, women with a bright headscarf. But these clothes were well on the way to becoming items of picturesque folklore: on dry land in Srinagar, Clare and I passed shops offering to take a photograph of visitors sporting "traditional Kashmiri dress."

Paul—the English artist who had shared our carriage on the train to Istanbul—was not wearing Kashmiri costume when we met by chance in Srinagar. "He's been in the mountains of north India," I wrote in my journal, "tanned, leaner, with sideburns and a short chin-beard. Much toughened up." The Hippie Trail gave travellers the opportunity to run into the same Westerners in different parts of Asia. This was not always a pleasure, though we were delighted to see Paul again.

Back at the Miami I noticed dark streaks on my teeth. Asia was writing itself on my body: I had lost weight and my hair had begun to thin. I also worried about hepatitis: in 1978 an outbreak in Kashmir, provoked by untreated sewage in Dal Lake, killed seventeen hundred people. Having escaped *Death in Venice*, were we wandering through *Death in Srinagar*? But Clare's nasal congestion and cough had improved. The house-boat's nightly infusions of mutton curry may have fortified her. Feeling more energetic than at any point since we left Iran, she asked me to trim the bangs she wore over her forehead— her "fringe," she called it in the British English I occasionally failed to grasp. I found a pair of scissors and attacked with enthusiasm. Two minutes later, the fringe was so short that Clare's forehead was exposed and her mood was one of fury. I felt too ashamed to tell her this was the first time I had cut anyone's hair.

Could Lord Shiva set matters right? We climbed a few hundred steps up Shankaracharya, the hill that looms over

Srinagar, in the friendly company of Hindu tourists or pilgrims. Their destination was a stone temple at the top, built in the ninth century or even earlier. I joined the others in walking around the shrine—the big metal *lingam* had flowers strewn on top and coins at its base—but mainly I just wanted to see the view. The lavishly crafted wooden houses a thousand feet below; the sun-spattered, boat-busy lake; the Afghan-built fort atop another hill... My attention strayed to the dozen eagles circling above our heads. The lowest-flying had a piece of wire embedded in its belly. It was making dog-like calls of distress. These sounds disturbed the other birds, and one—its mate? its mother?—kept veering past the injured bird and feinting, as though that could somehow dislodge the metal. The wounded eagle refused to land, but by twisting its body in flight, it finally managed to peck or rip away the wire. All the birds soared off then, leaving Lord Shiva behind.

To glimpse a little of what the eagles effortlessly saw every day, we went on a couple of gentle mountain treks. At Gulmarg, west of the city, not far from the Line of Control, we rode well-behaved ponies up to what a guide described as "meadow of skiing." In late May it proved to be a pasture of wildflowers: daffodils, daisies, tiny blue gentians, and pink, sweet-smelling dogwood. In the distance rose the white expanse of Nanga Parbat, known to English-speaking climbers as "Killer Mountain"—more than twice the height of any peak in the Canadian Rockies. Clare and I were drinking chai at a rickety outdoor table when the sky burst open: hailstones assailed us and spears of lightning lit up a snow-striped mountain freshly emerged from cloud. The rain continued until we had to dash for the bus back to Srinagar, soaked. At sunset, the air still damp, the fields of Kashmir shone with a strange greenish-yellow light, mild and almost sickly.

We needed our warmest clothes on a trip to the hill station of Sonamarg ("meadow of gold"). The bus passed the Oxford Tea Stall in the valley before climbing east toward the Tibetan Buddhist enclave of Ladakh — unfortunately, the highway into Ladakh would remain closed until sometime in June. The news came as no surprise: even on a fifty-mile journey, the bus had to ford three rivers in spate. The light drizzle of Srinagar thickened into moderate rain. In Sonamarg hundreds of sheep and horses were grazing wild. The land's colours were a rhapsody, or a raga, in green: the paleness of birches and sycamores, the darker shades of conifers, the luminous glow of moist and springy turf. Above all this, clouds washed and rinsed the Himalaya.

We were making for the glacier of Thajiwas. But as we climbed, the rain intensified. Clare, feeling miserable, seized a guide's invitation to finish the journey on a spare pony. I had a sudden flashback: she had told me, somewhere in Turkey, "I must say I like nice scenery, but I like *things* better." I stubbornly kept on walking, at first through the steep wet meadows, then — stymied by rushing streams — along the main path. The advance guard of a party of Calcutta schoolboys — fifty-eight of them, along with six teachers — caught up with me there. The cool breeze had accelerated into a bitter, gusting wind.

"Kashmir is paradise of India!" one of the boys shouted.

We reached the glacier's ragged edge: a hundred yards away, Clare and a few other people were sitting in open tents, steam rising from mugs of tea. The ponies were tethered nearby. I ventured onto the glacier, searching out stones and fragments of branches to prevent myself from slipping on the grey ice. And as I did so, a Calcutta schoolboy called out: "Sir, do you have whisky for sale?"

THE PARADISE OF INDIA is no more.

Is that an exaggeration? Dal Lake still exists—although, like so many rivers and lakes in Iran, Pakistan, and Afghanistan, it is ill and shrinking fast. Houseboats survive on its clogged surface; but in an effort to save the lake and its dwindling stocks of fish, courts and local authorities have banned the boats' construction, even their repair. One reason for the decline of Dal Lake is the volume of sewage that houseboats pump into the water. When Clare and I stayed in Srinagar, three thousand of the vessels were afloat. Just over nine hundred are now allowed. Yet the lake is still at risk of becoming a septic tank: the impacts of sewage and agricultural chemicals are worsened by road-building and other sorts of "development" that block the influx of fresh water from springs and streams.

Beyond and above the algae-ridden, weed-choked lake, global heating is rapidly taking effect. Thajiwas and other glaciers are losing their ice—Kashmiri glaciers have shrivelled, overall, by more than 30 percent since Clare and I travelled there. Some of the green fields we saw near Srinagar would turn mauve and purple later in the year, before farmers harvested the world's most valuable spice: saffron. To produce a pound of saffron, you need seventy thousand crocuses. The flowers must be picked by hand. But with the encroachment of drought and climate change, saffron crops in the Kashmir Valley are a small fraction of what they were.

In Srinagar the absence of houseboat maintenance has accompanied a lack of business: even before the COVID-19 pandemic, foreign travellers were choosing to stay away. The reduction of tourism is a minor side effect of a chronic political disease. Ever since India gained its independence, Jammu and Kashmir had been the only state with a Muslim majority. It enjoyed a degree of autonomy. But a violent insurgency against Indian rule began in 1989, and it has not yet ended. As Muslims suffered at the hands of Hindus elsewhere in India, Kashmiri Hindus came under repeated attack in their beloved valley. Nearly all of them fled. Finally India's government dissolved the statehood of Jammu and Kashmir and made it a Union Territory, ruled from New Delhi.

How long can a pressure cooker go on heating before it explodes? Half a million Indian troops are now ensconced in the region, using hotels as barracks; even the old Afghan fort above Srinagar fulfills a military purpose again. An Armed Forces Special Powers Act gives soldiers the power to search, arrest, and fire on anyone they suspect of rebellion. "Kashmiris," wrote the historian Tahir Kamran in 2021, "are condemned to live in terror of informers, double agents, and triple agents who could be close relatives or childhood friends." Pakistan has trained and financed a guerrilla force since the insurgency began; it calls the Union Territory "Indian-occupied Kashmir." Likewise, India refers to the northernmost parts of Pakistan as "Pakistan-occupied Kashmir." The Line of Control slithers and wiggles through the beautiful land — Nanga Parbat, the great mountain we saw from Gulmarg, rises in Pakistan. Meanwhile China has tightened its murderous grip on Tibet, and its troops have engaged in lethal hand-to-hand battles with

Indian soldiers on the border of Ladakh. War is always and only a mutual blunder away.

Clare and I were told that the Emperor Jahangir had a Persian-language couplet inscribed in a pavilion above Dal Lake, amid the tall fountains and fragrant terraces of Shalimar Bagh. The lines express his love of Kashmir: *If there is heaven on earth, / It is here, it is here, it is here.* After seeing its snow-veiled peaks and daffodil meadows, its forests and glacier-fed waters, I could appreciate the feeling. But the truth of the tale lies in shadow. Whether the couplet was written by a Sufi musician who lived centuries before the Mughals reached India or by a courtier who served Jahangir's son, almost certainly it did not refer to Kashmir. The poet, in all likelihood, meant to flatter Delhi.

WE LEFT FOR DELHI on a night train. Jammu's railway station was only three years old, and already a tent city had grown up beyond it: a slum with no apparent sanitation, a waste ground where children and adults in rags clustered around makeshift fires. At the station a large family hugged their loved ones a long and emotional goodbye. We bought tickets for a three-tiered sleeping compartment allowing me to stretch out my sleeping bag on a wooden slab. I dreamt of Persepolis in the depths of a desert canyon, ziggurats covered by plastic sheets. When I woke in the milky light, vultures in a field beside the tracks were feasting on I don't know what.

Delhi meant business: the General Post Office for mail (hearing from Annie: "joy, joy, joy," I wrote in my journal, "like the lifting of a millstone from round my neck"); a bank for cash;

the Royal Nepalese Embassy for "single journey" visas to the Kingdom of Nepal; the offices of Iraqi Airways to confirm our eventual flight back to London. Otherwise, we poked around the city. I noticed a sticker on a rickshaw: "Beauty is not to be touched." Five monkeys, including a mother and baby, gambolled among the shops and stalls on a side street near the Red Fort. A stone tablet at the imposing Kashmiri Gate paid homage to British troops who lost their lives here in 1857 during the Indian Mutiny (or, if you prefer, the First War of Indian Independence). No tablets commemorated the slaughter of unarmed civilians that followed the British recapture of Delhi.

Mixed in with the vendors of food and clothing in the cluttered bazaar by our hotel were a good number of "lady doctors" and "sex specialists," even a "sex and gas specialist." The posters for Bollywood films were lurid enough to give me gas: one of the hit movies of 1978 featured a terrified girl, a macho hunk, and a bloody knife, all displayed in frenetic green. It was ridiculous for us to imagine we could grasp a city the size of Delhi in just a few days. It was equally absurd to hope we could somehow escape the sporadic bursts of traffic chaos in which trucks, buses, cars, motorcycles, bicycles, rickshaws, horse carts, ox carts, cows, and pedestrians all had a role to play.

I had to accustom myself to a new decibel level and a different sense of personal space. But difference works in both directions. When the Indian writer Nirad C. Chaudhuri travelled to England for the first time in 1955, he felt baffled by the British need for private space. "In the buses of Delhi," he wrote upon his return, "all of us make use of one another for bodily comfort. In northern India people have very great difficulty in keeping steady in moving vehicles, and therefore they lean against one another or put their arms round a fellow passenger. Nobody is so ill-natured as to mind being used as a cushion." If anyone objects, Chaudhuri added, "he is asked in offended tones, 'What harm is there in it, you are not a woman?'" A shrewd perception, except that "all of us" must refer to Delhi men, "people" are evidently male, and "fellow passenger" excludes half the human race.

One evening in Delhi, I was the only passenger in a bicycle rickshaw coming back to the hotel. The driver stopped at a long traffic light and a man stuck the remnants of his right hand toward me, somehow clutching a tin bowl in what remained of his left hand. (*Who are you?*) The leper's skin was dark. I looked in his eyes: he was my age, more or less, somewhere between twenty and twenty-five. He had a handsome face, open, smiling. For at least ten seconds he stood beside me, waiting, saying nothing. I did not give. (*Who are you?*) He stepped over to the next rickshaw, where a woman with a *bindi* on her forehead quickly found a coin. The leper came back and stuck his ruined hand toward me again. And still I did not give.

Why? What were Pakistan and India doing to me? No, that's the wrong question. What were Pakistan and India showing me about myself?

WHAT CLARE AND I most wanted to see in Delhi were the museum dedicated to Mohandas Gandhi and the site of his cremation, Raj Ghat. I revered Gandhi for his commitment to pacifism. In Saskatoon, a few years earlier, I'd spent an evening arguing with a young Maoist who tried to persuade me of the need for revolutionary violence. My main defence against his dry harangue was the success of Mohandas Gandhi in the peaceful combat for Indian freedom (I knew almost nothing about the contributions made by Jawaharlal Nehru and other political leaders). Gandhi continued to serve as a symbol and an inspiration — not that the prairie Maoist was convinced. But people all over the world treasured his memory. On a trip to India in 1959, Martin Luther King asked to spend a night in the bedroom of Gandhi's old villa. Over the next decade he would model his American campaign of civil disobedience on what Gandhi ("the guiding light") had achieved in India.

Raj Ghat, beside the Yamuna River, had the air of a pilgrimage site. A black marble platform, set into a sunken walled lawn, marked the place where Gandhi was cremated the day after his assassination in January 1948. An undying flame burned at one end of the platform. Orange and yellow marigolds bedecked the marble slab. Clare and I walked barefoot around it, our voices scarcely more than a whisper. The Indian visitors were equally quiet. A few of Gandhi's sayings had been inscribed on the low wall in Hindi and English. The sayings were both idealistic and demanding: "I would like to see India free and strong so that she may offer herself as a willing and pure sacrifice for the betterment of the world." Suggesting a nation be a sacrifice so that others will benefit: not a recipe for popularity.

The Gandhi Memorial Museum displayed the bloodstained white clothes he was wearing in the hour of his death and one of the three bullets — so small, so ordinary-looking — that killed him. It takes so little metal, I thought, to end a life. Along with the hallowed relics — his watch, his sandals, his favourite copy of Tolstoy — we saw pieces of the yarn Gandhi had spun during the lengthy pursuit of independence. Under his leadership the spinning wheel became a symbol of Indian self-reliance, its homespun cloth a physical reminder that his country did not need to import textiles made on machines in England. A black-and-white photograph showed him lying down in a bed as a six-year-old Indira Nehru (two decades away from her marriage to the unrelated Feroze Gandhi) sat confidently beside him. He was, at the time, on one of his frequent hunger strikes. He looked so frail, so unlike a patriarch, yet across India people called him "father of the nation." Through the entire world he came to be known by the Sanskrit word *Mahatma*: "great soul."

The eleven vows that Gandhi famously made in 1930 were inscribed on the museum walls in all their ferocious integrity. Truthfulness, fearlessness, non-violence toward all living beings, use of local products, equality of all religions: so far, so good. But the non-enjoyment of food, the abstinence from sex, the discarding of all personal possessions... The puritan zeal of his beliefs disturbed me, and I began to ask how fair it was for me to pick and choose from the list of vows, concentrating on what I admired while ignoring everything else. How much, I wondered, are Gandhi's teachings all of a piece? Did he allow for compromise and outright dissent, or did he expect all-or-nothing allegiance?

Those are old doubts, and they are not the kinds of questions now being raised about Gandhi. More urgent issues have arisen. Africans and people of African descent have lit upon the racist statements he made during his years as a lawyer in Durban and Johannesburg; statues of him on that continent have lately tumbled. Feminists have criticized him for gender bias and for his "experiments in celibacy" that were, to say the least, peculiar. And as the novelist Arundhati Roy has eloquently shown, Gandhi believed, throughout his long life, that lower-caste Indians should be content to remain in their divinely appointed lot. Though he deplored the cruel effects of "untouchability," he also used cunning and charisma to help the caste system endure.

Such critiques come, in general, from the political left. Yet in contemporary India, most of the attacks on Gandhi's memory have been of a very different nature.

When Clare and I visited Raj Ghat and the Gandhi Memorial Museum, I didn't know who his assassin was, and I had no particular desire to find out. The man, I assumed, was deranged. India had gained its independence five months before the shooting: who would want to kill the nation's father? Gandhi was seventy-eight years old when he died, and he had maintained the practice of hunger strikes: extreme violence between Hindus and Muslims had preceded and followed the partition of India, causing him anguish. A proud Hindu, Gandhi showed discerning respect for other faiths. He addressed his final campaigns for justice, tolerance, and peace not to the British but to his fellow Indians.

The name of his assassin may, alas, be better-known today than at any time since 1948. Nathuram Godse was a militant Brahmin: he hated partition because it had torn away chunks of India to create the new nation of Pakistan. Godse yearned for a warrior Hindu state in which members of other faiths, especially Islam, would be subservient. Or banished. In a long statement written between his arrest and his execution, he accused Gandhi of "a pro-Muslim mentality" and declared, "My shots were fired at the person whose policy and action had brought rack and ruin and destruction to millions of

Hindus." Foreigners looked on Gandhi as a model for a blood-racked globe. Godse saw him as insufficiently masculine: a paltry excuse for a Hindu leader; an embodiment of weakness and surrender.

The breakneck growth of Hindu nationalism in recent decades has led many Indians to venerate Godse's memory. He has, like Udham Singh in the Punjab, become an assassin with a rosy afterlife. In 2021, a library and "knowledge centre" bearing his name opened in the city of Gwalior: a leader of an extremist Hindu party explained that the library aimed "to put before the world the true nationalist that Godse was. He stood and died for an undivided India. The purpose of the library is to instill true nationalism which Godse stood for in today's ignorant youth." Hindu militants revere the murderer as both a hero and a martyr. Calls have emerged to rename cities in his honour and to celebrate the day of Gandhi's assassination as "Bravery Day."

Gandhi's ashes, carefully meted out, were sent all over India and beyond. In 2019, on the 150th anniversary of his birth, one or more people broke into a memorial in the central Indian state of Madhya Pradesh and stole an urn containing some of those ashes. Across a portrait of Gandhi, the word "traitor" was scrawled in green paint.

A SOFT KNOCK. Clare and I were staying in the Pink City of Jaipur, just about to head off into a broiling afternoon. I opened the door to find a middle-aged man clutching a pen and an official-looking form. When we had checked into this government-run "Tourist Bungalow," a desk clerk had taken our passports and scoured them for information. What more could a civil servant want?

"Excuse me," he said. "Tell me, please, has your room been cleaned?"

"Yes, it has."

"Has your room been flitted?"

Flitted? I looked at Clare helplessly.

"Oh, yes," she said.

"Has your linen been changed?"

"Yes, it has."

"Was the morning tea delivered on time?"

"Yes, it was great. Thank you very much."

"Excuse me, do you have any suggestions?"

I thought of telling him the peacocks had wailed so loudly, they woke me up in the middle of the night—but neither Clare nor I said anything more. The man thanked us and backed out of the room, the palms of his hands pressed together. "I like India," I wrote that evening in my journal. "It tries so hard. It has so many bits of paper. It means very well."

The truth is, I was trying to keep myself from feeling overwhelmed. The relentless heat shortened our tempers and our stamina: here in the desert state of Rajasthan, the monsoon rain might be weeks away. When I confronted my torso in a mirror, its paleness appeared odd and wrong. Clare and I had lost our appetite for food. We sniped at each other. She accused me, more than once, of being morose. My presence reduced the chance she would suffer assault by Indian men, but it also impeded her from engaging in private conversations with Indian women.

I was prepared, up to a point, for the rich and complex

sights of India, and for its pungent smells. But the volume of
noise was wearing me down: loudspeakers and radios, stray
dogs and roosters, car horns and engines, children yelling and
laughing, grown-ups arguing and lecturing...Again, I wish I'd
read Nirad C. Chaudhuri. "Among us gregarious life is not just
contented and speechless adjacence as among cattle and the
English people," he wrote, "it is a demonstrative exhibition of
kindliness as well as bad temper, accompanied by a good deal
of sound...For us noise is as essential a condition of cheerfulness as is the warmth of the sun." By now India was on my
skin and under it.

The Ram Niwas Garden in Jaipur forced me to think not
just about India but about the colonial heritage I was still reluc-
tant to own up to. The garden contained a zoo established
under the Raj, and some of the cages looked as though they
hadn't been altered since 1877. A wolf paced back and forth,
back and forth, back and forth. In speechless adjacence, a single
chimpanzee crouched behind iron bars. A bear languished in
a bearpit. The zoo encapsulated a spirit of hopeless control: it
kept wonder at bay with dark iron. We had seen nowhere in
India more organized.

The Albert Hall Museum, also located in the garden, showed
not the brutality but the complexity of imperial power. An
English engineer had designed the building in what I thought
of as a neo-Mughal style—the proper term, apparently, is
Indo-Saracenic—intending it to serve as Jaipur's city hall. It's
a flamboyant edifice with dozens of arches and unexpected
balconies. Murals around the central façade depict scenes from
other great cultures: Persia, Egypt, China. Inside the galler-
ies, busts of Homer, Marcus Aurelius, and assorted European

worthies stare down on the gaudily painted miniatures, the Rajasthani costumes, the camel-hide handicrafts. The museum's red-and-white exterior, chock-a-block with turrets and domes, pillars and cornices, pays tribute to the Indian past. But it also embodies a supreme confidence: the British Empire, it suggests, was both the inheritor and the culmination of all that went before. It emptied the past and filled the present; it was large, it contained multitudes.

Then its agents packed up and went home. The Albert Hall Museum remained. And so did the shocking pinkness of Jaipur, the main buildings having been painted that colour in 1876 to celebrate a visit by Queen Victoria's eldest son. For Jaipur, a colonial choice of decoration had become a proud identity.

Women clothed in shawls, bright scarves, and heavy jewellery were watching children at play in the garden. Or perhaps they were watching us; but if so, they made no sign. The children didn't mind letting us know they found us funny: they pointed at us and laughed. I tried laughing at them in return, but the smile died on my lips.

The rest of Jaipur too had a slightly surreal quality—unless my sense of surreality was a product of dehydration. A sign at the Jaipur bus station announced a Police Out Post. We passed a car dealership named Swastika Automobiles—the swastika is an ancient Hindu symbol for wealth and good fortune— and a Booking Office for Elephants and Cars. Thanks to a power failure, Clare changed money in the State Bank of India by candlelight. The Palace of Winds boasted a top layer that seemed to back onto nothing but air: the building stood on a hill, a pink impenetrable honeycomb full of latticed windows and staircases that led nowhere in particular. Two sterling silver vessels in the City Palace looked impossibly big; they were forged so that a maharajah sailing to England in 1902 could drink water from the River Ganges everywhere he went. He did not stay abroad for long: eight thousand litres proved enough.

Most haunting of all was the Jantar Mantar: an outdoor collection of instruments to measure the sun and other stars. We learned that an enlightened Rajput king devised the observatory in 1732 long before the British seized control of Rajasthan. Jai Singh II was a devout Hindu, a mathematician, and an astronomer; thanks to him, work by Euclid was translated from Greek into the sacred and even more ancient language of Sanskrit. After founding Jaipur and naming it after himself, the king had observatories built there and in four other Indian cities. Latitude, altitude, longitude, time; distance, diameter, meridian, zenith: the Jantar Mantar assesses them all. Its nineteen instruments include the largest sundial on Earth, accurate to within two seconds. As I was unable to tell my azimuth from my declination, the observatory felt to me like a sculpture gallery dreamed up by an eccentric artist of genius. Yet if history had veered in a wildly different direction, Jaipur Mean Time might have reduced Greenwich to irrelevance.

Clare and I wandered alone through the Jantar Mantar. The sundial's gnomon loomed high above us. Having been troubled by the raucousness of India, I now understood the power of silence. It would be strange, I thought, to spend a night amid these huge mathematical devices, far from the squawks of cars and peafowl. I would not be trying to measure the world; the world would take the measure of me.

"WHAT'S THE MATTER, MISTER?"

I was strolling past a brick-red building, constructed in the eighteenth century, now a jewellery shop in Jaipur's inner city. The voice emanated from the darkness just inside the door.

"You come look, don't buy."

"I don't think so," I said.

"Looking is free…"

But I didn't go in. The stresses of the trip had left me wary. Meeting anyone new, my first thought was *What does this person want from me?* Every day overflowed with fresh impressions and revelations, but the journey had turned into an endurance test. It obliged me to wash my sweat-stained clothes every night. It required me to stay continually on guard.

Leaving Oxford, I had vowed to remain open to the world. I had hoped to be unlike the person I feared I was becoming.

WE DIDN'T EXPECT TO run into politics in Agra. The home of the Taj Mahal, we thought, would be above and beyond politics.

A pleasant fantasy. There was protest on the wind, slaughter in the air. We had not avoided politics in Turkey, Iran, or Pakistan. Why should India differ?

A month before our arrival, dozens of people broke into a magistrate's office in Agra and were arrested. A hundred or so demonstrators tried to block their transfer to police cells. The police attacked with *lathis* — batons in Indian English — hoping to disperse the crowd. But the conflict worsened. Buses and scooters went up in flames. People on housetops threw bricks at the police, who shot and killed a protester. As the disturbances grew, rioters tried to burn the post office, a fuel depot, and a power station. The police again resorted to guns. Peace resumed only after the declaration of a curfew and a deployment of the Indian Army. Five people were killed by police in Agra that day; thirty-four were injured seriously enough to need hospital care.

I've lifted the above details from remarks made by an Indian cabinet minister during an emergency debate in Parliament a few days later. He saluted a "timely intervention by the police" against "miscreants" who were "indulging in rowdyism." But the tenor of his statement is open to question. An opposition member blamed "the ruffian forces" of the Agra police for "this slaughter and bloodbath." He described the demonstrators as "downtrodden, neglected, and humiliated." They belonged to the Scheduled Castes; they were *dalits;* they were the lowest of the low in India, the people formerly known as "untouchable." Oppression was their daily bread.

The curfew had been lifted when Clare and I arrived in Agra, but tension overhung the city, almost as palpable as the heavy smog. "People are not trusting Janata," a rickshaw-wallah told us on our way from the bus station. Indira Gandhi having been defeated at the polls a year earlier, power belonged to an awkward coalition by the name of *Janata* ("people" in Hindi). The driver was a Muslim; he wanted to see Mrs. Gandhi back in office. He dropped us at a low-cost hotel that proved to be a magnet for wildlife: we put our backpacks down in a room inhabited by a mouse, a lizard, a gigantic dead spider, a plump-bodied spider that was very much alive, a dead cockroach, several big ants, and innumerable tiny ants. After we left the fauna to its own devices, we passed scores of policemen on the streets.

Agra is a bustling and mostly Hindu city dominated by the memory of Muslim death. The Taj Mahal is only the most sumptuous example. Tombs of Mughal emperors and their loved ones provide Agra with the same mixture of green space and spiritual (or psychological) nourishment that poets' tombs do in Iran: the wealth and grace of the past mollify the unruly clamour of the present. I loved the Itmud-ud-Daulah, a small mausoleum for one of the Emperor Jahangir's many fathers-in-law, its marble walls encrusted with lapis lazuli, its interior geometries echoed in star-shaped flowerbeds outside. The Yamuna River—once pure, still holy—separates the mausoleum from the wheezing lungs of Agra. On the morning we saw the Itmud-ud-Daulah, the sky was a curious non-colour: too blue to be white, too white to be grey, too grey to be blue. Soldiers in a barracks were firing practice rounds.

The tomb of Akbar, the most tolerant of Mughal emperors, is near the city's edge—an amalgam of white marble and red sandstone in a style much influenced by Hindu temples. His third wife, Mariam-uz-Zamani, grew up as a princess in a Hindu kingdom. Clare and I watched blackbucks grazing in the big park around Akbar's tomb, their spiral horns stretching into the air, their pale legs ready to skitter at a moment's notice. A committee of white-rumped vultures surveyed us with interest: at least forty were clustered on a trio of palm trees, weighing the branches down. Their bald heads and necks emerged from portly, dark-feathered bodies.

"They look like Oxford dons in gowns," Clare said with relish.

At the time, up to eighty million white-rumped vultures lived in India. Soaring through a territory that stretched from

Iran to Vietnam, they may have been the world's most abundant bird of prey. Today they are almost extinct: across their vast range, only a few thousand remain. The vultures were poisoned by a chemical that farmers in the 1980s and '90s fed to cows: Diclofenac helps cattle recover from wounds and inflammation. It heals mammals but even in tiny amounts kills vultures. India officially banned the product in 2006, yet Diclofenac can still be purchased there, and the birds have failed to recover. The white-rumped and three other species of vulture are now classed as "critically endangered."

Dead cows in the birds' absence are devoured mainly by rats and feral dogs. Their numbers have shot up. So has the incidence of rabies and other diseases that rats and dogs, unlike vultures, carry. Across the country, wells have been contaminated — this in a land whose most ancient scriptures, the Vedas, rejoice in the power of water: "May the Earth pour out for us delicious nectar, may she bedew us with a flood of splendour... On whom the running universal waters flow day and night with never-ceasing motion, may she with many streams pour milk to feed us." It took a massive amount of dying for people to realize how elegantly the vultures managed death.

IN ITS IMMACULATE GRANDEUR, the Taj Mahal poses a few inherent challenges. Some ardent Hindus see it as a disgrace that the most beloved symbol of India is a Muslim building. An Indian author with the improbable name of P. N. Oak found a cure for the disgrace: he wrote books and articles in Hindi, English, and Marathi propounding the notion that the Taj was originally a temple to Shiva, one the Mughal emperor

Shah Jahan disguised and repurposed. Oak thereby joined a rich tradition of charlatans and purveyors of fake news—he would also claim that St. Peter's in Rome, the Kaaba in Mecca, and Notre Dame in Paris had all been Hindu shrines. In the 1960s, when he began to publish his theories, people everywhere saw them as a bad joke. But his writings would be translated, republished, debated, restated. Today, thanks to the internet and the growth of Hindu nationalism, they enjoy a wider currency than ever before.

An urge to glorify India has led some politicians to utter extraordinary claims about the country's technological prowess in the remote past. In 2014, the prime minister, Narendra Modi, peered back thousands of years and stated, "We worship Lord Ganesha. There must have been some plastic surgeon at that time who got an elephant's head on the body of a human being and began the practice of plastic surgery." Four years later, a junior education minister asserted that a venerable Indian epic, the *Ramayana,* speaks of airplanes. Then the chief minister of the state of Tripura declared that the *Mahabharata,* an even longer epic, mentions the internet. While it's easy to scoff at such delusions, an authentic hunger lies behind them: the desire to see India recognized around the world for its accomplishments, not its poverty.

The Taj Mahal also presented a challenge to impressionable travellers on the Hippie Trail. In North America and Britain during the 1960s, the standard cliché about India was that it's a very poor country, full of surplus cows and malnourished children. "Eat up everything on your plate, just think of the starving children of India." Mothers repeated the admonition—almost a mantra—to their puzzled sons and daughters. India did, and

still does, contain millions of hungry children. But this of all
nations transcends clichés (among them the image of the Taj
on countless postcards and posters). To many young travellers
the Taj threw into question a belief system that lay at the heart
of everything they'd learned in school: the doctrine of progress.
Their minds were blown by an "underdeveloped" country that
in some respects was more developed than anything they knew
at home. While the streets of Agra lay far out of their comfort
zone, the Taj was simply far out.

When they left home, bursting with goodwill and curiosity, few overlanders knew that India is a complex multilingual
civilization, one whose gifts to global culture—in architecture,
poetry, philosophy, theology, sculpture, painting, linguistics,
and much else—far exceed those of, say, the United States
(let alone Canada). The Taj Mahal gave pause to even the least
introspective. How could a city that reeked of human shit in
the late twentieth century have produced a building so majestic
and serene more than three hundred years earlier? Or, to turn
the question around, how could a city that had generated such
an awe-inspiring edifice be so rancid and chaotic now?

I and most other Western travellers suffered from a severe
ignorance of history. We did not realize that India had long
been renowned for its wealth. I thought the British Empire,
despite all its faults, had exported not just railways and cricket
but a modest level of prosperity. It came as a shock to learn the
truth: when ships of London's East India Company first reached
the Arabian Sea and the Bay of Bengal, India accounted for a
much higher percentage of the global economy than Britain
did. By the end of the Raj, the proportions had been reversed.
Much of the wealth of Victorian Britain stemmed from its

exploitation of India. The total value of goods and money that Britain took from India—some economists prefer the word "stole"—may be in the dozens of trillions of pounds. An unimaginable sum. Unimaginable to me, anyway.

The colonial masters were always on the lookout for a good bargain, and in 1831 the Governor-General of India, Lord William Bentinck, drew up a plan to demolish the Taj Mahal. He thought the marble would fetch a good price, and a Jain entrepreneur in Bombay agreed. "By what authority does the Governor-General offer the Taj for sale?" protested a Welsh writer named Fanny Parkes. "Has he any right to molest the dead? To sell the tomb raised over an empress, which from its extraordinary beauty is the wonder of the world?" A wonder of the world in her eyes, but a fat dollop of marble insolence to some of those who believed in the natural superiority of the Christian religion and the white race. Parkes, who spent twenty years in India, had been appalled to find British officers and their wives dancing quadrilles in front of the central tomb while a brass band played on the terrace. Fortunately Bentinck's plan fell through and his successors showed no desire to revive it.

I went to the Taj Mahal three times, twice with Clare, once on my own. I was hoping against hope to catch the sound of a flute. In my mind I could hear the cool, birdlike cadences of *Inside*, a 1969 album recorded in the Taj Mahal by the American musician Paul Horn. It captured a classic moment on the Hippie Trail: an improvised fusion of flute and human voice, Horn's jazz-inflected fragments of melody intertwining with and swirling above the echoing chants of an Indian man. East had met West after closing time at the Taj, giving rise to a bestselling harmony. I loved the music when I was younger, and it didn't bother me then that the singer on the album is unidentified—and, no doubt, unpaid.

But when I visited the Taj Mahal, no flute was in evidence. I had to be content with the sight of a hoopoe in the fountainous, peacock-filled park. I had to be content with a dawn breeze rustling through the marble latticework. I had to be content with rippled lamplight, reflected, floating high into the dome. And I was.

THE ENGLISH I HEARD and read in India was unlike anything I knew from Britain or Canada. Clare and I travelled on its rickshaws, buses, and trains before Salman Rushdie, Amitav Ghosh, Arundhati Roy, and other Indian novelists sprang into the literary consciousness of the English-speaking world, and at times I felt disconcerted, even threatened by the unruly burgeoning of a language I liked to have at my full disposal. Words had taken on different nuances here: Who was I to say these nuances were wrong? "Gratifications Are Not Permitted"—a notice board near the Taj Mahal. "No person is greater than the nation and none commands more respect than the public convenience"—a sign in a railway station. "English Piggery Products"—an advertisement in the heart of Delhi. I took refuge in what I saw as quirks and oddities. My use of words had a bashful, law-abiding accuracy that shrank in the face of the unkempt exuberance of Indian English.

I thought I had a wide vocabulary. My Asian journals are studded with terms like "hyperbole" and "refractory." But in India my vocabulary turned out to be inadequate. Could a *dacoit* also be a *yaar*? And how many of them would make a *lakh*? For centuries Indian English has swallowed terms from local languages with glee and abandon. Its outpouring of new words, its twists and turns of phrase, have both engorged and subverted the juggernaut of mainstream English. This chapter contains more than forty words that originated in Hindi or Sanskrit. They include not just the obvious examples like *yoga*, *guru*, and *sitar* but also some less predictable ones: *bandana*, *candy, jungle.*

THE TRIP FROM AGRA to the little town of Khajuraho began on a congested train; Clare and I had tickets but no seat reservations. I spent some of the journey standing in the aisle and some of it squatting on my backpack. Beside me stood a convict in handcuffs, escorted by two soldiers. The convict grinned at me. The soldiers did not. The train trundled through Gwalior and deposited us in Jhansi, where we discovered that the next bus to Khajuraho would not leave until the following morning at 6:30, 8:30, or 9:30. Nobody could say for sure. With its reliance on rumour and surmise, the journey to the east occasionally felt like a plunge into the void.

Faced with an unexpected overnight stay in a mid-sized Indian city, a different kind of traveller would have sought out local company, and a different kind of travel writer would now feel free to invent a revealing encounter or two. But I'm hamstrung by what Clare and I failed to do — and by my refusal, or inability, to concoct the past. *Ram Naam Satya Hai*: the name of Ram is truth. The saying honours the most virtuous of Hindu gods; it inspired Mohandas Gandhi. And the truth is that in India, most of the conversations we had with local people were transactional: buying tickets, changing money, checking times, ordering food and drink, finding hotels, asking directions, and so on. We seldom spoke about politics, religion, art. I wish we had.

In Jhansi, smothered by damp heat, I drank three small bottles of mango juice, a glass of lassi, a cup of chai, and a bottle of some fizzy, lime-flavoured beverage in less than an hour. Soon I felt thirsty again. "A few more months in India," I said to Clare, "and I'd look like the Fasting Siddhartha." Neither of us found the joke amusing. We spent an uneasy night in the Hotel Central, where I tried to repair a sandal with string—the strap had broken in the Taj Mahal while I was feeling exalted. I could do nothing, however, about my newly stopped watch. Clare's watch had given up the ghost in Iran.

Despite our uncertainty about time we made it to Jhansi's bus station by 6 a.m., half an hour before departure but still too late to obtain seats to Khajuraho. A grey-haired man relinquished his aisle seat for Clare and then groped her from above and behind. Ever since we crossed from Iran into Pakistan, she had suffered these occasional assaults. Maybe I should have spoken up, shaming the old man in public. But I never liked to cause a scene, and I had confidence—perhaps too much—in Clare's skill at withstanding trouble. She managed to move beside a window and immerse herself in a book. Having been assigned a "squatting place" on the arm of another seat, I spent ninety silent minutes perching in sweaty discomfort until a passenger alighted at a wayside stop. Then I could sit down at last.

The bus lurched and puttered through flat, sandy country-side for five and a half hours. And I thought to myself, *Now I know why so many travellers prefer the Magic Bus—they can get*

*from Notting Hill to the Pudding Shop to Freak Street without
suffering all this.*

But who was I to complain? This was what I'd signed up for.
I was innocent enough to crave "the real India," not a mani-
cured, curated version. And compared to Clare, I had it easy:
nobody was sexually harassing me. After we reached our hotel
in Khajuraho — another Tourist Bungalow, this one with a pale
grey mongoose on the driveway — we slept the afternoon away.
I dreamed my father stood waiting to meet me at a concrete bus
station I did not recognize; my pleasure at seeing him turned
into grief when I clambered off the bus and he told me both
our cats had died.

When I woke up, night had fallen. The mongoose had gone
off on its travels. We ate at the Raja Café, run by a Bengali
woman and her tall Swiss husband, and slept some more.
Trying to insert a hard contact lens next morning before sunrise,
I dropped it somewhere on the sheets. I searched for it with
increasing frustration: the overhead fan must have blown it
across the room. Five hours later Clare noticed the lens on a
threadbare carpet, undamaged.

Khajuraho seems a nondescript place now, but a thousand
years ago it was the headquarters of a small kingdom whose
rulers respected, and seem to have practised, both of India's
oldest faiths, Hinduism and Jainism. At some point they shifted
their capital elsewhere and dwindled out of history, the temples
they left behind becoming overgrown and forgotten. A British
Army engineer rediscovered them, wrapped in jungle, in 1838.
Less than a third of the original eighty-five temples survive. But
together they make a unique collection of religious architecture
and erotic art.

Row upon row of carvings adorn the temples: a sandstone panorama of daily and heavenly life. Gods and goddesses are here, lushly naked, often engaged in acrobatic sex. Not all the sculptures are erotic—elephants and horses are here too. So are musicians and dancers, lions and parrots, death's heads and battle scenes, most of them aligned to face the rising sun. I bought a small paperback to help me figure out what I was seeing. Its title page said *Latest Khajuraho Guide: Romantic & Hilarious.* Sometimes the text by the nameless author embodied both of the subtitle's adjectives: "With her at midnight the Moon had dalliance." Elsewhere the prose was merely functional: "There are many administrative gods and goddesses in Jain mythology."

Only in India, I thought, does the civil service revel in the pantheon—to attain immortality, those gods and goddesses must have earned a fistful of diplomas. They must have lined up in the vaulted offices of holy mountains to sign forms in triplicate... Yet I don't mean to sneer. But for *Romantic & Hilarious*, I would have understood even less about Khajuraho than I did. I would not have known why Vishnu can have eleven heads. I would not have known why a swan would dash at a goddess's wet hair. Nor would I have been sure which structures were Hindu and which were Jain.

One of the Jain temples had a rank animal smell. We discovered why as we wandered behind the sanctum. A colony of fruit bats was roosting there, twenty or thirty hanging from the low dark ceiling as if practising yoga headstands in thin air. Their size shocked me—one of them was fluttering a pair of translucent wings whose span exceeded the length of my arm. The nearest animal was just a few steps away. I told myself not to be scared: vampire bats, I knew, live only in the Americas. Even so a sudden, primal desire to escape overcame me. If we disturbed the bats I feared the whole colony might quit the temple, flying a few inches above our heads. My heart was making its presence felt in my chest. We retreated fast.

Clare liked the stone elephants of Khajuraho and what she called the "cuddly" sculptures, ones that evoked love as well as athleticism. I was intrigued by some of the others. How in the world—or out of the world—could a goddess or a courtesan perform fellatio upside down while balancing on a single arm? Both Clare and I were missing intimate physical contact. The orgasmic bliss depicted in a shoulder stand was far in excess of anything I'd imagined in my Oxford yoga class. The unlikely and spectacular contortions on Khajuraho's erotic sculptures are alien to Western notions of religion—India, as ever, goes its own way. But if renunciation offers one path to the divine, as some Indian traditions assert, joyful participation in physical and sexual life can provide another.

Such is the allure of Khajuraho, and it had an obvious appeal for overlanders who believed in making love, not war. Yet a few of the temple carvings depict war, not love. Hinduism— indeed, India—defeats generalization. I'd been reading a slim Penguin selection of the Upanishads, among the most ancient of Hindu scriptures, and finding some of them deeply congenial: "What cannot be spoken with words, but that whereby words are spoken: Know that alone to be Brahman, the Spirit; and not what people here adore." In 1978 that mixture of elitism and abstraction suited me—though I was also captivated by the sensuous finesse of the temple carvings.

A solitary Tamil man, youngish and long-haired, noticed

that Clare and I had a guidebook and followed us around. He asked me to explain the significance of a male figure whose distorted body seemed to trap him forever in an arduous yoga pose, decidedly non-erotic. The man also wanted me to "make small notes" for him on two big-breasted goddesses. He drank most of our water. He may have been stoned. We left him gazing at a temple dedicated to the goddess Parvati with, as *Romantic & Hilarious* remarked, "loose loves" unfolding languidly across its highest frieze.

Khajuraho's temples are built on high stone terraces, accentuating their strength. Their pinnacled roofs are said to emulate the Himalaya—the sacred mountains where the gods reside and great rivers are born. The moon was new when we visited and, as the birds of night began to call, darkness came in a rush. Dry thunder crackled, but no rain fell. We saw dozens of men and boys carrying lights as they walked to a building still in use: a temple dedicated to Lord Shiva, the god of transformation. Clare and I watched the procession from a distance. There seemed too many people to fit inside. Yet they found a way.

AS A TEENAGER IN western Canada, I kept a poster of an impossibly hirsute George Harrison on my bedroom wall. His sitar-playing had been essential to Beatles songs like "Norwegian Wood" and "Within You Without You," and he continued to use the instrument in his solo career. Harrison bought his first sitar on Oxford Street in 1965 and soon decided to seek the best instruction he could find—which meant flying to India. He spent a few days on a Kashmiri houseboat in the company of Ravi Shankar, a master of the instrument. As his sitar skills improved, Harrison also became drawn to Indian meditation and philosophy. All of the Beatles (even Ringo, briefly) fell under the spell of the Maharishi Mahesh Yogi, who served as the group's unofficial guru. Paul Horn was among the many Western musicians who followed in their wake. The Beatles composed much of the *White Album* while staying on the Maharishi's ashram by the Ganges.

If I couldn't make a guitar gently weep like the quiet Beatle, I could at least try to meditate like him. And so, one afternoon in Saskatoon, I sought initiation into the Maharishi's trademarked brand of Transcendental Meditation. The local headquarters — an elm-shaded house near the university campus — were a haven of candles, joss sticks, and cut flowers. A young woman with a beatific smile and a long floral dress disclosed a mantra, supposedly ideal for me, and made me promise never to divulge it. Through a summer and into a fall I sat alone for twenty minutes every morning and evening, repeating the meaningless syllable, until one day I didn't. But if I'd come up short on the path to enlightenment, I blamed my teenage self and not the Maharishi.

Like millions of other young Westerners in the 1970s, I saw India as the epitome of cool. It seemed the natural home for travellers in both time and space, as Led Zeppelin put it in "Kashmir." Recalling the song one morning aboard the houseboat on Heaven Canal, I'd been puzzled by its trance-like evocation of a desert: the singer's eyes fill with sand as he scans a wasted land. I didn't know that Robert Plant composed the lyrics after a journey in southwestern Morocco. He and Jimmy Page had visited Bombay, but none of the band had set foot in Kashmir. Details of geography didn't matter to Led Zeppelin;

what counted was the languorous, dreamy mood the name "Kashmir" evoked.

"Would you call yourself a refugee from the materialistic values of the West?" an Indian reporter asks a British pop star in *The Guru*, a 1969 film by Ismail Merchant and James Ivory.

"Come again?" the pop star says.

He has flown to India to learn the sitar from one of the instrument's masters — the film is very loosely based on George Harrison's initial days with Ravi Shankar. But contrary to the reporter's severe inquiry, most of the young Indians in the film care less about the traditions of sitar-playing and discipleship than they do about Western pop and glamour. To many Indians, the European and American thirst to idealize their homeland caused surprise, even consternation. "The seduction lay in the chaos," Gita Mehta wrote in her acerbic 1979 book *Karma Cola: Marketing the Mystic East.* "They thought they were simple. We thought they were neon. They thought we were profound. We knew we were provincial...Into the vacuum of our unsatisfied desires the great Western marketing machine disgorged peasant skirts with hand-printed mantras, vegetable dyes, and lentil soup."

Harrison moved on from the Maharishi to sit at the feet of other gurus and to worship with the Hare Krishna movement, but he did not become disillusioned with Hindu spirituality. Words from the *Bhagavad Gita* appear in the notes to his final album: "There never was a time when you or I did not exist. Nor will there be any future when we shall cease to be." After his death in 2001, his family took his ashes from California to India, where they were scattered in the Ganges and Yamuna. Harrison's devotion was profound and lasting. Westerners, though, tended to recoil from his kind of faith. Having begun by expecting too much from the East, many grew resentful about receiving too little.

Mehta quotes an aging blonde woman she met in the 1970s in a Bombay café: "'We discovered these places, Afghanistan, Nepal, Goa. When we arrived everybody loved us. Now the whole damn world is on the trail we opened up, and the same people who loved us, fucking hate us.'" The monumental arrogance of those words — the idea that "we" could somehow "discover" places in Asia with long histories and rich cultures of their own — annoys me so much, I struggle to admit the truth underlying her bitterness. But the Hippie Trail was indeed a Pandora's box; it unleashed curses. "In search of a lovely simplicity, Westerners saddle the East with complexities; in search of peace, they bring agitation." Pico Iyer wrote these words more than thirty years ago, and his diagnosis of foreign travel in Asia remains astute. "As soon as Arcadia is seen as a potential commodity, amenities spring up on every side to meet outsiders' needs, and paradise is not so much lost as remaindered."

Unlike small countries like Nepal and Sri Lanka, India was so vast and multifarious, its tensions so many, its contradictions so flagrant, that no one could easily mistake it for paradise. Yet so many God-hungry overlanders poured into India that, for a while, the demand for enlightenment far exceeded the supply. You could argue there was nothing new about the quest: European and American authors had been fascinated for centuries by India's spiritual traditions. But only in the 1960s did the allure of India go mainstream. And only in the 1970s did India export guru after guru, men (and they were all men) who knew how to captivate a Western audience.

They faced a problem of translation. Over the centuries a host of Sanskrit religious terms had filtered into English: *avatar, dharma, karma, nirvana*... The accepted meanings of these words in London and Los Angeles sometimes diverged from their meanings in India. And these concepts entered a language whose speakers had other ideas embedded in their minds—such as heaven, hell, blasphemy, sin—ideas that do not exist in Sanskrit and are foreign to Hindu thought. "For example," wrote the scholar P. Lal, "Indian philosophy has no word for 'miracle' in Sanskrit or any of the Indian languages. Miracles cannot happen because nothing in this world of matter and karma operates outside the orbit of matter and karma. Hindu gods have notoriously clay feet and are subject to the laws of cause and effect as are we poor mortals. The gods we worship are the gods we create; we cannot worship the God who creates us."

Some of the most famous gurus of the era turned out to be deeply corrupt; it was as if the gurus the Westerners worshipped were the gurus they created. Charges of sexual abuse, financial misdealings, or both would swirl around Swami Muktananda, Sathya Sai Baba, Kripalu Maharaj, Bhagwan Shree Rajneesh, and many others. The orange-robed Swami Satchidananda opened the Woodstock Festival in 1969, calling music "a celestial sound... that controls the whole universe"—but a generation later, news emerged that he had far too little control over his earthly desires. Rajneesh, in particular, proved all too adept at stretching and adapting certain Hindu teachings to the fantasies and appetites of Americans. "My followers have no time," he told a reporter for *Time*. "So I give them instant salvation." Addressing those followers directly, he said, "Yes,

I teach you selfishness. Service is a four-letter dirty word." Rajneesh's worship of luxury—he owned more than ninety Rolls-Royces—took religious materialism to its extreme and far beyond.

"Get high on the music," Ravi Shankar once said. "It is enough!"

IN THE HOLY CITY of Varanasi—or Benares, to use one of its old names—Clare and I found ourselves in a Classical Music Centre. The self-appointed guide who took us there would have earned a commission had we booked a lesson or bought an instrument. The musician on site—an unshaven, pot-bellied man with tangled hair—appeared to be wearing a red towel and nothing else. He played a couple of short pieces on a sitar, five-finger exercises of great loveliness and simplicity. I would have loved to hear more, but we had no intention of making a purchase and he had no intention of giving a free recital. The guide also led us toward a large temple dedicated to Shiva but, with a sign declaring "Gentlemen not of the Hindu religion are not admitted," we saw it only from a nearby roof.

A man standing outside another temple gave us marigolds, wished us long life, and demanded a small payment in return. This kind of transaction would have pissed me off at the start of the trip, but I had grown used to the idea that looking and listening are only sometimes free. We came upon a mosque with a pool of goldfish and discovered, down a warren of lanes, a Hindu temple in the style of a Nepali pagoda, rich in carvings made of heavy wood. Dogs, monkeys, and white cows roamed the city as if it had been made for them. I was prepared for the sight of Varanasi's brick walls, narrow streets, and wide stairways: weeks before I left Oxford, I had watched Satyajit Ray's film *Aparajito*, much of it set in the city during the 1920s. But the film, about the child of an impoverished Hindu priest, is shot in a moody, grainy black and white. The images that lingered in my mind left me unready for Varanasi's blaze of colours and its din of sound.

Another guide — "I am student, not guide" — picked us up on a street corner with practised flair and brought us past a pair of wrestling schools to a shop that sold silks, saris, and brocades. There his older brother awaited us or any other likely customers: the Mehta brothers were mentioned in a French guidebook to India that the younger man proudly showed us. A cow was pondering something or other in the small inner courtyard. We took our shoes off at a door and climbed a staircase to an upper level where we could recline on a pillowed mattress; a third brother, still a boy, arrived with tea. A portrait of a goddess hung on the wall beneath a fluorescent light. The oldest brother put on an elegant show, lifting each silky item from a colourful stack by his side, displaying it to catch the light, then withdrawing it from view. The more I saw, the more I worried: time was money, time was passing, and I had no desire to buy a sari or anything else. Clare expressed delight in a long piece of gold-green fabric, which the man removed from his pile and hung over a railing for us to contemplate further. But her delight fell short of an actual purchase. Finally she decided on a gorgeous headscarf, buying it for fifteen rupees: a mere pound in British currency. The brothers had expected more.

"We're on our way to Kathmandu," I said. (This was true.) "We'll be returning through Varanasi." (Not true.) "And when we're back here, Clare and I will buy one of your saris." (Even less true.)

The Mehta brothers were intelligent young men, and they must have been aware I was spinning them a fantasy. But it served its purpose: it allowed us to depart on smiling terms, with everyone maintaining their dignity and self-respect.

Next morning we rose early, aiming to reach the Ganges by dawn. The sky was cloudy, the sunrise gradual, and the long *ghats* leading down to the water already busy. Varanasi is an ancient city, and the home of countless stories: one of them identifies it as the place where the Ganges washes Shiva's feet. Another tells of how the god Brahma sacrificed ten horses here. Devout Hindus look on it as both the city of light and the birthplace of time.

We hired a ferryman and he rowed us away from shore into the boat-filled water. The salty estuary lies hundreds of miles away in Bangladesh, but even here the Ganges is immensely wide. Stretched out before us, along the muddy edge of the sacred river like figures in a living frieze, were pilgrims immersing or drying themselves, people climbing the broad steps of the *ghats* or descending them, washermen slapping clothes on stones, a child shouting, an aged man alone and motionless on a stair, women bearing jugs of water, customers buying drinks at a tea stall, a goat poking its nose into something nutritious by the shore, a man rocking back and forth in prayer, and a handful of tourists taking pictures of life and death.

A single body was on fire by the shore. A pile of cinders flickered.

After noon we trudged through the sticky heat to one of the city's biggest *ghats*—two of them are dedicated to cremation.

An orange-clad *sadhu*, his hair far longer than mine, stood near the top of a stairway, smearing ashes on pilgrims' brows. *Ram Naam Satya Hai*... Incense hanging in the air mixed with other smells, less alluring. Below the steps, on some open ground, several bodies were burning; two more awaited their turn. Vultures revolved in slow circles high above a scrawny, yelping dog and a flat-bottomed boat, packed with branches to feed the pyres.

The dead men we saw lay covered by a white shroud; dead women wore a shroud and a bright sari. The corpses rested neatly between layers of wood: no one's flesh could escape this fire. Before a cremation began, each of the bodies would be anointed with clarified butter, and a son or other relative would walk around the corpse three times, bathing it from a clay pot full of Ganges water. Then, having let the pot fall, he would light the pyre and, not looking back, the family members would leave. A fragrance of sandalwood sweetened the young flames. A wreath of marigolds had fallen near a few smashed pots.

Clare and I stood and watched all this through clouds of smoke, human smoke. Occasionally a cloud changed direction and drifted toward us, stinging us with its heat and odour. "India is probably the only country in the world," Gita Mehta observed, "that allows the tourist to treat death as a spectator sport." I felt both privileged and ashamed: What right did I have to witness a stranger dissolve under my gaze? I had never seen a dead body before, and here was a woman's broken skull turning black. Her left foot and ankle were still unburnt; a minute or so went by, and they snapped off from the leg. A low-caste attendant, dressed only in white trousers, shaven-headed except for a topknot, picked up the foot and ankle and rearranged them on the pyre. Before long they too were charred. The woman's stomach burst and shrank, fluids dripping out onto the dwindling pile of wood. She was becoming a skeleton.

Soon she would be not even that. The attendant, smoke on his skin, wiped his face with his hand. He looked across the flames and met my eyes.

"JUST CLAY, A LEAKING POT, a nine-holed jug": that's how the poet Kabir described the human body. All through northern India, he's regarded as a saint. Yet almost nothing is known about him; the only certainties are that he lived in Varanasi during the fifteenth century and that he wrote subversive poetry. He grew up in a caste of Muslim weavers — in India, even Muslims are split by caste. Kabir denounced the caste system and criticized both Hindus and Muslims. Yet Muslims and Hindus alike exalt him, and a few of his poems and songs, elliptical and questioning though they are, appear in the Sikh scriptures. Varanasi has several temples dedicated to the man. It's said that after he died, both Hindus and Muslims tried to claim his corpse. A fight erupted. The lifting of the shroud revealed no sign of Kabir's body: flowers lay in its place. Sikhs tell the same story about Guru Nanak, the founder of their faith.

Kabir's legacy of irreverence and dissent is, like the political legacy of Mohandas Gandhi, now under siege. Since 1978, India's economy has been transformed: instead of being patterned along socialist lines and constrained by countless regulations, it has flung itself wide open to global capitalism. Large numbers of people have done well from the changes, some becoming fabulously rich; an even larger number of others have not. The shorthand term is "liberalization," a word that makes sense in the realm of bankers and entrepreneurs. Yet for artists, intellectuals, freethinkers, India has become less and less liberal. Arundhati Roy, in a 2022 interview, described her country's leadership as "intrinsically fascist" and said that "we are in the process of becoming" a fascist state. In India, as in Afghanistan and Pakistan, Iran and Turkey, the unorthodox and the irreverent are now under duress.

The tale of the shroud and the miraculous flowers suggests that Hindus and Muslims were often at each other's throats in Kabir's day. Since then the mutual rancour has waned and grown, waned and grown, without ever going away. It would be wrong, though, to see it as the dominant thread in India's tangled history. In her biography of the Mughal empress Nur Jahan, Ruby Lal evoked a culture "in which you could be Shi'a or Sunni Muslim and yet marvel at the esoteric message of Sufi mysticism or Hindu asceticism, question Jesuits about the life of Jesus, or tease a youthful monk about the pleasures of the flesh, all of which Nur Jahan did. Nur, a Shi'a Muslim woman, married a Sunni king who had a Hindu mother and both Hindu and Muslim wives and concubines." The regal pluralism of the seventeenth century would be unthinkable for India's rulers today.

Despite the 1947 loss of lands that became Pakistan and Bangladesh, India remains the home of the third-largest body of Muslims in the world. The rise of Hindu nationalism has made their lives burdensome, as if their faith somehow disqualifies them from being true Indians. Muslim names have disappeared: the state government of Uttar Pradesh, for example, imposed a new identity on a metropolis known since the Mughal era as Allahabad. Buildings are as vulnerable as names—buildings like a sixteenth-century mosque in the small city of Ayodhya. A well-organized mob tore it down in 1992. Leaders of the riot justified the act by saying the mosque occupied the birthplace of the Hindu god Ram. A mastermind of the demolition, Narendra Modi, would go on to become India's prime minister. Like his contemporary Recep Tayyip Erdoğan in Turkey, like Ayatollah Khomeini and General Zia before him, he has sought to fuse religion and national pride, as if his country's honour relies on a single faith.

With Modi in office, India's enormous TV and movie industry has had to tread carefully. A Netflix adaptation of Vikram Seth's novel *A Suitable Boy* ran into legal troubles in 2020: it showed a Muslim boy kissing a Hindu girl (nothing racier than that) with a Hindu temple in the background. A leader of the youth wing of Modi's political party complained that the scene could encourage "love jihad"—a conspiracy theory that accuses Muslim men of seducing Hindu women so as to convert them to Islam. The government was much happier about *The Kashmir Files*, a violent Bollywood movie that became a box-office sensation in 2022. It demonizes Muslims and wildly distorts historical facts. Yet as he praised the movie, Modi said: "Those who live for the truth have a responsibility to stand with the truth." Hindu nationalism of the kind whipped up by *The Kashmir Files* threatens the Gyanvapi Mosque, one of the largest in Varanasi: a Mughal emperor ordered it built on the site of a demolished Hindu temple. Militant Hindus want the mosque destroyed. Barbed wire now surrounds it, a watchtower overlooks it, and police keep a regular patrol.

I couldn't have imagined all that on the morning we took a short bus ride from Varanasi to Sarnath, hoping to explore both a temple and a garden. The name *Sarnath* (taken from a Sanskrit word for "lord of the deer") commemorates an ancient king who refrained from killing a doe, creating a wildlife sanctuary instead. Clare and I saw no deer among the flame trees and purple-flowered bushes, but we did pass some nilgai—bulky, short-horned Indian antelope—browsing in an enclosure they shared with peacocks and pheasants. The male nilgai had a strange blue-grey pelt, akin to the colour of the Buddha's hair in the Japanese wall paintings decorating Sarnath's main temple.

For this is a Buddhist site, one of the most significant anywhere: it marks the spot where the enlightened Buddha, having understood the folly of extremist religion, began to expound the Middle Way. At Sarnath he made his vision public. Here his long years of teaching began. Here—perhaps 2,400 years ago, perhaps 2,600, perhaps even further in the past—he preached his first sermon, warned against the two extremes, set out the four noble truths, explained the eightfold path, and developed the twelve insights that stem from those four truths...My head was spinning with arithmetic. In the Sarnath Museum we looked at a silver casket that held sacred relics from Taxila, and a four-lioned sculpture, carved out of sandstone, that symbolized the power and wisdom of the Buddhist emperor Ashoka. India's first prime minister, Jawaharlal Nehru, made the lion sculpture the emblem of his newly independent country.

Thousands of years earlier, it's said, the king had spared the doe's life because a Bodhisattva—a kind of Buddha in training—transformed himself into a deer and asked the king to shoot him instead. Thinking about the tale, I recalled the Byzantine monk whose story we had come across in Turkey: the monk befriended a bear. I thought of the hoopoe who leads the Sufi flock in *The Conference of the Birds*, and of the reverence given an elephant and a monkey in the pantheon of Hindu gods. And I thought about the fruit bats we'd seen at a Jain temple in Khajuraho—Jains are strict vegetarians who go out of their way to avoid killing any animals, even insects, and their doctrine of *ahimsa*, or non-violence, entails rules for animals' proper treatment. Buddhism is by no means the only faith that has dared to conceive a different relationship between the human and non-human realms. Even the ancient Hittites glimpsed the need to prevent their lands from being shattered by floods, droughts, and fires. If only the wisdom embodied in these stories could affect how people treat what remains of the natural world today…

One of the abiding mysteries of Indian history is why Buddhism, having spread to many other countries in Asia, all but vanished from its birthplace. The teachings of the Buddha fell into shadow; the edicts of Ashoka were forgotten. Armies loyal to the Muslim warlords and sultans who dominated the region eight hundred years ago wrecked dozens of Buddhist monasteries and slaughtered countless monks; in India, destructive zeal is a very old affliction. Yet by the time of the Muslim conquest, Buddhism had already given way to Hinduism through most of the country. Even Sarnath, which has a strong claim to call itself the wellspring of the faith, had no place of Buddhist worship— merely a sprawl of stone and brick ruins—until 1931, when a Hawaiian convert, influenced by a Sri Lankan monk, funded a temple graced by Japanese frescoes.

Twenty-five years later a scholar, lawyer, and politician named B. R. Ambedkar made a very public conversion to Buddhism. He had helped write India's constitution and had served under Nehru as the first justice minister of an independent India. But Ambedkar was also a *dalit*, an "untouchable," and he disputed Mohandas Gandhi's acceptance of caste as intrinsic and necessary to Indian society. As he neared the end of his life, he grew more and more despondent about the injustice and entrenched force of the caste system. "To the Untouchables," he wrote, "Hinduism is a veritable chamber of horrors." The egalitarian teachings of the Buddha, he hoped, could light up a new road for his people. When Ambedkar converted, hundreds of thousands of *dalits* did the same, rejuvenating Buddhism in its ancestral home. He died less than two months later.

All this was not, presumably, on the mind of Indira Gandhi in 1974 when, under her prime ministership, India detonated its first nuclear weapon. She received a coded message from the Rajasthan desert, assuring her of success: "The Buddha has smiled."

BACK IN VARANASI THE streets were their usual tumult. The Beat poet Allen Ginsberg—an inspiration to many wanderers on the Hippie Trail—lived here in the early 1960s, feeding his lungs on cannabis and his eyes on the daily commotion of the *ghats*. In Varanasi a multilingual Indian poet by the name of Nagarjun—a Brahmin who had converted to Buddhism, then Marxism—introduced Ginsberg to the harmonium. The plangent, droning sound of the instrument, European by origin, had become a staple of Indian classical music. Ginsberg took a small harmonium back to the United States and used it to accompany his readings.

Over chai Clare and I talked to a young man from Vancouver—not one of the best minds of his generation—who was repelled by India's pungent chaos and had found Calcutta as dismal as its reputation; but he loved Indonesia, and he'd "had a good time" in Bangkok. I didn't ask him to define "good time." We were staying at a budget hotel named the Empire; our spacious bedroom contained a gasping fan, strips of peeling paint, and a window devoid of glass. In the late afternoon, as we walked into the lobby, Sandeep, the desk clerk, rushed out from behind the counter.

"Will you come to a wedding party tonight?" he asked. "It will be my honour."

Why did he invite us?

"Yes!" we said. "Of course!"

We opened the door of our room to find a small lizard creeping down the wall: it lunged forward and grabbed a jumbo cricket off a bedside table. I removed my shoes and sweat-damp shirt and lay down to rest. After a while, when I turned toward the table, I saw three or four of the insect's legs still twitching out of the lizard's jaw.

A few hours later—we'd left our inept watches in a repair shop, and our concept of time was fuzzy—Clare and I were perching in the back of a taxi heading down a main road in Varanasi. Sandeep and his cousin sat in front near the driver. The bride was the cousin's wife's sister: I think that's what Sandeep said. I kept my elbows pressed to my sides; with us in the back were a slightly older English couple and their five-year-old son, Gabriel.

"He's a good traveller," his mother said loyally, "and every-where we go, people keep giving him presents. Although in Nepal, for some reason, people were a bit afraid of him."

The taxi slowed and turned onto a dark side street, then another, then an alley; then it could go no further. It had reached a sort of courtyard. As soon as we spilled out, we could hear bugles and drums. In front of us, people had gathered in a loose circle to watch teenage boys dancing with kerchiefs or bandanas in their mouths. Lights were suspended on chains. On the far side of the courtyard hung images of gods. A man rushed by, squirting a perfumed liquid over the crowd. I got very wet.

And then the dancing stopped: the groom was arriving in a carriage, led by a pair of brightly garnished ponies. He sported a gold turban, adorned with a brooch and a single feather. Clare and I and everyone else were shouting and clapping when Sandeep reappeared. We followed him up two flights of stairs to the roof, giving us a terrific view of a fireworks display.

From atop the building, we could see Varanasi's pitted skyline: hidden in the darkness, beyond all the shops, homes, factories, and temples, the Ganges flowed on. We could also peer down onto a mid-level terrace that held other wedding guests. Children surrounded us: thirty of them, maybe more, dressed in their finest clothes. A few reached out, giggling, to touch our hands and legs. The adults gazed at the rockets, emerald wheels, and Roman candles, applauding the most spec-tacular; but to the kids, fair-haired Gabriel was now the centre of attention. For the moment, he took their laughter in stride. His family, Clare, and I were the only Westerners in evidence.

"I have twenty-five sisters," a boy told me.

I raised my eyebrows.

"Please, give me twenty-five rupees?"

A minute later he had five sisters and six brothers, and this may have been the truth. I wondered what, if anything, the boy knew of Canada. Did he dream it was like the United States: a nation of golden sidewalks? The flecks of silica in American pavements had made some immigrants think the roads were built of gold, and in excitement they spread the illusion to relatives back home.

Sandeep's cousin asked us to come and meet the bride. Along a corridor, down another set of stairs, we entered a windowless, lantern-lit room with family members bustling to and fro. Reena, ensconced on a chair in temporary splendour, looked no more than seventeen. She wore a gold-embroidered, lemon-coloured sari that could, for all I knew, have come from the Mehta brothers or the descendants of Kabir. Clare and I bowed and smiled. Reena bowed and smiled in return. I wished her a joyful marriage. Her mother looked as though she were worrying about a thousand things at once.

Later, sitting on mats, we drank a rosewater-flavoured beverage and ate a vegetarian feast. Our plates were big leaves. Family members served the food from buckets: tomato and potato curries, daal, spiced rice with green peas; rotis, chutneys, and mango pickle. The candies had a tooth-numbing sweetness. Children watched us, none of them rude enough to inquire why the pallid strangers were dining first. The party would go on for hours, Sandeep told us; the wedding, at least one more day.

Shortly after eating, we said a round of farewells and slipped into the night: Gabriel was having trouble staying calm or awake. Or both. On our ride back to the hotel, I felt too stunned and humbled to say much. Varanasi's streets were almost quiet.

I have no idea why we were honoured like this.

THE NIGHT AFTER THE wedding party, our watches keeping time again, we set off by steam train toward the Nepali border. We must have had a reason for making the trip in three zigzagging stages. Perhaps it was the cheapest way to get there—our money was beginning to run low. But did we forget to consult a map? Or had the heat addled our brains? "Do not try to rush on Indian trains," *Student Guide to Asia* advised us. "They seem to have been put there to slow down Western minds. Just curl up and watch the world go by."

The train left Varanasi at 10:30 p.m. We had a sleeping berth for the first leg of the trip, and arrived in the city of Gorakhpur before dawn. At Gorakhpur we transferred to a Janata Express heading southeast to Sonpur, away from the border. The word "Janata" was accurate—this was indeed a train for the people—but it could hardly have been less of an "Express." During the first four hours of the fourteen-hour journey, we had to stand. Then some passengers left the carriage and we nabbed a pair of adjacent seats. Clare was suffering from heat rash. We reached Sonpur at 9:30 p.m. The connecting train to the shabby border town of Raxaul was supposed to leave at 11:40 p.m.; it moped into the station shortly before dawn. We made our destination just after 1 p.m., having spent a night, a day, a second night, and half of the next day travelling to a place that is, as the grey-necked Indian crow flies, only 163 miles from Varanasi.

The Janata Express had no fans, no lights, no food, no drink, and no toilets. Or rather, it did have a single toilet at one end of the carriage—but the toilet, like the four compartments and the corridor, was crammed with more women, men, and children than I believed possible. Each compartment provided enough room for eight travellers to sit in modest discomfort; halfway to Sonpur the carriage held, at a conservative guess, at least ninety people. Those who couldn't find a space on one of the wooden benches remained standing, leaning, squatting on the floor, or living dangerously on the roof. Clare and I did not find it easy to curl up and watch the world go by. I tried to recall why we'd resisted buying tickets to ride a European bus with psychedelic shapes and colours swirling along the sides and a peace sign plastered on the rear...

"I am admirer of Percy Shelley. Are you?"

Bibek taught English at a Catholic school in the tea-growing hill station of Darjeeling. A crow could have flown there in a day.

"Tell me, please, what is the sound of a skylark?"

On a coal-fired train wheezing through the buffalo-filled plains of Bihar, one of India's poorest states, I laboured to explain why the poet had compared a skylark to a golden glow-worm, a highborn maiden, and a deflowered rose.

"Percy Shelley was cremated," Bibek remarked. "Are all English people cremated?"

Clare assured him they were not. He seemed a little disappointed.

"What is the most poetic word in English language?"

The steam engine was having as much difficulty in pulling the train as I was in answering the teacher: it would chug along for a mile or two and then, for no apparent reason, stop. Once, while it was motionless, I watched children swimming in a dark, tree-shaded pond while a paradise flycatcher swooped back and forth over the water. Then the engine started up again, the train lurched forward, and a small man squatting on the floor shouted at me. My backpack had fallen against him. Whether he was rebuking me in Hindi, Bojhpuri, Maithili, Bajjika, Angika, Magahi, or one of the many other languages of the region, his words were lost on me. He glared and spat. I glared too. Clare was biting her fingernails in agitation. Finally I mumbled an apology in a language the man may or may not have understood.

But that was an exceptional moment. For the most part, the travellers bore the annoyances of the trip with good humour and equanimity. Many dozed away the hours. A man sitting across from us kept his eyes open: the whites of them were not white at all but a strange pinkish-yellow hue, almost certainly a result of hepatitis. Occasionally, when the train hissed and creaked to a stop, I would hear some *tsk-tsking* and notice some head-shaking. But nobody launched a sustained complaint in any language. This was Janata Express. This was Indian Railways. This was Bihar. This was life. Why give way to anger?

I had arrived in the country with the hope, or at least the dream, of attaining some kind of mystical rapture. Nowhere in India had I risen to those elusive heights. But India was teaching me, even on a hugely overcrowded train, especially on a hugely overcrowded train, a more important lesson: patience, endurance, resilience. *Be Here Now*, wrote Baba Ram Dass, previously known as Professor Richard Alpert of Harvard University. "Be Here Now," sang George Harrison. Well, I was here now.

When we reached Sonpur—a few dim lights above the long platform allowed us to read the town's name—the corridor was a breathing wall of passengers and the only way we could leave the train was by clambering through the window. Clare went first, balancing nervously on the frame before jumping down into the night. I tossed her backpack after her, then my own, and finally scrambled out myself. At last we could stretch our legs, use the toilet, drink some tea. I had no appetite for food; I was now thinner than I had ever been in my life. A station official took pity on us: he invited us to shower in a building off limits to most travellers.

He did not extend this generosity to the Indigenous tribespeople waiting on the same platform as ourselves. I noticed one of them — a man with long grey hair and a beard, very dark skin, a short dhoti, and a staff in his right hand — hobbling up and down, peering at a motionless, unlit train. He decided to climb aboard only when the train coughed, whistled, shook, and inched forward. A woman dressed in long rags attempted to follow. The train meandered out of Sonpur at an ox's pace, but the woman had missed the first open door and in the darkness she could not find a second. As she stood on the suddenly empty platform, her shoulders sagged. For a long time she didn't move.

On the final stretch of the journey, I began to write a poem addressed to my own skeleton. "Mind is the source of bondage," I had read in the Maitri Upanishad, "and also the source of liberation. To be bound to things of this world: this is bondage." At Raxaul the international border was a faded signpost and a pair of sheds. "To be free from them: this is liberation."

5.

Nepal

"Where is your home?"

A week before her fatal overdose in 1970, Janis Joplin covered the soul hit "Cry Baby." Her version — ragged, heartfelt, jittery — adds some lyrics to the original, lyrics about walking around the world and looking for an end to the road. And where could that be, if not a heroin-filled hotel room in Hollywood? The road, she cries out, will end in Kathmandu. Joplin had never been there, except perhaps in her dreams.

Neither had the Michigan rocker Bob Seger, who enjoyed a minor hit in 1975 with "Katmandu." The song is a curmudgeonly thank-you letter to the United States — he mentions four regions of the country, praising them all — yet Seger insists he is about to leave. He says that nobody in America loves him. It's hard to believe the man, and even harder to believe he means to fulfill his fantasy of hightailing into the mountains, all the way to Kathmandu. He stutters over the letter K as if firing an automatic weapon.

Cat Stevens never went to Kathmandu either. He wrote his plaintive "Katmandu" (both Stevens and Seger use an odd spelling) while recovering from tuberculosis and a collapsed lung, and after reading an item about the city in *Rolling Stone*. The song appeared in 1970 on the young Englishman's third album. His "Katmandu" is a dream of escape: from a grey, cold morning on which a lake drinks up the sky to an elusive, flute-haunted place that allows its visitors to enter a strange and bewildering time.

I listened to that song on the sound system of Aunt Jane's in Kathmandu while I was munching a water-buffalo burger. Or did we hear "Katmandu" follow "All I Want" on a radio station in the New Hungry Eye? Or wait, maybe the manager at Tibetan Cock Crows had a cassette of the entire Cat Stevens album. At the end of the road (or nearly) things were getting a little...blurred. Was I living on Easy Street? No, in the Blue Angel off Freak Street. In Nepal, for almost a week, I stopped keeping a journal. In Nepal, I relaxed.

BUT NOT AT FIRST. Birgunj, a trading town on the Nepali side of the Indian border, boasted a long line of tailors' shops and thick mosquito clouds. Clare and I walked to a bank as soon as we arrived, and the teller politely declined to cash her travellers' cheques. He wouldn't cash mine either. We drooped at the counter, exhausted by the trip from Varanasi, backpacks on the floor in front of us, a line of people growing behind, and argued our case without success. I reached below my loose shirt to fumble in my money belt. Any pound notes inside? There were — enough to get us to Kathmandu on a bus the next day. We trudged back to the bus station amid a clatter of sewing machines and checked in at the Hotel Delight. It did not live up to its name. In the street, a man was picking lice out of someone else's hair.

Birgunj is eighty-four miles south of the capital. "Your journey will take seven hours," we were told. It took ten. I had left England thinking of time as a fixed and steadfast quantity; travel in Asia was teaching me to look on it as variable, elastic, fluid. Crossing the border from Raxaul, we'd moved our watches ahead by ten minutes: Nepal maintains a secluded time zone of its own. It also keeps its own calendar. Five calendars, to be exact; one of them lags behind another by 802 years. We had arrived, according to the official Nepali calendar, as the month of Asar began in the year 2035. I found myself more than three decades in the future beyond the date of the satirical piece of futurism that had made the present trip possible in what now seemed like the distant past.

The bus advanced through flat, wet jungle in the morning and drenched foothills in the early afternoon, our luggage safe—we thought—under tarps on the roof. Clare's backpack got wet despite the tarps, and our big water bottle disappeared. (The Donald Duck bottle had vanished weeks earlier.) Monsoons had caught up with us at last. I felt a wild voracious joy in the rain, as though a physical need was finally being satisfied. Between cloudbursts thundering in my ear, the bus drew to a stop in a hamlet—the middle of nowhere to me, the heart of the world to its few families—and the driver and conductor shared a bowl of rice and lentils near the brink of a green gorge. Girls and boys splashed barefoot through the mud. They were pursuing a crested lizard, laughing and screaming at the thrill of the chase.

I might have called the scene idyllic were it not for the human excrement underfoot and the police checkpoint ahead. "A village is made of a single scene," Dhruba Chandra Gautam would assert in his novel *Unwritten*: "Smoke, dust, secrets, poverty. A village looks like someone standing with his waistband full of holes or patches." Gautam was born in Birgunj in 1943; he knew the south of Nepal well.

Our bus switchbacked up a mountain, the road rising to a pass nine thousand feet high, lost in drizzle long before the climb ended. The summit in question belongs to the Mahabharat—the world's only mountain range, as far as I know, named after an epic poem. (Call it the Lesser Himalaya if you must.) June is the worst month in the Western calendar to look north and see the Greater Himalaya: swirls of heavy mist and rainclouds wrapped the peaks. But the fog could not obscure a skein of ridges, terraced hills, and valleys striped by barley fields. Brick, wooden-windowed houses looked as red as the lush earth. Corrugated iron topped some of the homes; other roofs were thatched. I would have seen more, a lot more, except I was sandwiched between Clare and a dozing Indian gentleman whose oily head had slipped onto my chest. Just when I thought I couldn't take any more, the bus reached the entrance to the Kathmandu Valley and the long and winding road slid down.

It led us into a city like nothing I had seen or imagined. Streets alternated with rice paddies. Turn a corner, and we'd find a dome or a crumbling brick wall painted with giant eyes. Turn another corner, and we'd see banners strung above a temple and a bull reclining in front, possibly sacred, possibly dangerous, possibly neither, possibly both. Clare and I wandered the muddy roads and alleys keeping watch on the windows above: as in medieval Europe, householders on the second or third storey would toss out their slops. Durbar Square, ringed by wooden palaces and temples, overseen by tall pagodas, hosted casual games of frisbee. Rain fell so intensely there one evening that Nepali children played a game of ducks and drakes across pools that had formed on the pavement, skimming plastic sandals over the water instead of flat stones. A statue of the monkey god Hanuman guarded the gate to a palace courtyard. The god wore a scarlet cloak. Night and day, rain or shine, he squatted beneath a black umbrella.

Above all, Kathmandu came as a relief. For us, as for most of the overlanders, India had proved overwhelming. It challenged our minds, tested our bodies, exhausted our senses. Now we found ourselves in a city that offered — to privileged foreign travellers, I mean — most of India's rewards and far fewer of its trials. The temperature was milder here, the crowds smaller, the noise level lower. One evening in Durbar Square, Clare and I sat for hours looking at the Taleju Temple, serene and almost mountainous, framed by a full moon on the left and a massive fig tree on the right. The tree's airy roots grew above a domed stupa. Our breathing slowed. Our lungs rejoiced.

We smiled freely at passersby in Kathmandu. They smiled freely at us.

PEOPLE IN THE KATHMANDU VALLEY, I thought, had adjusted quickly and successfully to Western travellers: so successfully I found it hard to believe that little more than a generation earlier, Europeans and North Americans were all but unknown in Nepal. The country had never been colonized. Whereas Westerners had traipsed across India for centuries, marvelling and complaining in equal measure, Nepal remained isolated — even more cut off from the outside world, for long periods, than its famously inward-looking neighbour, Tibet. Until 1951, Nepal's borders were closed, and only the luckiest or most intrepid travellers made it through. Then, at roughly the same time that Chinese troops invaded and overran Tibet, Nepal reversed its policies and began to open up to foreign tourism. In 1953, a Nepali Sherpa named Tenzing Norgay and a New Zealand beekeeper named Edmund Hillary climbed to the summit of a mountain known in Nepali as *Sagarmatha* (sky goddess) and in Tibetan as *Chomolungma* (holy mother) — and with their "conquest of Everest," Nepal found itself figuratively as well as literally on the map.

A decade later Kathmandu had become renowned for its laid-back acceptance of Western counterculture: drugs were legal, food was cheap, and the views were beyond magnificent. Young travellers in Kathmandu could elude the past and imagine the future — peaceful, mellow, aromatic. Was there a better place to feed your head? Through the 1960s the backpackers who poured into Nepal in ever greater volumes knew little about the country; its many languages and complex history remained a closed book. They ignored its rigorous caste system and its lack of political freedom. But they loved the vibe.

Nepalis were, to say the least, taken aback by this sudden influx of long-haired visitants from faraway continents. Some of the travellers wore little clothing, even when poking around sacred Hindu and Buddhist sites. Others eagerly bought funeral shrouds and wore them as scarves. "They are dirty, ugly, without shoes," a Kathmandu businessman told Mark Liechty, the author of *Far Out*, an excellent study of tourism in Nepal. "I mean, 'What kind of people are they? It must be a joke.' But slowly we talked with them, day to day, and found that, yes... white people are not like supermen. They are like we are. They make mistakes, they do stupid things, they sometimes cheat us, they are not always rich men, sometimes they beg from you." The spectacle of Westerners panhandling in the streets of Kathmandu jolted Nepalis who had equated tourism with wealth.

The city served as the principal setting for a Bollywood blockbuster, *Hare Rama Hare Krishna*, which was released in 1971. Its hero, Prashant, catches a plane to Kathmandu in search of his long-lost sister Jasbir, who has taken up with a bunch of Western ne'er-do-wells — young Bubbly would soon do the same in the Pakistani film *Miss Hippy*. One of the foreigners makes a living by stealing and selling ancient Nepali artifacts of the sort Clare and I saw for sale in the city. All of the travellers are liable to recede from view behind a veil of hash. A catchy song called "Dum Maro Dum" — or "Take Another Toke" — became immensely popular in India, and propelled *Hare Rama Hare Krishna* to vast profits. The movie portrayed Kathmandu, like the hippies themselves, as both desirable and dangerous; or rather, the danger lay in the desire. Prashant retains his virtue in the face of temptation. Jasbir — renamed Janice by the dope-smoking freaks — eventually feels so ashamed of her behaviour that she takes her own life.

No mainstream Indian movie could have glorified the foreigners who were engulfing south Asia, smashing taboos with innocent glee. A little finger-wagging was clearly in order.

But like the anti-drug commercials that North American TV stations were broadcasting in the same era, *Hare Rame Hare Krishna* demonstrated the allure of what it supposedly warned against. Even as some Nepalis reacted with dismay to the casual sloppiness of Western travellers, others were drawn to the music and the material objects those travellers brought with them. Another of Liechty's informants—he had been a teenager in the 1970s—recalled that "People like me, we looked at hippies and didn't see dharma seekers. We didn't see revolutionaries. We looked at them and saw Levis. We saw guitars. We saw records. And we wanted that stuff!"

Freak Street—*Jhochhen*, to use its Nepali name—allowed both sides in the exchange to quench their thirst. Its restaurants, shops, and budget hotels embodied young foreigners' dreams of Asia and young Asians' fantasies of Western counterculture. Yet its heyday was a brief one. Cannabis had flourished in Nepal for millennia but, in 1973, under pressure from the United States, the government outlawed all recreational drugs. No longer would stores along Freak Street openly sell cannabis—the Hashish Ganja Shop, the Eden Hashish Centre, and other such businesses changed their names or shut their doors. No longer would the menu of the Cabin Restaurant promise "marihuana puding" and "ganja coffee." In practice, drugs continued to be easily available; many foreigners in 1978 still smoked openly. Clare and I were sharing a table at New Style Chai and Pie one evening when a dreadlocked man across from us produced a needle and a plastic bag full of white powder: heroin in its purest form. A young American woman at another table was lamenting— or bragging—that she used to spend thirty dollars a day on opium. Most Nepalis would have needed two or three months to earn such a fortune.

At least one Western musician did write a song about the real Kathmandu, not an imagined version: the Canadian singer Bruce Cockburn. "Tibetan Side of Town," released a decade after I visited the city, summons up Kathmandu at sunset:

> *To hold that last shot of red sun through haze over jumbled roofs*
> *Everything moves like slow fluid in this atmosphere*
> *Thick as dreams with sewage, incense, dust and fever*
> *And the smoke of brick kilns and cremations...*

He goes on to mention the "laughing kids with hungry eyes" that he noticed from the back of a motorbike. A disabled beggar on a skateboard was grinning too — but why? Cockburn doesn't pretend to understand.

Tourism had rapidly become vital to Nepal's flimsy economy: no other industry or activity produced so much foreign exchange. It took some years for the country to catch up with what Westerners expected — as our *Student Guide to Asia* noted, "Kathmandu is not one of the world's healthiest cities and dysentery (at the very least) seems inevitable. Water should always be boiled." Dumbfounded at first by the unlikely hordes on the Hippie Trail, the Nepali government soon decided to pursue a more lucrative type of foreign guest. It realized that entrepreneurs could reap much greater profits than would ever be made by the small-scale merchants of Freak Street. The early 1970s, accordingly, saw Nepal rebrand itself. The regime was tired of welcoming frugal rebels who arrived in a battered van or a coughing bus, intending to keep on truckin'; now it sought affluent professionals who would fly into Kathmandu, stay a few days, and head out trekking. In economic terms this was a desperately poor nation, and the shelter, guides, food, and equipment required by trekkers would put far more rupees in circulation than young overlanders could afford to spend. And so Nepal adopted "adventure tourism" as a strategy and an ideal. The tallest mountains on Earth, apart from being sacred, were a tangible asset.

Before long, trekkers and would-be adventurers dominated Nepali tourism. And perhaps this was a blessing. Were it not for foreigners willing to pay a premium to explore a couple of national parks in the lowland jungle near the Indian border, poachers would have butchered the last tigers and rhinos in the country. Tourists had the inadvertent power to protect forests that illicit logging would otherwise have ravaged. Clare and I had reached the country at a pivotal moment. During our time in Nepal—we saw new hotels under construction in several districts of Kathmandu—freaks and trekkers roamed the streets in roughly equal numbers, each group glancing at the other with suspicion, even scorn.

"Hello, bye-bye, one rupees?" Kathmandu children would say to us with a grin, their eyes bright, their hands outstretched. I had the disturbing impression that some of their faces were too old for their bodies. "Where you from, England? Capital Londons...one rupees?" In Kathmandu, just as in Kayseri, hope is the bread of the poor.

A Nepali rupee was worth less than five English pence. Instead of giving the children a coin, I would stretch out my hand and playfully shake theirs. The children went on smiling. They didn't seem to mind. Or so I wanted to believe.

"Have just been watching a Nepali boy of 12 or so unsuccessfully but persistently try to get money from a pair of Americans with a guide," I wrote one morning in my journal. (After some days off, I had assiduously taken it up again.) "To think that all my sympathies would once have been with the boy! He just made a half-hearted try for me."

SMILES AND EYES ARE at the crux of a caustic short story published by the Nepali writer Shankar Lamichhane in 1962 — a moment when Westerners were just becoming a common sight in Kathmandu. The story would be translated into English under the title "The Half-Closed Eyes of the Buddha and the Slowly Setting Sun." In the first part, an enthusiastic tourist addresses a local guide. He waxes lyrical about a culture he does not understand, erroneously praising *momos* — steamed Tibetan dumplings — as a typical Nepali dish. In his mind this is a land of harmony, free of the very notion of ownership. He applauds his guide for living in a house like a temple, although he thinks the guide could never appreciate its beauty. The more whisky the visitor consumes, the more he compliments Nepal.

The tourist loves how local people smile at him. He believes their smiles are full of wisdom. But even more than the country's many smiles, its many eyes impress him: "The eyes of the carved lattice windows, the eyes painted on the door panels. The eyes on the *stupas*, the eyes of the people. And the eyes of the Himalaya, which peep out from the gaps between the hills like those of a neighbour's boy when he jumps up to see the peach tree in your garden. This is a land of eyes, a land guarded by the half-closed eyes of the Lord Buddha." Before he staggers off for the evening, the tourist implores the guide to show him a pair of eyes he will never forget.

The second part of the story takes place the following day. It's written in the voice of the guide. They go up a hill to a part of town few visitors ever see. The guide bypasses a temple whose prayer wheels celebrate the jewel at the heart of the Buddhist lotus. Instead they arrive at a cramped house where a farming family lives in the utmost poverty.

A child is lying inside the house, a child who will never jump up to look at peach trees or anything else. He is so badly afflicted by polio that he can neither walk nor crawl. The boy is unable to speak; he cannot even chew his food. Only his eyes sporadically move. The guide has arranged the visit by lying to the boy's parents. They believe the foreigner is a doctor, and they smile in the hope he will heal their son. Even the wary grandmother beams at the guest. But, the guide warns, the family's smiles will be extinguished when the tourist turns to depart. Smiling is an act of will, a performance.

Lamichhane leaves us to guess at the tourist's response. Compared to the loud, self-confident tones of Westerners, Nepali voices often go unheard; but in the second half of the narrative, only the guide gets to speak. The story ends with his sardonic exaltation of the paralyzed boy's eyes: "These are eyes surrounded by mountains; their lashes are rows of fields where rice ripens in the rains and wheat ripens in the winter. These are the eyes that welcome you...Look! They are just as beautiful as the setting sun's reflection in the eyes of the Buddha!"

I WAS STANDING IN the main square of Kathmandu when Lord Vishnu appeared.

Or rather, King Birendra, educated at Eton, Tokyo, and Harvard, and looked on by some Nepalis as an incarnation of Vishnu. Paunchy, mustachioed, despotic, he was thirty-two years old. Not far from middle age, I thought. Before entering the country, I had imagined Nepal to be mainly a Buddhist nation; I knew that a village in the forested lowlands west of Birgunj is recognized as the Buddha's birthplace. It surprised me to learn that the vast majority of Nepalis are Hindu. In 1978, the country was a Hindu monarchy—the only one in the world—and the king commanded the status of a god. In consequence, Birendra could never visit a temple just outside Kathmandu. Its beautiful statue of the sleeping Vishnu is revered as another incarnation, and if the king saw it he would surely die. Birendra did have the right to meet the Kumari, or virgin goddess: a little girl who spends her childhood inside a brick-and-wood palace in Durbar Square, until the blood she sheds in her first period makes her mortal again and creates a vacancy for a new goddess.

Clare and I had devoured *momos* and apple pie for lunch—since the earliest years of the Hippie Trail, Kathmandu restaurants had given pleasure to travellers by the juiciness and size of their fruit pies—and were doing nothing much outside a temple in Durbar Square when we noticed a crowd gathering. We joined it and waited—afternoons here could stretch out placidly as they never could in Delhi or Lahore—until eventually a royal motorcade cruised by. Queen Aishwarya, big-haired and lavishly jewelled, rode beside her bespectacled husband in a black sedan. Yet the Nepalis in the square, unlike the Iranians we'd seen in Shiraz when the Shah swept by, remained silent.

I sensed a subdued excitement as the couple passed; a healthy chatter broke out afterwards. But nobody cheered the king.

His family, both large and rapacious, were widely believed to be raking in huge profits from the illicit sale abroad of drugs and antiquities. Since 1960, the Nepali monarchy had kept a monopoly on power; the previous king, Birendra's father, had outlawed political parties. In 1990, faced by dissent and fury, Birendra would reluctantly accept a transfer of authority to elected leaders. Even so, the royal family retained great wealth and prestige.

Among Western travellers Nepal enjoyed the image of a safe haven — in some minds, indeed, a safe heaven — but the image stood at some distance from the facts. Clare and I heard rumours, perhaps untrue, that the sudden death of an American resident, Jane Martin, had been a murder; Aunt Jane's, the restaurant she founded and managed, long outlived her. At Christmastime in 1975, Charles Sobhraj — a French serial killer later nicknamed "the Serpent" — flew into Kathmandu with his girlfriend and an accomplice; within days of arrival, they murdered a Canadian and an American backpacker. A decade later a Peace Corps volunteer named Nancy Hart disappeared while trekking in the Himalaya; her body was never found. These were a few of the famous deaths — famous in the West, that is. More obscure, indeed largely unknown, are the seventeen thousand Nepalis who died in a Maoist insurgency and civil war that began in 1996.

King Birendra and Queen Aishwarya were assassinated as that conflict raged — though not by Maoists. Their eldest son, Prince Dipendra, burst into a family dinner at the royal palace on the first day of June 2001. Dressed in military clothing, he was toting a submachine gun, an assault rifle, and two other weapons from his extensive collection. The crown prince may have been drunk; he may have been stoned; he may have been psychotic. He was almost certainly enraged at his mother for refusing to approve his choice of bride. Whatever the motive, Dipendra killed his father. He killed his mother. He killed his sister, his younger brother, and five other members of the royal family. He wounded several more. Finally he shot himself. He survived in a coma for three days, during which he was proclaimed king and became, in some eyes, a god.

Dipendra's uncle, Gyanendra, had been away at the time of the massacre. He hastened back to the traumatized capital and ascended the throne. In a ceremony to exorcise King Birendra's troubled spirit, an elderly Brahmin priest broke his lifelong vegetarian vows by feasting on meat; then, wearing the dead king's clothes, shoes, and glasses and carrying some of his belongings, the priest rode out of Kathmandu on a decorated elephant. Grieving crowds chased them from the city. This exquisitely Nepali ritual was the last of its kind: faith in the monarchy was evaporating. A government-owned newspaper, *The Rising Nepal*, tried to reduce the massacre to "an unanticipated incident." Gyanendra, who was disliked by almost everyone, asked his subjects to believe that the royal deaths had resulted from "the accidental discharge of an automatic weapon." The insurgency grew until, in 2008, Gyanendra abdicated. Nepal remade itself as a republic, its new prime minister a Maoist.

ONE MORNING CLARE AND I rented bicycles—black, one-speed, one-size-fits-all—and set out for Gokarna, a wildlife sanctuary east of Kathmandu. It had served as the hunting forest for Nepal's kings. Where the city petered out into countryside, the route to Gokarna wasn't obvious and, having ridden a couple of miles, I stopped on the roadside to check the foldout map. Clare pulled to a halt behind me. A Nepali Army van was parked in front. And while I studied the map, the driver put the van into reverse. It lurched backwards and slammed into my bike.

"Hey!" I shouted. I wasn't injured but the bicycle was—as I instantly discovered, the front wheel wouldn't turn. I climbed off. The van began to drive away.

Nepali bystanders were shouting too. The driver, a young man in military green, stopped the van. He got out to inspect the damage, or to inspect me: a gesticulating, shouting foreigner in no sign of physical pain. Then, without a word, he got back into the vehicle and drove away. The bystanders *tut-tutted* and shook their heads. They did not appear surprised. "The knife forgets," a Nepali proverb has it, "but the wood remembers."

Clare rode back to the Blue Angel. I wheeled the bicycle to the rental agency past diesel-spewing vehicles and marigold-shrouded shrines, complaining loudly to the universe—in Asia I had become less self-conscious about making a scene. A policeman in baggy khaki shorts looked at me curiously. The agency charged me sixty rupees for repairs. In my aggrieved state, this seemed a lot of money. I hurried off to a tourist office to write a formal complaint; a clerk sent me to the national headquarters of the Department of Tourism. Kathmandu was not a large city; the headquarters were only a block or two away. It had begun to occur to me that I might be overreacting — sixty rupees were less than three British pounds — but I persisted. I told myself it was the principle that mattered. The ramshackle hut had a sign on its front door: "Department of Tourism. Only for Tourist. Please Push It." I pushed it. A young woman behind the counter smiled at me; she bowed and sympathized. But she did not refund my sixty rupees. "Namaste," she said as I left, her palms pressed together. Having filed an official report, I strode back to the hotel feeling as if, on Nepal's oddly shaped crimson flag, the sun was eclipsed by the moon.

The Blue Angel — clean, spacious, and splattered with peace signs — came equipped with a library of paperbacks, mostly in English, from which I borrowed Graham Greene's *The Quiet American* and read it in a day. We breakfasted on the hotel's succulent pancakes: in Kathmandu my hair stopped thinning, my teeth stopped darkening, and I put back a little of the weight I had lost in the previous months. The Blue Angel even supplied a lunatic in the hall — or at least, a stoned Australian who attempted to do a handstand outside our room one night at 1 a.m. The lock being faulty, the Australian succeeded in kicking our door open. He fell backwards onto the floor with an oath and a loud apology. The heyday of the Hippie Trail was over, but the aftermath had its moments.

Three days later I tried for Gokarna again: same rental agency, different bike. This time Clare stayed behind to do some shopping; wildlife reserves held less appeal for her than for me. Once out of the city, I rode through rugged farmland wet with rice or tall with corn, passing a settlement that boasted a Public Welfare Tibetan Palmist and Clinic and a yellow stupa with undulating eyes. A crew-cut monk — he wore a yellow shirt beneath his red robes—had the face of a Westerner no older than me. From the top of a stone pillar twice my height, a sculpture of a gold-headed cobra oversaw the women, men, and buffalo at work in the fields. A man walked past me in the opposite direction, so bent over by the basketload on his back—firewood, was it?—that I could not see his face.

Gokarna itself was the quintessence of lushness: nature at its most ebullient. I followed a path up a leafy hill to survey the sanctuary. Instead I found myself *listening* to the sanctuary: peacocks crying, parakeets screeching, rhesus monkeys clattering through the high, wind-tossed canopy. Elderflowers grew in creamy clumps on bushes just too tall for me to peer over. I laughed out loud; I prayed out loud. It was an enormous relief to be on my own amid more kinds of birds and plants than I could ever identify. But why was my left sock pink?

I looked down in puzzlement—my other sock remained its usual off-white. It took me a couple of seconds to realize it was my own blood that had turned several inches of fabric pale red. I rolled down the sock and found a tiny wound above my ankle. Even though the leech had dropped off, my blood continued to trickle. After a few seconds I laughed again: nothing hurt, and the joy I felt in Gokarna overrode any anxiety.

Then I heard the sound of drums, punctuated by chants and shouts. Could the armed forces be conducting manoeuvres in a wildlife reserve? I wasn't sure where the clamour originated: all around me, oak and walnut trees shimmered into hills that vanished in the low clouds, and the drums seemed to reverberate from every direction. I walked down a path toward the road where I'd left the bicycle and noticed a flat area of open land in the distance. A large, blue-spangled butterfly skittered by. As I approached the meadow, I saw a man clutching a drum and two long, curving drumsticks. A second man held a pair of cymbals.

They were the only musicians. But a dozen men and women kept them company: dancers, a few in jeans, several wearing elaborate red and yellow robes. One sported a crimson head-dress that made me think of a lampshade. The dancers whirled to the percussion's beat. Sometimes they stopped and sang. Sometimes they spoke loudly in a language that sounded noth-ing like Nepali. For a while they maintained a circle around a man holding a black umbrella. On the far side of the meadow, at the forest's edge, about thirty people, some of them children, stood watching. A herd of spotted deer browsed by a hillock, unconcerned by the humans on display.

Two Westerners emerged from a low building beside the road. I went over to them, hoping they wouldn't stare at my socks.

"What's happening?" I asked.

"Hey, it's a Tibetan dance troupe," said a girl with luxuri-ant chestnut-coloured hair and a University of Oregon T-shirt. "They live here."

"Will they perform in Kathmandu?"

"No, it's for July 6th," she said. "The birthday of His Holiness. Hey, what happened to your leg?"

Less than twenty years had elapsed since the Fourteenth Dalai Lama fled his home in Lhasa, the capital of Tibet, crossing the Himalaya by an arduous pass to reach safety in northeastern India. He was far from alone: by the end of 1959 a hundred thousand Tibetans had left their country in the wake of a failed revolt against the Chinese occupation. About a fifth of the refugees walked into Nepal. At the time, they were welcomed.

On that warm, breezy morning amid the peacocks and the deer, I thought the American girl meant the Dalai Lama would visit Kathmandu in early July. But in fact, he has never been to Nepal. Every Nepali regime, whether royal or republican, understands his presence in the country, however fleeting, would infuriate China. And that's the last thing any official in Kathmandu wants. On July 6th, in countries around the world, Tibetans honour the Dalai Lama's birthday with all the splendour, longing, and hope they can muster. Wherever they gather, a white silk scarf adorns his photograph on an empty chair that substitutes for a throne.

I watched the Tibetans rehearse for a time — in Nepal, I found time had lost much of its power — and then cycled back to the city to meet Clare for a late lunch. Every few hundred yards I rang the bike's bell to warn pedestrians or scare stray dogs. On trays by the roadside, chili peppers were drying, blood-dark. The rippling fields made an ocean of green.

If I looked for those fields today, I would find asphalt and concrete. Over the past half-century, the Kathmandu Valley has seen intensive population growth. The Maoist revolt and civil war lasted for a decade, driving many thousands of rural Nepalis into the capital; sheer unremitting poverty led countless other villagers and farmers to make the same decision. Trees around the city met a saw or an axe. As glaciers throughout the Himalaya shrink and recede, Kathmandu has only a quarter of the drinking water it needs; in some weeks its residents choke on air even more polluted than the air in Tehran, Delhi, and Beijing. The city of two hundred thousand people where Clare and I relaxed in 1978 has swelled to a metropolis of more than two million today, its slender rivers little more than sewage canals. Thanks to a flurry of road-building, forests in some of the most remote regions of Nepal are being erased.

Yet the nation is now a democracy of sorts; life expectancy has doubled since the 1950s; incomes have risen; a far lower proportion of women die in childbirth. Believers in the doctrine of progress can point to Nepal with pride, sidestepping all doubts as to whether the progress is sustainable. Is it sentimental—is it even colonialist—if I or any foreigner mourn the erosion of its diverse cultures and the ruin of its wild spaces: meadow-rich mountains, free-flowing rivers, rhododendron forests, and an abundance of plants and animals unique to the country? I have no right to tell a Nepali farmer to stop cutting down trees. But neither can I repress my sorrow: the snow leopard, once gone, will never reappear. Nor will the red panda, the spiny babbler, the Himalayan yew. Nor will the shrines and temples sacrificed to the god of development. Nor will the languages fallen silent, the stories no longer told. Progress is an engine that operates on heavy, tainted fuel.

Gokarna survives, in a sense. No longer is it a wildlife sanctuary. By 2022, it had become an upscale private resort specializing in "corporate retreat and team building." Its website holds out the promise of "immaculate cuisine and luxurious accommodation," an eighteen-hole golf course, an indoor swimming pool and jacuzzi, a spa and health club offering serenity massages—and some "exotic" birds you are "guaranteed to spot" if you buy a guided tour through the "enchanted forest grounds."

THE CONVOLUTED JOURNEY TO Kathmandu had convinced
us we should return to Delhi by plane. My spurious grumbling
in *Punch* could pay for my travels no longer: even though the
flight to Delhi would be cheap, I didn't have enough money to
buy a ticket. But we had the privilege of borrowing, in extremis,
from the Bank of Clare's Father. Having booked a date and time
in advance with the state-owned telephone company, she waited
beside a black device in a large hall while a Nepali operator put
the call through. There were fewer than ten thousand phones
in the entire country.

The line to England was terrible and six pounds bought
only three minutes. Clare spent them explaining that she
needed the money telexed to Nepal Bank Ltd., Banking Office,
Kathmandu, NP 200. I listened as her voice grew sharper and
louder: "Nepal, Nepal! Nepal—the country! NEPAL! Banking.
Banking—what you do in a bank. BANKING!" I stood guard
nearby, gesturing helplessly at people amused or miffed by the
volume of Clare's voice. Thanks to her father, I would not have
to brave Indian Railways again.

My relief and gratitude mingled with powerlessness and
shame. I had neither wanted nor expected to be financially
dependent on her. "Is Clare good for me?" I wrote in the
last of my notebooks. "I feel so much chafing. But maybe
it's necessary for me to be with someone who laughs at my
pretensions, who doesn't take me so seriously, who won't let
me build everything up on no foundations." In retrospect,
I wonder what I was trying to build up. The chafing went in
two directions—many things about me annoyed her, apart
from my lack of money. We engaged in some verbal sparring:
a form of play ("Fish face!" "Flounder flesh!") with a nasty

edge. Once, while dealing with officialdom, Clare referred to me as "beloved husband." She went on to use this phrase in a later sneer.

I spent an entire afternoon analyzing our relationship in my journal. "I don't want to malign her," I wrote, and then filled two single-spaced pages with a sour tirade. Some of my complaints — but only some — were a defence against her repeated attacks on me for being "deeply serious," "gloomy," and "morose." She knew how to wound me. "Were you ever young at heart?" she inquired one day. Her taunts and jeers kept blowing like a circle around my skull. Pride, she told me, was my greatest sin. I think she was right.

Clare and I had been through a lot together, but we had not drawn closer as a result. We had grown weary of each other's face and voice, opinions and jests. After nearly three months, we wanted to be apart. Nepal allowed this more than anywhere else we had travelled — although even a stay in Nepal came with risks. Both of us were now looking beyond the last days of the journey into the unwritten future.

ELEVEN YEARS LATER, I would take part in a conference of the international writers' group PEN. It held some of its 1989 congress in Toronto, some in Montreal. On a train between the two cities, I began to chat with a small man with intense black eyes and a ready smile. He introduced himself as the vice-president of a newly established PEN Centre in Kathmandu and, as I soon learned, he worked as a short-story writer, film director, playwright, TV scriptwriter, and newspaper columnist. First and foremost, however, Dhruba Chandra Gautam was a novelist. *Alikhil*—it would be translated into English as *Unwritten*—had won Nepal's highest literary prize.

"From my childhood," he told me, "I always wanted to be a writer. My wife says this is the only gift I have." I knew the feeling.

He seemed pleased that I had visited Nepal. But he didn't want to listen to my smiling memories of Kathmandu or Gokarna or even his birthplace, Birgunj. He wanted to impress on me what I'd merely glimpsed or had failed to see altogether.

"I write against the society's evil," Gautam said. "What I write shows the inner side of Nepal. Poverty, separation, empty bellies." By separation, he meant the remittance system that turns millions of Nepali men into long-term migrants, toiling away from their families for years without respite, wiring money home from the likes of Abu Dhabi and Dubai. "Not what the tourists see."

Nepal was a country, he explained, lacking in both fairness and freedom—a country where "it is not dignified to be a writer." In 1989, authors were forbidden to criticize King Birendra or to call for changes in the political system. They sidestepped the prohibition by a reliance on allegory and myth. In one of his books, Gautam had retold a fable from the *Mahabharata*, intending it to carry political resonance for his own time and place. He thought most of his audience got the point: writers need to believe in their readers.

Near the end of *Unwritten*, a village disappears—it mysteriously vanishes. The characters come up with various explanations. "Actually it was destroyed," the wisest of them suggests, "because there was no spirit of revolt. When the spirit of revolt dies out in a people, that's the end of the checks upon cruelty; one day it's bound to be destroyed."

Meeting writers from far-off countries at the PEN gathering had emboldened Gautam. "Mostly," he said, "I feel very pushed up. I will be more daring in the future, perhaps. I will take more risks in my writing." But his use of the word "perhaps" revealed this was not an easy promise to make. Ten Nepali journalists had been arrested in a police raid that year; months after their initial detention, three of them still languished behind bars. Some of the writers Gautam approached to join the PEN Centre in Kathmandu had declined, fearing censorship or worse.

"We want to read!" he told me, stopping to peer out the grimy window. "But have we arrived? Where is this?"

Our train was pulling into Montreal, a city named for a mountain that Dhruba Chandra Gautam would have regarded as a very low hill. It is a metropolis that contains, on a Nepali scale, unimaginable wealth. Yet it is also a place of cruelty and lingering poverty: an abode of migrants, solitude, and empty bellies. This is not what the tourists see.

A GODDESS STOOD ON a turtle. We did a double take. Clare and I were looking at a palace in the venerable city of Patan — in 1978 it had not yet been swallowed by Kathmandu. Patan has at least three alternative names; this would have surprised me in most countries, but not in Nepal. By then I had also accepted the truth that in Nepal, sculpted gods come with a multitude of arms holding different objects and pointing in different directions. Surrounding Patan's central square and palace courtyards are dozens of temples, both Buddhist and

Hindu, many of them in the form of pagodas. Nepalis say that pagodas originated in the Kathmandu Valley; only later was their design exported to Tibet, China, Korea, and Japan. The country is defined by low hills, high hills, low mountains, and impossibly high mountains, a context in which pagodas make perfect sense: a tiered architecture that embodies the steepness of the shifting land. We were grateful to discover they also provide good shelter in a monsoon.

A short walk from the square we found a Buddhist monastery, the Hiranya Varna Mahavihar, known in English as the Golden Temple—a catchier name, I suppose, than the more accurate Gilded Copper Temple. The scent of incense suffused the shrine to roughly the same degree that we'd found the fragrance of hash imbuing one or two other temples in the valley. A guardian showed us frescoes of the Buddha but forbade us from looking at Tantric relics and images. This would have annoyed me at the start of the trip, when I felt I had a right to see everything. Instead we nodded and left. I feasted my eyes on stone dragons, lions, elephants, and crocodiles. In Patan my eyes could have gone on feasting for days.

As they could in Bhaktapur, eight miles to the east. The palaces and temples around its main square astonished me. I marvelled at an elaborate peacock carving that jutted out from a window frame—Nepalis long ago perfected the art of carving wood with incredible strength and delicacy. Around a corner from the Palace of Fifty-Five Windows stood the Vatsala Durga Temple, built not of wood but of grey stone. A hulking silver bell near its entrance once tolled a nightly curfew for the citizens of Bhaktapur. In the National Art Museum—housed in a small palace guarded by further gods and lions—we contemplated paintings and sculptures of Bhairava, the fearsome aspect of Lord Shiva, and Kali, the goddess of destruction.

Closer to Kathmandu we climbed to the Buddhist shrine of Swayambhu, one of the oldest settlements in the entire valley. The winding path up a hill to the temple complex led through monkey-busy woodland. After a wet morning the clouds had begun to disperse, and snow peaks to the northeast flickered in and out of sight. At the foot of the main stupa, a great pale dome — it represents the world itself — shone like a glacier in the sun. I noticed Clare smiling at an inquisitive child with a pierced nose and kohl around her eyes. Lamps of pungent yak butter were burning in a Tibetan monastery, a recent arrival at Swayambhu. Vendors just outside the monastery tried their best to interest us in prayer wheels and turquoise beads, cymbals and demon masks. Necklaces were made of string and bone; a cup had begun life as a human skull. A few of the red-robed monks walking purposefully back and forth could have been no more than nine years old.

If they continued to chant and work at Swayambhu, those boys would have been middle-aged monks in April and May of 2015, according to the Western calendar, when Bhairava and Kali descended on Nepal with the utmost force. Or, to put the matter in seismological terms, the country experienced a 7.8 magnitude earthquake, followed days later by a 7.3 magnitude aftershock. Nine thousand people lost their lives. Nearly three million were displaced, their homes damaged or ruined.

The devastation of Nepal's built heritage was extreme. When I looked at photographs taken a day after the quake, it shocked me to find that the magnificent central square in Patan had become a jumble of debris, broken masonry tossed and tumbled with broken carpentry. The pictures showed crushed pieces of stone and wood draped by plastic sheets in an initial effort to protect the remnants. An unharmed pair of life-size stone elephants watched over the havoc. The Vatsala Durga Temple in Bhaktapur collapsed like a toy — although its silver bell survived, as did the Palace of Fifty-Five Windows. A statue of the Lord Buddha was up to its waist in fallen bricks. While part of the Swayambhu complex remained intact, thirteen monuments were badly affected there; some of them crumpled into rubble and dust. In the core of Kathmandu, the ancient, three-tiered wooden pavilion — Kasthamandap — that gave the city its name was among the buildings that disintegrated.

Many of the architectural treasures that Clare and I saw had been restored or remade in the wake of previous disasters. The country has suffered this kind of loss before — indeed, an earthquake in 1934 killed an even larger number of people in Nepal and northern India. With the gods and seismologists appeased for a generation or two, there should be ample time for temples and palaces, homes and shrines to rise afresh. So be it. All things fall and are built again, and those that build them again do so, sometimes, with love.

That's the optimistic view. A morose assessment would focus on the corruption, the political infighting, and the unwise rebuilding methods. "Kathmandu continues to operate as a city on the loose," wrote the scholar Urmi Sengupta several years after the earthquake. "The reconstruction is often an assault on [Nepalis'] personal and collective identities...A great sense of injustice has arisen over the way building contractors have ignored local techniques and values."

TELEVISION HAD NOT REACHED the country in 1978, but Kathmandu did have an English-language newspaper named *The Rising Nepal.* The local values it reflected were those of the monarchy. I found the lead article on every front page gave a blandly positive image of Nepal, highlighting the progress of the nation or the labours of King Birendra, usually both. A smattering of global news and sports appeared on the inside pages, along with reports of ministerial speeches and earnest delegations. A list of foreign exchange rates routinely omitted the U.S. dollar. The editorial page featured a "thought for the day," a comic "tailpiece," and a sententious sentence by the king. Only in its choice of features from abroad did the paper hint at issues confronting Nepal: an article on the impact of mass tourism in Sri Lanka, another on a belated push to preserve a threatened Buddhist site in Java.

"I think I'll head over to the British Council library," I said to Clare over breakfast one day.

"Good idea," she replied. "I won't be joining you."

So I spent a happy morning going through newspapers and magazines from England and India. I devoured a two-week-old copy of *The Times,* skimmed a three-month-old *Times Literary Supplement,* and browsed an issue of *Poetry Review* published two years earlier. A Delhi newspaper, much more up to date, told me what *The Rising Nepal* had neglected to mention: UNESCO had warned the Nepali regime about the smuggling of antiquities and the decay of ancient buildings in the Kathmandu Valley. Like the *Tehran Journal, The Rising Nepal* prevented its readers from hearing any criticism of the nation's king.

Unlike its Iranian counterpart, *The Rising Nepal* liked to print the occasional folktale. Maybe the editors or their government censors believed these stories could help knit the country together. Its official language is Nepali—part of the enormous Indo-European group, like English, though written in a very different script—but Nepal also has 128 "national languages," many of them related to Tibetan. Tourists, diplomats, and foreign businessmen were not the only readers; the newspaper aimed to reach educated Nepalis too. I read with fascination a tale that appeared there in Asar 2035, the month Clare and I were in the country. The story comes from a district of western Nepal near the Buddha's birthplace.

It describes a rich farmer called Titibincha. He owns a large herd of goats and sheep, buffalo and cows, and he takes them up a mountain to graze in a verdant meadow. One day, while he's napping, an ogre steals the animals. "I am ruined," moans Titibincha when he opens his eyes. "What shall I do now?" He runs along the trail, hoping to catch the thief. But instead he comes across two eggs arguing between themselves. The eggs see Titibincha in tears and ask why he is so distressed. When he explains, they stop quarrelling and agree to search for the missing herd. Soon Titibincha and the eggs meet a pair of squabbling needles. They too stop bickering when the farmer recounts his loss. Before long he has gathered not just eggs and needles but two peas, two snakes, and two rams. All of them abandon their own disputes and accompany Titibincha down the path.

In the evening, exhausted, they arrive at an empty house and find the stolen animals grazing in a meadow. Titibincha and his surprising friends go inside to rest. Late at night, the ogre returns home. But when the eggs wake up, they blow charcoal into his face and blind him. The snakes bite the ogre;

the needles pierce his flesh; the peas, who were perched on a staircase, make him lose his balance and fall. Then the rams gore the wounded ogre to death.

The story is not a sermon or a Bollywood movie—it doesn't impose a moral. But I think it contains one anyway: no matter how small and insignificant you may feel, you can overcome any obstacle if you join forces with others. Ogres are never as mighty as they seem. Teamwork can accomplish great things.

Doubtless this is a valuable lesson. It fosters confidence; it instills hope. Yet the ogre in the story did nothing more terrifying than abduct a farmer's herd. He didn't have the power to melt a glacier or annihilate a culture.

ON OUR LAST FULL day in Nepal, Clare and I rose early. We had a bus to catch, and even at 6 a.m. the streets of Kathmandu were vibrant with activity. Three mynas squawked and whistled, as if holding a sardonic conference of the birds. Outside the General Post Office a crowd had gathered near an elephant whose trunk kept waving to and fro. On its back sat a pair of felt-hatted riders, each of them sipping an early chai. When the men had finished their drinks, the elephant set off toward Durbar Square at a fast trot. Time for us to board the mail bus to the Tibetan border.

It was the food bus, too, bringing bags of rice to villages in the Himalaya. No other Westerners were on board. Every few miles, as the landscape grew wilder and the road steeper, the bus would stop at a settlement. The conductor—an affable young man with a mean scar on his chin—would saunter off to deliver letters and rice. Not the fastest way to travel, but I thought we had plenty of time. On the map, this looked like a modest journey: we should be back in the capital before evening.

We had been on the bus for nearly four hours when the driver abruptly braked. The highway was snaking along the edge of a mountain. I peered ahead and saw rocks and boulders strewn across the road. Occasional rocks were still plunging down, some of them adding to the mess, others bouncing and dropping all the way to a brisk, white-flecked river on our right. I climbed out. We all climbed out.

Could this mortal planet be any more lavish with ferns, bamboo, rhododendrons? Could the pine-tingling air be more exhilarating? I felt as if I'd traded the earthy fragrance of patchouli in Freak Street restaurants for the pitch-pure fragrance of the Earth itself. "Hello," said a teenage Nepali boy, interrupting my reverie. "Where is your home?"

"In Canada," I said.

"Canada." He paused for a second. "What is Canada like?"

I told him it was very large. I told him much of it was very flat. He could perhaps imagine the size — India and China are also big countries — but I feared the notion of vast flatness eluded him.

Clare and I were the only passengers who betrayed anxiety about the rockslide. The Nepalis understood it would be cleared, sooner or later. They joked and smoked; they chatted to each other; they didn't have a plane to catch the following day. A young man scrambled forty or fifty feet up the pathless mountainside, pursued by one of his friends. They began to augment the rockslide by heaving further debris down, laughing every time a rock stayed on the road. Farther back we had passed a retaining wall built above a long section of highway to prevent minor landslides, especially in the monsoon season. The wall-builders had uprooted so many trees that landslides grew more frequent. Or so the conductor told us.

The need to protect forests in Nepal is neither a new idea nor a Western one. Ram Shah, a Gurkha king who ruled much of the country during the early seventeenth century, issued an array of edicts on topics ranging from the payment of debts to the wearing of gold on the feet. Two of those edicts are about forests. "If there are no trees," the king wrote, "there will be no water whenever one looks for it. The watering places will become dry. If forests are cut down, there will be avalanches... Without forests, the householder's work cannot be accomplished. Therefore he who cuts down the forest near a watering place will be fined five rupees."

A bulldozer arrived from somewhere and set to work. Before long the bus driver asked everyone to reboard. The last to do so were the men who had kept busy tossing rocks down the mountain.

The rockslide had, after all, meant a delay of less than an hour, and the bus kept a steady pace after that. We passed a narrow field being plowed by a man and a dark-furred yak, its long horns curving up toward the heavens. A few women going about their daily chores belonged to a minority group related to Tibetans; their breasts were bare.

Although their breasts were covered, a pair of Tibetan-looking girls behind us were being mercilessly teased and prodded by some Nepali men. Clare and I thought of intervening, but what could we say or do? We were guests in the men's country, passengers on their bus, tongue-tied in their language.

"That's how men behave," Clare said with a scowl.

"Not all men," I weakly replied.

Yet I knew, even then, a feeling of sexual entitlement can puff up the weakest and most vulnerable of men. Clare had experienced this to her cost in Turkey, Pakistan, and India. *Nepalese Customs and Manners*, a book first published in Kathmandu in 1976, advises its readers that "while a husband may never be given food contaminated by his wife, she considers it a special privilege to eat his leftovers."

The bus inched delicately around scree on the road, proof of a further rockslide. But some of its slowdowns and halts were planned. At one stop I left the bus and scrutinized a rickety table holding copies of Mao Zedong's poems in Chinese, English, French, and German. The English paperback, issued by Foreign Languages Press in Beijing, included a frontispiece of the sunlit author gazing at an alpine vista. The poet had ruled China for twenty-five years. I handed four rupees to the cigarette-puffing bookseller.

> *Seize the day, seize the hour!*
> *The Four Seas are rising, clouds and waters raging,*
> *The Five Continents are rocking, wind and thunder roaring.*
> *Our force is irresistible,*
> *Away with all pests!*

A strident feeling of inevitability is among Mao's legacies to China—that, and a willingness to define anyone else as a lethal pest. The book's final poem is a dialogue between two birds. The last word goes to the one who says, *Stop your windy nonsense! / Look, the world is being turned upside down.* Mao took pride in doing exactly that.

Mist was rising from a crane-slim waterfall just inside Nepal. Clouds fluttered like prayer flags in the undivided sky.

We reached the Tibetan border just before 2 p.m., nearly eight hours after leaving Kathmandu. From here, the highway would cross the Sunkosi River far below—its glacier-born water would eventually find welcome in the Ganges. The Nepali village of Kodari had no café or restaurant, but we were lucky: the scar-faced conductor invited us to join him in a private house whose owner regularly brewed up tea for the bus company's staff. He led us down a littered alley and into a small, dim room with mud walls and an earth-packed floor. A pot of water bubbled over an open woodfire: the smoke deterred the flies.

Fortified by Indian-style chai—not the yak-butter tea of Tibet—Clare and I strolled to the Nepali checkpost to get our passports stamped. The stamping policeman had little work to do: in 1978 private crossings were hard to arrange and traffic across the Friendship Bridge was light. Traders had once moved freely through passes in the Himalaya, bringing salt and wool from Tibet into Nepal and hauling rice in the reverse direction. Then Chinese troops invaded Tibet, and small-scale trading stopped. But with the passage of time, Nepal's dependence on China grew; the highway on which we were travelling, broad enough to carry battle tanks, had been constructed with Chinese "help." Not coincidentally, Nepal's readiness to admit Tibetans shrank. No Tibetans escaping their homeland have been allowed in since 1989, and many of the original refugees have moved on from Nepal to India.

The bridge is a short one: I could have picked up a stone and hurled it into a different country. Clare waved at a gun-toting Chinese soldier on the far side. He did not wave back. Beyond a large red flag, an empty highway snaked into the mountains. A thousand feet up and a mile or two distant, the corrugated roofs of a new settlement glittered in the Tibetan sun.

We had not exactly walked around the world. But for Clare and me this was, at last, the end of the road.

I WAS TWENTY-THREE AND still greedy for enlightenment. Asia had given me all the experiences and impressions I could ask for, but I was a glutton: I wanted more. On that sunlit afternoon I could only gaze across a dark, snow-fed river tumbling through the Himalaya. I vowed that in the future, somehow, one day, I would see Tibet.

I wanted to explore the Potala, a 999-room palace atop a hill overlooking Lhasa; apart from being a castle, a pilgrimage site, a monastery, a school, a storehouse, a mausoleum, and the seat of Tibetan government, it was the winter home of ten Dalai Lamas. I wanted to see Tashilhunpo, the home of ten Panchen Lamas, a monastic city within the city of Shigatse. "If the magnificence of the place was to be increased by any external cause," wrote an English diplomat named Samuel Turner after a visit in 1783, "none could more superbly have adorned its numerous gilded canopies and turrets than the sun rising in full splendour directly opposite. It presented a view wonderfully beautiful and brilliant; the effect was little short of magic." I wanted to look on Mount Kailas, never climbed to the summit, revered as holy by worshippers in four religions; streams that rise in the shadow of its massive, icy flanks are a source for the Indus, the Ganges, the Sutlej, and the Brahmaputra. The most devout are said to believe that on Mount Kailas, there are stairways to heaven. I wanted to visit the Sera Monastery and the Norbulingka Garden and Lake Manasarovar, into whose turquoise waters some of Mohandas Gandhi's ashes were strewn.

As the years passed I would meet Tibetans in exile—men and women who, unlike me, would never see their homeland again. They would live and die below a remote northern sun. I became friends with a few of them in Montreal: tough-minded, dedicated, humble people who had kept their spirit intact in the midst of unthinkable loss. A history was inscribed on their minds and bodies. A culture survived in their imaginations. Inspired by the Fourteenth Dalai Lama, they refused to give in to despair.

His Holiness took to the airwaves and the skies, hoping to find support for Tibet in foreign capitals. Everywhere he went, he spoke of kindness as a higher value than righteousness, compassion as more necessary than any type of political or religious purity. He visited my country several times, urging the Canadian government to advocate for Tibetan rights and freedoms. One year, when I was writing for the *Montreal Gazette*, I interviewed him in a hotel suite near Parliament Hill in Ottawa. After he had answered my questions, I said the émigrés living in Canada were a credit to their nation and to him. His Holiness nodded and beamed even before a young accompanying monk had translated my words into Tibetan. His evident pleasure at my remark was nothing compared to the delight I felt.

In middle age I was becoming less and less preoccupied with any God-shaped emptiness still lurking inside me. To gain at least a smidgen of enlightenment, I finally saw, I didn't have to probe the Himalaya or any other distant lands. But I would need to listen. I would need to give.

I had no desire by then to inspect the ruins of Ganden. Established in 1409, famous for its dozens of chapels, its imposing statues, and its three-dimensional mandalas, Ganden had been the home and workplace of thousands of monks. Chinese soldiers laid waste to it in 1959, an act of brute revenge following the Dalai Lama's escape to India. Seven years later the Red Guards assaulted Ganden again, first with guns, then with dynamite, leaving only rubble. No earthquake could have done a more thorough job. The Jokhang Temple, founded in the seventh century and blessed with even more extraordinary architectural marvels, met a similar fate. A scattering of ancient chapels escaped demolition only to become a pigsty, an abattoir, a barracks. Indeed, between 1959 and 1976, the People's Liberation Army and the Red Guards wrecked nearly all of Tibet's monasteries. Their gold sculptures, melted down or sold to collectors in Hong Kong and Tokyo, funded Mao's regime. Their sacred books, the ones that escaped burning, were torn apart and used as footwear or toilet paper. *Away with all pests!* Tibet was plundered in those years, its lands and wildlife ravaged, its people shackled and starved.

Nor did I have any wish to tour a museum erected by the Chinese just below the Potala to celebrate the fiftieth anniversary of their "peaceful liberation of Tibet." I felt no urge to sleep in their Shangri La Hotel Lhasa or their Intercontinental

Lhasa Paradise. I didn't want to go anywhere near the "Qing Government in Tibet Grand Minister Administrative City Former Site." I didn't even want to see the rebuilt versions of Tashilhunpo, Ganden, Jokhang, and other great monasteries and temples where a sanitized form of Buddhism is now tolerated but all traces of free expression are outlawed.

I revised my earlier vow: barring a political miracle, I will never set foot in Tibet.

IN THE BORDER VILLAGE of Kodari we began the journey back to Kathmandu. But something had gone wrong with the bus: Clare and I listened with concern to a coughing, scraping noise coming from a rear wheel. Soon the vehicle juddered to a stop and, once again, everyone clambered out. The driver and conductor got down on their knees and peered at the wheel; two or three male passengers joined them. They removed the tire and examined the axle. An hour later they had fixed nothing and the bus remained immobile. Clare had bitten her fingernails down to the quick, and both of us had exhausted our supply of four-letter words.

"It will be another three hours, maybe," the conductor said with a shrug.

"Will there be another bus?" Clare asked.

"Not today. Tomorrow morning a bus will come."

"So what are we supposed to do?"

"In the next town there is a Jeep for hire, maybe."

The next town, Barhabise, was about twelve miles away—maybe—and Clare and I began to walk there. We comforted ourselves by saying the road would be mainly downhill. I'm not sure we were thinking clearly. While this may have counted as adventure tourism, it was not the sort the government of Nepal wished to promote. To stay immobile beside the stricken bus, as the Nepali passengers were calmly doing, would have required a level of faith and confidence we did not possess. If we waited to catch the promised bus, we would miss our flight to Delhi. And if that plane left without us, we might also miss the London flight. Time had regained, in our anxious eyes, every scrap of its power.

"Is that really a car?" Clare said after we had walked in silence along an empty stretch of highway. The blue-black swallows were flying lower now, and a scent of juniper imbued the damp air. Droplets of rain had begun to fall. A chunk of sky looked ominously dark.

In the distance a white van was approaching us, making for the Tibetan border.

"Let's flag it down," I said.

And so we were rescued by Drolma, the Tibetan goddess of liberation—I mean, by a German couple hoping to cross into Tibet over the Friendship Bridge. When we explained our predicament, they turned the van around and drove eleven miles back to Barhabise. Using most of our remaining Nepali currency, we managed to hire a Jeep. The driver, who spoke little English, took us straight to the Blue Angel, barely slowing even in monsoon downpours and not stopping once along the way. The night sky had cleared when we reached Kathmandu, in time to devour a final fruit pie and pay our last respects to the monkey god in his scarlet cloak.

The flight to Delhi on Royal Nepal Airlines required just seventy-five minutes for what could have filled three days by bus and train. Sitting on the right side of the plane, we enjoyed a spectacular view of Annapurna—elegant, pristine, glacier-clad—crowning a sea of fluffy clouds.

"The world will end," a Tibetan prophecy states, "when the mountains wear black hats."

Epilogue

I was standing outside a milk-white bungalow in New Delhi when Indira Gandhi appeared.

The bungalow was hers: it stood in the embassy district of the Indian capital, far removed from the hubbub of the old city. A Mughal tomb, a polo club, and a museum dedicated to her father, India's first prime minister, all lay within walking distance. So did India's parliament buildings. It's unlikely, of course, that Mrs. Gandhi walked to any of them. Even in the restrained environs of New Delhi, she would have been mobbed. She was the most famous person in the country, the object of both scorn and adulation. After eleven tumultuous years as prime minister—two of them embroiled in a national emergency during which she ordered the suspension of democratic freedoms and the arrest of opposition leaders—she had been voted out of office in 1977. Yet she remained in command of the main opposition party, the Indian National Congress, and by the time of our visit her political fortunes were looking up again. In 1980, as the Janata coalition fell apart, she would regain power.

Clare and I met her because we broke our own rule. Throughout the journey we had taken no guided tours, even in sprawling cities like Tehran and Lahore. But now the final day of June had arrived, our last full day in Asia, and the small, Indian-run hotel where we were staying promoted a small, Indian-run tour of Delhi, unlike anything sold by an international travel agency.

"We are not Thomas Cook, sir," said the desk clerk severely, looking at me over a pair of thick-rimmed glasses. (I hated being called "sir.") "You will enjoy an authentic experience."

Even in 1978 Delhi held more than five million people — it is four times bigger today — and stretched over a broad area. We'd glimpsed only a fraction of the city a few weeks earlier. A bus tour, we thought, would give us a chance to see its grandest temple, its tallest minaret, its oldest pillar...And so it did, although the mustachioed guide maintained such strict control — "Now you will look to the left. All eyes. To the left!" — that my frustration grew by the hour. Before we streamed out of the bus at the presidential palace, the guide told his captive audience: "You will not exceed five minutes. English time, not Indian time. Five minutes!"

Clare and I hadn't realized that our hotel, located in a warren beside a bazaar, catered to people from the south of India. The guide lectured them on the excessive number of children he suspected they must have produced. Nearly all the passengers on board — mostly men, a few women — lived in the states of Tamil Nadu or Karnataka. Hindi, the dominant language of north India, was foreign there: even if the passengers understood it, few of them would be fluent speakers. So the guide delivered his instructions in English. Apart from Clare and me, the only Westerner on the bus was Ulf, a lanky Swede who wore his camera like a snake around his neck.

By mid-afternoon I'd had enough of the compulsory staring at palaces, mosques, temples, mausoleums, museums, gates, forts, embassies, observatories, and ruins. But the other passengers were unsatisfied: they had ideas of their own about what to see in Delhi. Theirs was the part of India that had remained loyal to Indira Gandhi in the national election a year earlier. Some of them may well have been Congress Party activists. When the bus stopped on a leafy street not far from her bungalow, they all piled out—with a greater sense of urgency, I thought, than they'd shown at other sites. Two Sikh guards were standing beside a name-plated gate into the garden. We saw no trace of further security.

"Mrs. Gandhi is very busy," one of the guards said to our group. "Today she cannot see you."

His words induced a modest uproar.

"You will come back on Monday!" the guard shouted.

One of the passengers—a middle-aged man in a yellow shirt—took charge.

"Not possible!" he said in an equally loud voice. "We refuse to leave!"

Then he sat down outside the gate. Some of the other passengers joined him on the ground, or shuffled nervously as if they were considering it. The guide had fallen silent. Clare and I looked at each other in bafflement: Would the tour group really be allowed to enter?

After a few minutes the guards gave in—they hadn't needed too much persuasion, I thought. Perhaps they were used to all this. I remembered that decades earlier, Mohandas Gandhi had more or less created the sit-in as a force for political change. The yellow-shirted man stood up and led the way through the entranceway, past a little guard-hut on the right. Clare and I followed. The guide—I suspected he was used to this, too— escorted Ulf, Clare, and me up to a circular portico about thirty feet from the entranceway. The Indian passengers clustered together on two large carpets. We waited. I still couldn't believe Mrs. Gandhi would appear.

But there she was, smaller and more fatigued-looking than photographs usually suggest, emerging from the white house and stepping across to the men and women waiting on the carpets. She stood in front of them, wearing a pale, full-length sari, a purple shawl draped over her shoulders. Two or three members of her staff accompanied her, one of them holding a camera. As soon as his shutter had clicked, Mrs. Gandhi moved away from her Indian admirers. She strolled over to us.

"Good afternoon," she said. "Where do you come from?"

"From England," Clare said.

"And Canada," I added. "We are honoured to meet you."

I can't remember if Ulf put in a word.

"Are you students?" she asked.

"Yes, we're at Oxford University."

"Oxford!" she said. "You know I attended Somerville College myself."

We did not know this. Clare was clutching a copy of Mohandas Gandhi's *Autobiography*, and I had a sudden desire to ask the former prime minister to sign it. No: wrong Gandhi.

"And how long have you been in India?"

Glancing across the lawn, I realized that the bus passengers were staring at us with awe or annoyance, possibly both.

Evidently Mrs. Gandhi meant the world to some of them, yet she had idled at the carpets for only a few moments. Instead she was chatting with three scruffy young foreigners. Ulf wriggled free of his camera and handed it to one of Mrs. Gandhi's staff, who took a couple of further pictures. I was beaming. Clare was beaming. I imagine Ulf was beaming.

"I wish you very good luck," Mrs. Gandhi said. For some reason she emphasized the "very." Her words emerged from beneath a singularly long and bony nose. The famous white patch of hair above the right side of her forehead was still prominent, I noticed, although grey had begun to infiltrate the black locks elsewhere.

"You must excuse me now," she said and returned to her bungalow. Clare and I watched her go. I believe my mouth was hanging open.

"She may need the luck more than we do," I said.

Next morning Ulf appeared in the hotel's breakfast room with a look of fury on his unshaven face. He had taken the roll of film to a shop in the bazaar to be developed overnight. But a power surge or a power failure ruined the film.

Two years later, once again prime minister, Indira Gandhi would move to a grander house in the same neighbourhood. She continued to meet well-wishers from all over India — "You have no idea how tiring it is to be a goddess," she told a foreign reporter. One morning in 1984, as she strolled through the sunlit garden toward her nearby office, she would fall to the earth, her body destroyed by more than twenty rounds of ammunition. As a girl she had idolized Joan of Arc; she must have known she too could meet a violent death. Her assassins were two of her own bodyguards: Sikhs, bent on revenge. Earlier

that year Mrs. Gandhi had sent troops to storm the Golden
Temple in Amritsar—fervent Sikh nationalists had made it
their headquarters. Operation Blue Star, as it was called, killed
a large number of Sikhs (the figures are endlessly disputed)
and damaged the Golden Temple. I had loved the building
when we passed through Amritsar six weeks before meeting
Mrs. Gandhi, and in my innocence I didn't imagine it might
become a hotbed of revolt.

In response to her death, rioters in Delhi and other cities
murdered thousands of Sikhs. In counter-response, Sikh
extremists bombed an Air India flight from Montreal to
London, murdering hundreds of Indo-Canadians.

"WE TAKE NOTES," Gustave Flaubert complained in a letter
written in Egypt more than a century and a half ago. "We make
journeys: emptiness! emptiness! We become scholars, archaeologists, historians, doctors, cobblers, people of taste. What is
the good of all that?" The French novelist wondered what had
become, what would become, of "the heart, the verve, the sap."
I ask myself the same question.

Decades ago I spent a couple of nights under the stars in an
Iranian border town. I was on the rooftop of the Hotel Asia,
free to peer over the edge at the shopkeepers and soldiers, the
stray cats and students below. They were busy with their lives;
they had dreams of their own. I don't know what they thought
of the youthful Westerners smoking, chatting, or dozing in the
darkness overhead. Many of the travellers were keen to change
the world. We would discover, sooner or later, that the world
was changing us.

Shaggy-haired or clean-cut, spiritually questing or indifferent, politically radical or otherwise, we were in the midst of a journey that would affect the rest of our lives. Clare, for one, would spend many years as an educator at the National Portrait Gallery in London. But, as she wrote to me in 2021, "Our journey set me up for a lifetime of enjoying travel—I was so excited when I finally visited Nemrut Dagi, having wanted to go there for so many years after passing so close to it then. I think our journey influenced me wanting to join Voluntary Service Overseas and I was delighted to be sent to South Asia."

I can't say what the future held for most of the travellers Clare and I encountered. But I know that Paul, whom we met on the train to Istanbul, became a renowned painter, one whose vision of life would be profoundly touched by Sufism. I know that Hugo, who told us of his uncanny struggles in northeastern Iran, went on to be an anthropologist and a climate activist. My brother-in-law John, who enjoyed a distinguished career in tropical forestry, earned a doctorate in science—"but," he told me, "the degree that best prepared me to work in international research and development projects was the degree in life and survival I gained thanks to an overland trip from London to Nepal and back." Climbing down from the rooftop of the continent, all of us shared a mutual challenge: how to retain our idealism while discarding our illusions.

As for me, I wrote a boxful of articles and a handful of books. The first to appear in print was a work of literary travel based on a journey that required three months. Those travels took place in western Canada: I'd come to realize how little I understood about the region where I grew up. Oxford had encouraged me to swagger in my knowledge; Asia had taught me different lessons. I believed I would go back to India one day, probably to Istanbul, possibly to Kathmandu. I never did.

The impressions I gathered between Istanbul and Kathmandu abraded over time. For more than forty years I buried my tomato-coloured notebooks in a drawer, a filing cabinet, a closet. I earned a living, as people say. I moved on. I survived a bout of cancer. And at last, a desire grew to describe what I had witnessed in Asia and, perhaps, foreseen. The journals are what made this book possible: in their absence, I could have conveyed little more than haphazard facts and hazy impressions. Nor would I have recognized my younger self.

I wish the notebooks held more verve and sap: their densely scrawled pages are the dried-up skin of experience. Rereading them has left me, just as Asia did, with questions. I've tried to answer some of them in these pages; I've tried to re-create the heart of the journey. But the most urgent questions still give me pause. Can kindness survive ideology? How can religions avoid being twisted into vehicles of hate? What are the responsibilities that come with privilege? Above all, how can cultures survive — how can people live — if they leave the natural world in ruins?

The narrator of Hermann Hesse's *Journey to the East* never slept on the rooftop of the Hotel Asia. He never saw the Ganges or the Himalaya, never met a half-faced beggar on a Pakistani train or a young bride in Varanasi. Searching for the best way to tell his story, he stumbled: "I do not know. Already this first attempt, begun with the best intentions, leads me into the boundless and incomprehensible. I simply wanted to try to depict what I have remembered of the course of events and individual details of our journey." It wouldn't take long, he thought, my sweet lord.

ON THE AFTERNOON WE left Delhi, I bought fresh lychees and Clare bought fresh mangoes. Cows were striding purposefully through the clamorous streets. "The cows won't be sacred tomorrow," I wrote in my journal, "and England will seem underpopulated."

We reached the airport in the throes of a mauve, parakeet-speckled sunset. The airport—in a few years, it would be renamed to honour Indira Gandhi—proved as busy, loud, and hot as a typical Indian railway station. I cast an eye over the magazines at a newsstand. *Looking is free.* The cover story in *Onlooker*, illustrated by a picture of a whey-faced cabinet minister, asked: "Are Tantrics Behind Janata's Troubles?" As we waited in line to go through Immigration, I noticed a gigantic beetle sitting motionless on a wall. Could it really be bigger than the palm of my hand? Perhaps it had just arrived in India, or perhaps it too was ready to leave. *How many years you have this job to be tourist?*

At midnight we boarded an Iraqi Airways plane bound for Dubai and Baghdad. Climbing the steps onto the gleaming 747, I thought we'd left Indian soil behind. But Indian soil had not left me. *You wouldn't want to know.* I sat down, fastened my seatbelt, and felt something jump inside my T-shirt. A minute later I felt it again, behind my right shoulder. I reached back and grabbed hold, squeezing two folds of cloth together.

"Ew," said Clare. "What's that crunching noise?"

I'd killed a large cricket that had taken up residence on my skin. *Hello. Hello! Goodbye.*

Half the seats on the plane were occupied by Sikh men departing their homeland for jobs in the Persian Gulf. They were travelling to feed their families, I thought, not to search for enlightenment. A man across the aisle gave us his copy of *The Times*—a copy that was three days old. I dozed over dark lands and a sea. On a stopover in Dubai's pale, sumptuous airport, the music spilling from the loudspeakers featured, of all things, an early Simon and Garfunkel song: words were falling like the raindrops of a restless dream; amid the silence, a vision remained... In the wide and bright departure lounge a man in a white robe sat waiting to fly somewhere, a pink-clothed baby no older than three months on his ample lap. I changed out of my insect-sullied T-shirt and into an embroidered shirt I'd purchased in the Delhi bazaar. *Who are you?* And I wrote a final entry in my journal:

> Emotions of gratitude. I won't be sad at saying farewell to Clare, but the more I reflect lucidly on it, the more I realize my good fortune in travelling with her. Most of the time, we got on very well. Am I really as gloomy or as docile as she thinks? No, no. But there are certain qualities of Clare it might benefit me to develop. I know I worry too much.

We reboarded the plane for a short flight at sunrise above the oil-oozing sea and the green marshes of Iraq, controlled by a young strongman named Saddam Hussein. A hot wind blasted our cheeks as we strolled across the tarmac into Baghdad's airport. *How do you feel about this life?* The music playing in the terminal building—a mixture of Arabic and American pop—competed with a muezzin's call to prayer. While the battle raged, through it we heard a boarding announcement for the onward flight to Heathrow.

None of the flights were delayed. None of our luggage went missing. It was all very efficient, very straightforward. And

I realized that after the nerve-racking delay at the Yugoslav border, the nighttime passage through a Turkish city under martial law, the smuggling ride from Iran into Pakistan, my physical distress in the Khyber Pass, the lack of a seat on the train and bus to Khajuraho, the slow and clogged journey from Varanasi to Nepal, the rockslides north of Kathmandu and the breakdown of the vehicle coming back, I'd been steeling myself for a disastrous climax to the trip. No such luck. Far from enduring any last-minute turmoil or acquiring any last-ditch wisdom, I was being handed a tray of scrambled eggs and juice by a flight attendant in a blue hat.

"Would you like some coffee?" she asked with a professional smile.

I looked out at the vagabond wisps of cloud floating above western Asia. The young overlanders on the move thirty thousand feet below were travelling through a continent almost entirely at peace, a planet brimming with hope.

Clare was going home. *Where is your home?* I needed to create a home, somewhere.

Hours after we left Baghdad I stepped, heart thumping, lychee-laden, into the arrivals hall at Heathrow. It felt, by English standards, cacophonous. My face and hands were darkened by the sun. The Indian shirt fitted loosely over my lean frame. *Be here now.* I walked up to Annie. For a few moments she did not recognize me.

Sources

EPIGRAPHS

Tagore, Rabindranath (translator). *One Hundred Poems of Kabir*. London: Macmillan, 1915.

Hamid, Mohsin. *Moth Smoke*. New York: Farrar, Straus and Giroux, 2000.

Rimbaud, Arthur. Letter to Georges Izambard, 13 May 1871.

PROLOGUE

Perkin, J. Russell. *Politics and the British Novel in the 1970s*. Montreal and Kingston: McGill-Queen's University Press, 2021.

Said, Edward. *Orientalism*. New York: Pantheon Books, 1978.

Rhodes, Cecil J. *The Last Will and Testament of Cecil John Rhodes*. London: "Review of Reviews" Office, 1902. info.publicintelligence.net/RhodesLastWill.pdf.

Jenkins, David. *Student Guide to Asia*, 4th edition. Melbourne: AUS Student Travel, 1976.

Hesse, Hermann. *The Journey to the East*. London: Peter Owen, 1956.

I. TURKEY

Pamuk, Orhan. *Istanbul: Memories and the City*. London: Faber & Faber, 2005.

Marnham, Patrick. *Road to Katmandu*. London: Macmillan, 1971.

Leed, Eric J. *The Mind of the Traveler: From Gilgamesh to Global Tourism*. New York: Basic Books, 1991.

Shafak, Elif. *Three Daughters of Eve*. New York: Bloomsbury, 2017.

Çelebi, Evliya. *An Ottoman Traveller: Selections from the Book of Travels* (translated and edited by Robert Dankoff and Sooyong Kim). London: Eland Books, 2011.

Ancient Faith Ministries. "Our Holy Father Joannicius the Great, Hermit on Mt Olympus," *Saint of the Day* [Podcast]. ancientfaith.com/podcasts/saintoftheday/our_holy_father_joannicius_the_great_hermit_on_mt_olympus_8462.

Aragona, Jared. "The Myth of Telepinu, Hittite God of Fertility," *World Mythology*, Volume 1: Gods and Creation. open.maricopa.edu/worldmythologyvolume1godsandcreation/chapter/the-myth-of-telepinu-hittite-god-of-fertility/.

Wikipedia. "Xerxes I inscription at Van." Adapted. en.wikipedia.org/wiki/Xerxes_I_inscription_at_Van.

2. IRAN

Polo, Marco. *The Travels*. London: Penguin, 1958.

Safi, Omid. "Fake Hafez: How a Supreme Persian Poet of Love Was Erased." *Aljazeera*, 14 June 2020. aljazeera.com/opinions/2020/6/14/fake-hafez-how-a-supreme-persian-poet-of-love-was-erased.

Attar, Farid ud-din. *The Conference of the Birds* (translated by C.S. Nott). London: Janus Press, 1954.

Zakrzewski, Alex. "The Defense of Van." *Historynet*, 26 May 2016. historynet. com/the-defense-of-van/.

Ferdowsi, Alboqasem. *Shahnameh: The Persian Book of Kings* (translated by Dick Davis). London: Penguin Classics, 2016.

Hafez: I have adapted the few lines I quote from three published versions. Translations of Hafez can be fraught with controversy.

Foster Fraser, John. *Round the World on a Wheel*. London: Methuen & Co., 1899. The entire text is now available online at ia600202.us.archive.org/22/ items/cu31924023252707/cu31924023252707.pdf.

Leonard, John. "Review of Edward Said's *Orientalism*." *New York Times*, 1 December 1978.

Kapuscinski, Ryszard. *Shah of Shahs*. New York: Harcourt, 1985.

Smith, A.C.H. *Orghast at Persepolis*. London: Eyre Methuen, 1972.

Sofer, Dalia. *The Septembers of Shiraz*. New York: Ecco, 2007. Used with permission.

3. PAKISTAN

Rushdie, Salman. *Shame*. London: Jonathan Cape, 1983.

Hanif, Mohammed. *A Case of Exploding Mangoes*. New York: Alfred A. Knopf, 2008.

Kincaid, Jamaica. *Among Flowers: A Walk in the Himalaya*. Washington: National Geographic Society, 2005.

Hamid, Mohsin. *Moth Smoke*. New York: Farrar, Straus and Giroux, 2000.

Mishra, Pankaj. *Age of Anger: A History of the Present*. London: Allen Lane, 2017.

Anglo-Australian documentary, "An Asian Overlander" (Part 2). Produced by Top Deck Travel. youtube.com/watch?v=eDIWZ3s6H-k.

Shah, Idries. *The Way of the Sufi*. London: Jonathan Cape, 1968.

Bhutto, Fatima. *Songs of Blood and Sword*. London: Jonathan Cape, 2010.

4. INDIA

Tagore, Rabindranath. *Fireflies*. New York: Macmillan, 1928.

Singh, Teja. "The Sikh Religion: An Outline of Its Doctrines." Amritsar: Shiromani Gurdwara Parbandhak Committee, 1977.

Anand, Anita. *The Patient Assassin: A True Tale of Massacre, Revenge and the Raj*. London: Simon and Schuster, 2019.

Kamran, Tahir. "Bleeding Kashmir." *The News*, 7 February 2021. thenews. com.pk/tns/detail/785970-bleeding-kashmir.

Chaudhuri, Nirad C. *A Journey to England*. London: Macmillan, 1959.

Griffith, Ralph T.H. (translator). *The Hymns of the Atharva Veda*, vol. 2. Benares: E. J. Lazarus and Co., 1896.

Parkes, Fanny. *Begums, Thugs and Englishmen: The Journals*. London: Eland Books, 2002.

Mascaró, Juan (translator). *The Upanishads*. London: Penguin, 1965.

Mehta, Gita. *Karma Cola: Marketing the Mystic East*. New York: Simon & Schuster, 1979.

Iyer, Pico. *Video Night in Kathmandu*. New York: Alfred A. Knopf, 1988.

Lal, P. "Indian Influences on Western Literature." *Asia Society*, 2001. asiasociety. org/education/indian-influences-western-literature.

Kabir's succinct appraisal of the human body: These words are my adaptation of two published versions.

Roy, Arundhati. Interview by Karan Thapar, 12 February 2022, thewire.in/ politics/full-text-narendra-modis-star-is-falling-arundhati-roy.

Lal, Ruby. *Empress: The Astonishing Reign of Nur Jahan.* New York: W. W. Norton, 2018.

5. NEPAL

Gautam, Dhruba Chandra. *Unwritten* (translated by Philip Pierce). Kathmandu: Malla Prakashan, 1992.

Liechty, Mark. *Far Out: Countercultural Seekers and the Tourist Encounter in Nepal.* University of Chicago Press, 2017.

Cockburn, Bruce. "Tibetan Side of Town," *Big Circumstance.* Toronto: True North Records, 1988. Used with permission.

Lamichhane, Shankar. "The Half-Closed Eyes of the Buddha and the Slowly Setting Sun." In *Himalayan Voices: An Introduction to Modern Nepali Literature,* translated and edited by Michael James Hutt, ©1991 by the Regents of the University of California. Published by the University of California Press. Used with permission.

Sengupta, Urmi. "Kathmandu Locals Are Fighting 'Injustice' to Save Their City's Heritage, Years after Deadly Earthquake." *The Conversation,* 25 April 2019. theconversation.com/kathmandu-locals-are-fighting-injustice-to-save-their-citys-heritage-years-after-deadly-earthquake-115938.

Lall, Kesar. "Titibancha." In *The Origin of Alcohol and Other Stories.* Kathmandu: Ratna Pustak Bhandar, 1993.

Ram Shah's fourteenth edict: Used as an epigraph by Bista, Dor Bahadur. *Fatalism and Development: Nepal's Struggle for Modernization.* Hyderabad: Orient Longman, 1991.

Lall, Kesar. *Nepalese Customs and Manners.* Kathmandu: Ratna Pustak Bhandar, 1976.

Tsetung, Mao. *Poems.* Peking: Foreign Languages Press, 1976.

Turner, Samuel. *An Account of an Embassy to the Court of the Teshoo Lama, in Tibet.* Originally published in London in 1800; the full text is available online

at google.ca/books/edition/An_Account_of_an_Embassy_to_the_Court_
wof/17s6AQAAMAAJ.

Many books, articles, and websites assert that Yusuf Islam visited Kathmandu
as a young man before writing a song that bears the city's name. My doubts
about this claim were confirmed by listening to a rare recording of a concert he
gave in Berkeley in June 1971. There he performed "Katmandu" as an encore,
and he introduced the song by explaining that he wrote it after reading an
item in *Rolling Stone.* "It's not actually about Kathmandu," he said.

For the same reason that I refer to Yusuf Islam by his earlier name, Cat Stevens,
I also refer to certain places by the names they had in 1978. The city now
known as Kolkata, for example, appears here as "Calcutta."

I would like to acknowledge two remarkable works of nonfiction that moved
and influenced me many years ago and continue to do so today. Although I
quote neither of them directly, I hope their spirit infuses some of Chapter 5:

Matthiessen, Peter. *The Snow Leopard.* New York: Viking, 1978.

Avedon, John. *In Exile from the Land of Snows.* New York: Alfred A. Knopf,
1984.

EPILOGUE

Flaubert, Gustave. *The Letters, 1830–1857* (translated and edited by Francis
Steegmuller). Cambridge and London: Belknap Press, 1980.

Hesse, Hermann. *The Journey to the East.* London: Peter Owen, 1956.

Acknowledgements

I trust this book demonstrates that I am deeply grateful to all the people of Turkey, Iran, Pakistan, India, and Nepal who helped me on this journey. Their acts of kindness and generosity inspired me in 1978 and do so again now.

As will be clear to any reader, I owe a tremendous debt to my travelling companion, Clare Gittings. Somewhere in Asia I would have collapsed in a black-bearded heap were it not for her intelligence, her depth of knowledge, and her extraordinary resilience. More than forty-three years after we set out from Oxford station, she took the time to read a complete draft of the manuscript, to make some invaluable suggestions (and a few corrections), and to mail me her copy of *Student Guide to Asia*, safely preserved. I also thank the late Robert Gittings, not only for his willingness to help me catch a flight from Kathmandu but for his encouragement of my early poems.

My friend Harold Hoefle acted as the first reader of nearly every chapter. He freely offered countless good suggestions, a few warnings, and much reading material. Each page of the book has benefited from his insights, his enthusiasm, and his gentle wisdom.

My wife, Ann Beer, sustains, inspires, and challenges me on a daily basis. She provided me with books to read, ideas to consider, and a detailed critique. *Diolch yn fawr iawn, annwyl.* I also thank my daughter, Megan Abley, for her forthright and thoughtful remarks on a partial draft. Her criticisms and comments improved the book enormously.

David Homel and Mark Dickinson read an early draft of the first forty or so pages. The chapter about India and part of the epilogue received the welcome and necessary scrutiny of Shanta Acharya. My thanks to them all for their helpful suggestions.

My gratitude also goes out to Meera Kachroo for enlightening me about funeral customs in Varanasi, and to Mark Liechty and Chris Adams for helping me look into the background to the Cat Stevens song "Katmandu." For their encouragement or aid with specific points, I thank Thubten Samdup, Ronald Wright, John Beer, Paul Benney, Walter Krajewski, Jyotsna Custead, and Hedley Auld. Particular thanks — decades late — to Martyn Thomas and the late Shirley Thomas.

Steve Payne, the director of copyright and licensing at Red Brick Songs, approved my request to quote from Bruce Cockburn's song "Tibetan Side of Town." My relieved thanks to him, to Kevin Thompson of Round Hill Music, and to Bernie Finkelstein of Finkelstein Management for making this possible.

Bruce Walsh, the former publisher of House of Anansi Press, encouraged me to write this book on the basis of a very skimpy proposal. I am grateful to him and to my longtime agent, Jackie Kaiser. I am delighted that the book includes two maps by Bill

Nelson; I'm equally happy that John Kenney took the author photograph.

The manuscript received a trenchant and thought-provoking edit from Derek Fairbridge; I thank him warmly for his many terrific suggestions and forgive him for a small number of others. Thanks too to Tracy Bordian for her keen-eyed copy-edit. At House of Anansi Press I'm grateful to Shivaun Hearne and Jenny McWha for their calm and considerate handling of the project, to Semareh al-Hillal for her initial welcome, and to everyone else who played a role in launching this book into the world.

Over the past years I have been fortunate to receive a writing grant from both the Conseil des arts et des lettres du Québec and the Canada Council for the Arts. I thank and acknowledge the jurors and staff of these organizations, and also the Access Copyright Foundation, for their support.

Finally I want to thank Jake (2000–2019), Tabby (2000–2020), and Black Cat (2007–2021) for comfort and joy.

MARK ABLEY is a nonfiction writer, poet, and journalist. His many books include *The Organist: Fugues, Fatherhood, and a Fragile Mind*, a memoir of his father; *Spoken Here: Travels Among Threatened Languages* and *The Prodigal Tongue: Dispatches from the Future of English*, among other books on language; *Conversations with a Dead Man: The Legacy of Duncan Campbell Scott*, an unconventional look at the Canadian past; and several poetry collections and children's books. His work has won international praise and has been translated into five languages. He lives in Montreal.